Becky Bexley 5 The Child Genius

Expe
With a Blind Student

Diana Holbourn

Becky Volunteers to Help a Blind Student, and Learns a Lot as a Result

Windy Seaside Publishing

Experiences With a Blind Student

This is a work of fiction. Names, characters, places, and incidents either are the product of the author's imagination or are used fictitiously. Any resemblance to actual persons, living or dead, events, or locales is entirely coincidental.

Cover design, book design and formatting by Gareth Southwell (art.garethsouthwell.com)

ISBN (paperback): 978-1-7384578-1-6
ISBN (ebook): 978-1-7384578-2-3

First published 2024 by Windy Seaside Publishing

Contents

Chapter 1

Becky and Barbara, the Blind Student She Volunteers To Help

Becky Bexley's experiences of university had been fairly positive on the whole, even though she'd gone there at the age of only ten, being a child genius. It had helped a lot that she'd made a lot of good friends she often had fun and interesting discussions with. She lived at home, with her mum taking her home each night, since she lived nearby, so she wasn't often around students who were drunk and feeling boisterous or reckless. Most of her friends were only moderate drinkers, who in any case preferred quiet discussions and humorous banter to going out to drink and dance and find hook-ups and so on.

She was studying psychology and media studies, and although the work was a lot for a child of her age, she often got through it with some time to spare for some relaxation with friends.

In her second year at university, she did some volunteering to help a few students who had disabilities.

She started after she heard about others doing it and thought it might be a nice thing to do, and was introduced to a new blind student called Barbara who said she needed someone to help her.

Barbara had a computer with software that had an electronic voice that could read out loud to her what was on the computer screen, and she could make it read documents and books to her if she had them on file on her computer or they were on the Internet.

The less fancy websites were easier for her to navigate through and use; and Barbara preferred ones without pictures, because images that were just there for the purpose of making a page look more interesting would just come across to her as clutter that needed to be waded through before she could get to the next bit of text she wanted her electronic voice software to read, especially because for some reason, descriptions of images that were encoded to go along with them, apparently designed for software used by visually impaired people to detect and read out, were often repeated about four times, or even six, one after the other.

It did at least help that her screen reading software could be made to skip from one paragraph to the next, so she didn't need to listen to them in their entirety. It also made it easier if a website at least put a word like 'image' or 'illustrative' at the beginning of the lines of text that were part of an image description, so she would know what they were straightaway and wouldn't have to read nearly a whole line of text before it announced that it was describing a photograph like she did on some websites.

Most websites she came across were readable, at least, and most of the ones she browsed didn't have many pictures on them.

The electronic voice would read back to her what she typed too, so she could write her essays on her computer and listen back to them to check they were presentable. Her software could read just individual words or letters one by one if she wanted it to, so what she typed was easy to edit.

However, she needed someone to find the print books in the library that she needed for her course, and to read them for her, or at least the parts her tutors told her were the most important ones. The university had some recording equipment that Becky and other volunteers used to record the parts of the course books she needed to study, and sometimes Becky read chapters of them to her face-to-face. Becky found a lot of them interesting.

Barbara's tutors would give her notes telling her which pages of the books were the most important or relevant ones for the essays she had to write, and she would pass them to her volunteers, who would divide the work between them.

Barbara had a printer so she could print out her essays for her tutors, though she told Becky that one day she'd printed out what she thought was her essay, but the ink had run out or dried out in the printer and she didn't know, so she'd handed in a load of blank pages without realising. The tutor marking the essay had asked her if she'd meant to hand in paper with nothing on it.

One day Becky asked Barbara if she needed any help cooking or doing anything else in her room. Barbara said she was usually alright. After that she sometimes asked Becky if the clothes she was wearing went together colour-wise. But she said she'd gone to boarding schools for blind people and people who could see a fair bit but not fully – boarding schools because there were so few blind pupils in them that the catchment area was too big for it to be practical for parents to bring and collect them every day because for some of them the school was far away – and the staff had taught them to do things like cooking, though they'd learned to cook a lot of things in cookery she thought she couldn't imagine ever being bothered to cook herself.

She confided to Becky that she'd hated her cookery teacher, and had even joked about making a horror film about her where she was a monster. She said she should never have taught blind people, since she just didn't seem to have a clue about the problems they were up against, though no accidents ever happened. It was just that she was always being insulting. Barbara explained to Becky,

"A blind person often has to do things more slowly than someone who can see does to be safe. To give an example, when a blind person washes up, while someone who can see can just take something out of the sink and plonk it down on the draining board, a blind person has to feel around on the draining board to find a gap big enough to put the object down on, unless they're sure they know where one is, and then they have to put it down slowly so as not to accidentally bang it against the thing next to it hard enough to risk breaking it.

"Then if a blind person dries up, they have to do the same in the cupboard or wherever each thing belongs when they put it down. And they have to walk towards the cupboards where the cups and plates and so on belong quite slowly so they won't hurt themselves if they bang into them.

"Besides that, a lot of us won't want to carry as much at once as a sighted person would, because we need to keep a hand free to feel for exactly where the cupboard we want is and where there's a space to put the things down. That's unless we can be absolutely sure where there's one. I've carried heavy boxes with both arms before because I knew just where to put them; but when it comes to smaller breakable things, or drinks we might spill if we're carrying them to a table and don't want to risk estimating where to put them inaccurately so we put them down on something we'd rather not have, we have to be careful. So it helps to keep a hand free to feel just where to put them.

"Besides all that, when it comes to washing up, before taking things out of the sink in the first place, a blind person will likely want to feel quickly all around them to check there doesn't seem to be any dirt on them that still needs washing off before putting them on the draining board, whereas someone with sight could check at a glance.

"And when you've done all that for, say, twenty things, it's bound to take a blind person several minutes longer than it would take someone who can see to wash and dry up. Plus I like to rinse each item quickly after I've washed it to get the washing-up liquid residue off it, which isn't to do with being blind, of course, but some people might say it's to do with being fussy. I'm pretty sure it's recommended though.

"Another thing is that when a blind person chops vegetables, they can't so easily just go chop chop chop chop chop quickly with a knife, but they'll have to feel where the end of the vegetable is every time they chop it before putting the knife onto it, make sure they're chopping a bit the size they want by feeling how far the knife is from the end of it, do the work fairly slowly so if they do happen to catch a finger with the knife they won't do it much of an injury, and so on. The teacher seemed to have absolutely no understanding of things like that. Her favourite phrase she used to use when she was scolding me was, 'Hurry up! If you go any slower you'll be going in reverse!' There was never any advice from her about what I might actually be able to do to speed up; just insult.

"One thing she used to like to do when one of us made a mistake or didn't do something well enough for her liking was to say, 'You're a clot! What are you?' And she would expect us to dutifully reply, 'A clot.' She said that to me once, and I did my duty and replied the way she wanted me to, but at the same time I was actually thinking, 'I know this is what you think you're making me believe, but what you don't know is that I don't really believe it!'

"One day I was putting things away after having washed up, and I was standing just in front of the opening of a cupboard door I wanted to get to, so I shuffled two tiny steps backwards to get out of the way so I could open it. The cookery teacher saw me and scolded me for walking backwards! I thought, 'What was I supposed to do, turn around, walk forwards that tiny bit and then turn back around, just to get out of the way of the edge of a cupboard door? Is that what sighted people do? Don't you think that would have slowed me down?' It seems that she thought what I did was quite a sensational offence, but that she could have fun by exaggerating it. I'm not sure she did, but not long afterwards, my form teacher took me aside and said it seemed I had some problems, and that if I wanted to walk backwards twice round the cookery room, it was hopefully just a phase I was going through. I'm guessing the cookery teacher had told some of the other teachers I'd done that!

"I'll admit that there were one or two occasions, which I don't think she saw, when I walked backwards a few paces in the corridor after finishing a conversation with someone there, just to save myself the bother of having to turn around and walk forwards, when there was a door I wanted to go in a few paces behind me. I mean, I can't see where I'm going, so it doesn't make any difference to me whether I'm walking backwards or forwards ... at least if I'm only going a few paces. I still do that. I don't see what's wrong with it. It's just practical."

She grinned and said for fun, "Imagine if a teacher did her best to drum into her pupils that reversing a car was a gauche habit, and that yes, older people did it, but the cool, sophisticated thing to do, even if someone just wanted to reverse a few metres, was to drive forward to where they could turn round, even if it took a few minutes to get there, and then drive back to where they'd wanted to reverse to, and then drive on to somewhere else where they were able to turn back around and start driving to where they'd wanted to go in the first place, till they got to the next place where they wanted to reverse a bit, and then they should do the same thing.

"Imagine if the teacher was so successful at drumming that idea into some of her pupils that one day one was in his family's car, and his dad was reversing a metre or so into a parking space, and the boy said, 'Dad! Don't reverse! It makes you look so uncool! You're supposed to drive forwards all the time!'

"His dad might say, 'Really? So when I drive into the garage when we get home, instead of reversing out the next time I want to use the car, I should instead accelerate at speed and knock the back wall down to get out, should I? That's the cool thing to do?' "

Becky laughed.

Barbara continued, "There are times when walking backwards a few paces just seems to make most sense as well. Obviously I wouldn't walk backwards to a lecture, since imagine me trying to use my white stick behind my back! It would be a bit awkward trying to slide it along – I think my arm and shoulder might ache after a little while with the effort of trying to move it along behind me. ... Mind you, it probably wouldn't hurt as much if I fell over while I was walking backwards, since I'd land on my bottom, so I'd get a softer landing than I would if I fell forwards and landed on my knees. ... Of course the problem is that I might fall over in the first place when I wouldn't have done if I'd been walking forwards with it in front of me."

Barbara told Becky that one day she'd been running in the grounds when she was at school – walking would have been quite a bit safer, but she was in a hurry. She said she fell over because part of her foot went off the edge of the path onto some gravel several centimetres below it, and she sprained her ankle. She got up and started limping painfully and slowly. She heard the cookery teacher in the distance talking to someone. She thought with a mocking smile, "If I meet her, I'm going to say, 'Just think! If I go any slower I'll be going in reverse!"

But she said that since she'd come to university, she hadn't met anyone like her old cookery teacher; everyone was friendly and helpful and considerate.

When she told Becky about the sprained ankle incident, Becky didn't know whether to laugh, sympathise or cringe. She did a mixture of all three. Then she had a thought, and said, "I don't know if you were running just because you like running ..."

Barbara interrupted to say, "I think I was just late for dinner. I wouldn't run around here, because I know it would be dangerous; there are far too many people around and things to crash into."

Becky responded, "Well I was wondering whether if that cookery teacher had seen you have the accident, she would have criticised you for having gone too fast! You'd have thought, 'I can't win!' "

Barbara laughed. Becky continued, "There are a few things I'm not very good at, and I've learned that the people who make fun of you and try to make you feel stupid for not coming up to the standards they think you ought to come up to can be the exact same people who make fun of you or condemn you if you try to do things better because of what they said and make a mistake because of it! Like if you're doing something a bit too slowly for their liking and they complain, so you try to do things faster, and drop something or make some other mistake in your haste! So I think it's best to try not to take too much notice of insults like that if you can, although I know it's not always easy."

Barbara introduced Becky to some of her friends. A few had other disabilities. One called Susan was a bit deaf, though she had hearing aids that made things easier for her, at least if there wasn't much background noise. In the lecture theatres, there was a loop system where a little microphone was attached to the lecturer, and what they said was transmitted to hearing aids without any background noise; hearing aids could be set to a setting where they didn't pick any up, but only what the person with the microphone on was saying ... or doing. She found she could hear things more clearly that way, even when things were fairly quiet, because the hearing aids amplified background noise on their normal setting.

One day she told Becky a funny story, saying, "I was in a meeting at a conference for deaf and hard-of-hearing people one day before I came to university, and a bishop was speaking about making churches more disability-friendly, such as by setting up loop systems there. After his speech, he forgot to take the microphone off and walked out of the room. The people who couldn't hear well in the room and were listening to him via the loop system could still hear him. We heard him go into the toilet, talking to himself, and then we heard him weeing. We all laughed. The people who could hear properly so they didn't have hearing aids wondered what on earth we were all laughing about all of a sudden. I've so often heard people laughing when I haven't heard the joke properly so I haven't understood what they were laughing about that I thought it was fun that the deaf people knew what was funny that time when the others didn't."

Barbara was there when Susan told Becky that, and she told her a funny story herself, saying, "Once I was going somewhere with a few blind people, with people who could see as our guides, when one accidentally dropped her white stick down what seemed to be a manhole outside a building. She worried about what to do at first; but then a voice from underneath us called out, 'Don't worry, I'm coming up!' Then a man came up with it and said he was a dentist working in a basement room, and the white stick had come in and landed in a pile of false teeth he had waiting for patients."

One of Barbara's blind friends, Carol, told them, "My older sister's blind like me. She moved into a flat of her own not long ago. She likes it. But she said a couple of weeks after she moved in, one day she heard what sounded like abnormally massive raindrops pouring down on the window. She thought it must be raining unusually heavily, and opened the window a bit to hear what was going on better, only to discover that the noise was being caused by a window cleaner outside cleaning the window. She hadn't even been told window cleaners came round to the flats. She said ever since then, when he's been round, he bashes her window hard several times with his brush – or whatever he uses – probably to make sure she knows he's there and doesn't open the window again while he's trying to clean it. She said he bashes it so hard she worries he'll break it. She said he doesn't need to bash it though, since now she knows what it sounds like when he cleans the window, she wouldn't make that mistake again.

"She said she asked a neighbour if she could tell her when the window cleaner was due to come round after the embarrassing incident, but the neighbour said the other residents don't always know themselves."

Becky often found spending time with Barbara and her friends interesting.

Barbara told her more stories about things that had happened to her and to people she knew.

She said she'd driven a police car once. Becky had visions of a reckless criminal blind person somehow managing to wrestle her way into the driving seat of one and whizzing away with it, with complete disregard for the safety of any traffic or pedestrians that might be in the way! But Barbara explained that her local society for blind people, which arranged some social events for people with sight problems and helped them out in some other ways, had organised a trip to an aerodrome that wasn't being used at the time, where they were allowed to take turns driving a police car around it, with policemen in it giving them instructions and directions. She said she'd enjoyed it – though the policemen with her or some of the people outside might have been a bit nervous.

Becky grinned.

One day Becky asked Barbara if she'd thought of getting a guide dog. Barbara said she'd heard they could be a great help, and even remember the way to places after a while and take their owners there without commands sometimes; but she said she'd wait till she thought she might have to travel around more before deciding whether to apply to have one, because she didn't have a problem getting to the places she needed to go with her white stick at the time; someone had shown her the way to her lecture theatres and around the corridor where her room was when she'd first come to university, and she'd walked over the routes again and again with them till all the directions she needed to go in, and all the places where she needed to walk especially carefully because there were steps she could fall down or things she could bang into if she wasn't concentrating on using her white stick well, were firmly implanted in her memory.

Besides, she said, she was too much of a wimp to like the idea of taking a guide dog for walks in the snow and cold in winter or the rain.

Then she said to Becky, "I had a blind teacher at school who had a guide dog; but while a lot of guide dogs are very well-behaved, this one could be a bit naughty sometimes. One thing it loved to do was nibble the bottoms off ice cream cones. When the teacher was walking down the street with it, it would just suddenly nibble a child's ice cream, and the first inkling he'd get that it had happened was when he heard a child yelling, and he'd have to buy them another one. It never did that to any child at school because no one ever had ice creams in cones there. But once we had a Christmas party and it stole a mince pie from a trolley."

Becky responded, "Naughty dog! There would probably be a way of training it not to nibble ice creams though, like maybe if someone held an ice cream in front of it and shouted 'No' loudly and snatched it away every time it went to nibble it, again and again for about half an hour."

Barbara chuckled and said she wondered if that would work. Then she thought about it and said for a laugh, "The dog would probably explode with frustration after a while though, and then you wouldn't want the ice cream any more than you would have done if the dog had bitten it, because it would be covered in bits of dog. Anyway, if you held an ice cream for half an hour, it would melt all over the place, and you'd probably only have the cone left by the end of it, with just a bit of soggy ice cream in it and the rest slopped over the floor. The dog wouldn't care any more that the ice cream kept being snatched away from him, because he'd be too busy lapping it off the floor!"

Becky giggled. She hadn't thought of that when the idea of training the dog had popped into her head. She said with a smile, "True, there is that."

Then she said seriously, "There must be some way of training a dog not to nibble kids' ice creams though."

Barbara agreed that there surely had to be one, though she wasn't sure how it would be done.

She told another story when she was alone with Becky one day, saying,

"When I was about sixteen, the summer was pretty hot for a few weeks, and the only way I could be cool enough to be comfortable outside in it was by wearing my swimming costume, so I wore it in the garden all day. It was especially warm because the garden's a real sun trap, sheltered from the wind when it comes from the most common direction it comes from. I really like to sit in the sun, and I would take a little laptop computer outside that's got the software on it that talks in an electronic voice so it can read things out loud so I can work or find entertaining things on the Internet. Schoolwork's easier to concentrate on for me when something's making me feel better at the same time as I'm slogging through it, like sunshine. I've discovered I can get more done in the sun because of that.

"But my mum told me off one day, saying a neighbour had phoned her up and complained, telling her he didn't think it was appropriate for females to be sitting around in their swimming costumes showing off lots of bare flesh. My mum told me not to do it again.

"I was annoyed. I thought wearing more clothes would mean I'd be too uncomfortably hot to stay in the sun for very long, so I'd have to sacrifice a lot of my time enjoying the sun and working on my little computer in a place where I could concentrate better, all because of some nosy neighbour. I hadn't even realised neighbours could see into the garden! No one had ever told me before.

"The complaint about me had been worse because the neighbour had also spotted me in the front garden, which is more public than the back garden where I normally sit, because it faces a quiet road that other people's houses look onto. I'd come in the back door one day, and a gentle breeze was blowing in the front door which was open, and it had enticed me out the front; I just curiously wondered if there was still sunshine out there, since it's there in the early morning and then moves round the house, but I wasn't sure what time it would leave there; and since I've got no way of telling if the sun's shining unless it's shining down directly on me so I can feel the heat from it, the only way I could find out was by going outside, or sticking my nose up to the window in the front room to see if my face felt warm when I did that. But doing that's awkward because there are chairs in the way!

"I was only out the front for a minute or two; I discovered there was no sunshine there so I went in. But it was enough to bring the wrath of my neighbour down on me; he complained to my mum that I'd been standing in the front garden in my swimming costume, as well as sitting in the back garden with it on. I was told not to do such a thing again, although my parents had never said they minded before.

"The neighbour said the worst thing was that I'd been sitting there with my breasts showing! What had actually happened was that I'd dropped something in the back garden and bent down to get it, and unfortunately one of the shoulder straps on my swimming costume had fallen down, showing more than I'd intended to. I'd put it back a couple of seconds later when I'd picked up what I'd dropped, but the neighbour saw what happened, and must have made it sound to my mum as if I'd been sitting there committing a shocking indecency. Somehow it can't have occurred to him that it was an accident! He angrily complained to my mum that his wife was with him when it had happened, and she saw it too, and it had made him embarrassed. He said he didn't think it was right that such indecency should be on display for all to see.

"When my mum told me off about it, I angrily thought about how it wasn't fair that this neighbour, who's got so many more advantages in life than I have, would end up restricting my life even more by stopping me enjoying the summer so much. I thought about how he could easily stroll through the neighbourhood looking for somewhere private and cool to sit if he wanted, but I can't see even half a centimetre in front of me, so I'm not free to do any such thing. And I thought I'd consider it a huge privilege if suddenly I was able to see even just something as big as the house the neighbour lived in by looking in its direction; yet here was this man who can see not only just my house, but enough detail about its surroundings to be able to see a person sitting some way away from him, and even what they're wearing, not being grateful, but abusing the privilege by nosing into other people's gardens and then complaining! I got more annoyed the more I thought about it.

"My mum did later say I could try sitting in the garden with a vest-type thing over my swimming costume. I did, and that seemed to solve the problem most of the time, since I was still normally cool enough to feel comfortable sitting outside, and as far as I knew, there were no more complaints. I was still annoyed with the neighbour though.

"One of my family took me swimming in the local leisure centre soon after that, and I thought about how it seemed strange that the place must be full of women wearing nothing but swimming costumes, and yet men and their wives seemed to be able to tolerate it without a problem. I wondered why sitting in my family's garden was any different; and I couldn't understand what the problem was anyway, since I couldn't imagine for a moment that my flabby body could be filling any man with the temptation to go out and be unfaithful to his wife or anything like that, although not being able to look in a mirror, I can't get much of an idea myself about what impression I might be making on the world in anything I wear, let alone my swimming costume.

"But thinking about that gave me an idea that made me smile. I thought of a trick to play on the neighbour as retribution for making me have to sacrifice some of my time in the sun where schoolwork felt like less of a slog, because I thought I'd better stay indoors some of the time on especially hot days after that. A friend of mine agreed to help.

"I wrote a pretend letter from the local council. I tried to make it sound official and important, although I knew it wouldn't really look like an official council letter. I found the council's address on the Internet and put it at the top of it. I wrote:

> Dear Sir
>
> It has come to the council's attention that male sensibilities everywhere are being offended by females wearing nothing but swimming costumes. We are concerned about this, so we have decided this state of affairs must no longer continue. Therefore the council has issued this decree:
>
> To come into effect immediately, any male over the age of 14 years must wear a blindfold at all times when in the local swimming baths, so they won't be inconvenienced by having to see scantily-clad females. For reasons of health and safety, this means each male over 14 years old must be accompanied by their own female chaperone and guide in the swimming baths, who will show them the way to the steps of the pool they wish to swim in, and tell them when it's safe for them to start swimming at

the beginning of each length they do because no one's in front of them so they won't collide with anyone. We hope it will be understood that this order is being issued purely to prevent injuries.

If a male is unable to find a female chaperone to guide him, he is to keep clear of the swimming baths altogether, since naturally it would be irresponsible of him to risk either colliding with people in the pool, and bumping into them or treading on them on his way out, or offending his own sensibilities by not wearing a blindfold and seeing women scantily dressed.

Any male found to have taken off his blindfold or to be unaccompanied by a guiding female chaperone will be faced with an on-the-spot fine of £50. We thank you for your co-operation. We hope you understand that these measures are being put in place to benefit all the men in the area.

Yours Faithfully

Mrs P Supe
Leisure Department

"I printed out the message and put it in an envelope. I asked a friend of mine to write my neighbour's name and address on it and to put it through his letterbox. She waited till he and his wife seemed to be out because their car wasn't there, so she hopefully wouldn't be spotted, and then quickly went and posted it. I didn't want to risk doing it myself, because I wouldn't have known if anyone was watching, and I'm not sure of the way up to my neighbour's front door anyway, so I might have been faffing around for a little while trying to find it.

"A few days later, I found out what happened. The neighbour had thought the letter really had come from the council, and phoned them in a rage, saying their new ruling was absurd. When he asked to speak to Mrs P Supe, the person on the other end of the phone laughed, saying there was no one of that name there, and that she was sorry for laughing but it sounded as if he'd asked for someone called Pea Soup. He got even angrier. When he was told the council had no knowledge of the supposed new ruling about males having to be blindfolded in the swimming pool, and had no idea what he was talking about, he got embarrassed and realised someone must have played a trick on him. He suspected me and my family. He made an angry phone call to my mum. I hadn't told my mum what I'd done, so she was surprised and said she didn't have anything to do with it, and doubted I had.

"Later she asked me if I'd had anything to do with it, and I admitted what I'd done. When my mum told me what had happened, I thought it was hilarious. I didn't enjoy the stern lecture she gave me though about how I must never ever do such a thing again!"

Becky thought the stories Barbara and her friends told her were interesting and amusing.

Chapter Two

Becky Meets Barbara's Blind and Talkative Older Brother Tony and Their Parents

Barbara's older brother Tony was blind like her. Becky met him once when he came along with their parents, Rita and Jeff, who were bringing Barbara back to university after Christmas. Becky happened to meet them just after they arrived, having gone to the university on the Saturday before term started, hoping to go to the library and have a sneak peek at some of the textbooks the students on her psychology course were about to start studying, and to see if she met up with any of her friends. They all got chatting after they'd unloaded some luggage Barbara had and were taking it indoors.

A Bit of Good-Natured Teasing and Laughter Breaks Out

When they were about to go in, Tony said, "Wow, there's a gorgeous smell around here; it's making me want to eat some of whatever it is that smells so nice!"

Becky joked, "Maybe Barbara put perfume on today and it's that. Do you enjoy eating perfume ... or should I say drinking it?"

They all chuckled.

Barbara said for fun, "I don't wear perfume that smells of junk food! Do you, then? That's what the smell is. Yes, Tony, maybe it's Becky's perfume!"

Becky joked, "I don't wear perfume that smells of junk food either! My perfume smells of petrol, or sometimes baked potatoes."

Tony asked for fun, "Or do you sometimes vary it a bit so it smells of chips? Maybe you do wear junk food perfume on special occasions, just not normally? I think that's what I can smell – chips!"

Tony Confesses to Some Bad Behaviour, and Becky Gives Him Some Advice, and Talks About Something Similar She's Heard

They went into Barbara's room and sat down for a chat.

After a while, Tony's disability came up in the conversation. Becky told him she was learning a lot of interesting things on her psychology course, and he said he wondered if she could give him a bit of psychological advice in that case:

He said he'd been taught how to get from his house to his workplace, going over the route a number of times till it was all in his memory, but it still wasn't easy to avoid the dozens of obstacles in his way as he walked there – overhanging prickly bushes, lamp posts, shop signs and so on. He would walk with a white stick, which helped him to avoid quite a few obstacles because it would hit them first as he slid it over the ground in front of him, so he could tell they were there and walk around them. But sometimes, perhaps because he wasn't using it quite as well as he should have been, or because it would slip under an obstacle like a sign or a car, he would walk straight into something, such as a car that was parked partly on the pavement, or a lamp post or a shop sign or a tree, and hurt himself.

He said sometimes someone would come up to him and ask if he was alright, and he would answer them rudely, because he thought he'd made a stupid mistake and felt humiliated that they'd seen him. He said he knew it wasn't a nice thing to do, but he seemed to do it on reflex before he'd thought about it.

Becky replied, "Maybe it's partly the pain making you bad-tempered; but maybe you're annoyed with them for what you Think they must be thinking, rather than what they're really thinking; maybe you think they interpret what you've done the same way that you do, as a silly embarrassing mistake; but really, they probably aren't thinking of it like that at all; they're probably thinking, 'Ouch, that looks as if it was painful!' and they're probably just worried you've hurt yourself. So it sounds as if you're resenting them for something they're not guilty of; and maybe if you can manage to train your brain to think, 'Oh there's a nice person who's worried about me' instead of, 'Oh no, how humiliating, they saw that!' every time someone asks if you're alright, you won't feel annoyed with them any more. After all, if anyone does think you look stupid, they're probably not the ones nice enough to want to help you."

Tony said Becky's suggestion might be a good idea, and he'd have a go.

Then Becky started talking about an article she'd read. She said,

"That reminds me: Not long ago, I read an article by a disabled person who has to go around in a wheelchair, who said she was fed up of people coming up to her and asking her about her disability, partly because it seemed to her that it must mean that whenever they saw her, they just saw the disability, rather than thinking of her as a person with likes, dislikes, opinions, talents and so on. She said she felt demoralised because she thought that every time someone came up to her and asked her about why she was disabled, it must mean they thought of the wheelchair first and her second. But I wondered if at least part of the reason she got upset was because of the way she was thinking about it, not because of what they were actually saying. I mean, if instead of thinking they were only seeing her as someone in a wheelchair, she thought, 'Oh, this could be a new friend, for all I know, and they might be asking about my disability because it's an obvious conversation starter', then maybe she'd feel better about it.

"Mind you, I could understand her not being happy, to some extent; she said people often ask about her disability when she's trying to enjoy herself on nights out with friends, or when she just wants to get around the shops and get her shopping done, and it brings her down to talk about it, so it ruins her enjoyment or makes her less cheerful, especially because sometimes people want to confide in her about people they know who've had accidents and become disabled. Maybe they assume she must be a caring sympathetic person. If she thought about it like that, she might feel complimented so she might feel better about it. But I can understand her not liking people doing that when all she wants to do is enjoy her time out, or even just concentrate on what she's doing.

"She said she sometimes tells people to go away, and then they don't think she's very nice. Maybe she needs to find a politer way of phrasing things, because she said she thinks they start thinking of her as an angry disabled person after she's told them she doesn't want to talk to them."

Barbara said, "That's a pity! You might be right about how she'd feel better if she could change her perspective. I think I can understand how she feels though, to some extent. It doesn't happen to me here at the university – I think it mostly happens when I'm around old people. I've been to a few social events with relatives and one or two other people where I think just about every person who's come up to me to say hello has immediately started asking me questions about being blind, and they always seem to ask the same few questions as well, like, 'Were you born blind?' 'Do you do your own cooking?' 'Does someone come in to do your cleaning?' and, 'Can you see anything at all?' It's not that I mind answering questions like that – or at least most of them; it's just that when those are the only things people ever seem to want to ask me about, it gets a bit dreary and depressing.

"You know, when I go out, I want to try to have a nice time; I don't want to keep being reminded again and again of my disability, and to keep having to explain the same old things. It's not that I mind talking about that stuff; but spending most of the time I'm with other people answering questions about things I can't do that most people can, or can't do so well, or need help with, or things I have to do in different ways to the way most people do them, doesn't exactly make for an enjoyable day out for me. It wouldn't for you, would it! I mean, just imagine if all anyone ever wanted to ask you about was how you manage to reach the top shelves in the library, or whether the work here's too much for you and you get people to help you with it, since you're so much younger than everyone else, and whether you have to go to bed much earlier than most people so you get enough sleep, and that kind of thing."

Becky replied, "Actually, I do get a fair bit of that sometimes."

Barbara said, "Oh. You can probably understand what I mean then. I'd far rather people ask me questions like, 'How's your life going?', or better still, for people to tell me things about themselves, than to have everyone who comes up to me just ask me questions about how blind I am, and whether I can manage to do this, that and the other.

"I'm not faulting anyone for asking those questions; I mean, maybe for other people, that kind of thing's new and interesting, or they're really curious about it, because they can't imagine how they'd do it themselves; or maybe when most people want to just make conversation, they look for things they can comment on, and me being blind just seems like an easy conversation starter. It's just that when several people in a row have just seemed to want to ask me the same few questions about being blind, and only seem to want to talk about me being blind, it starts to feel as if people must think of me as just a walking talking heap of blindness; I mean, there's a lot more to me than being blind!

"I know the people asking questions like that won't know I've been asked them lots of times before, so it won't be their fault; and I'm probably just as bad myself for asking people about things they don't want to talk about. Maybe everyone does that to other people. And it's at least nicer to have people coming up to talk to me than it is when no one talks to me, which has happened quite a bit in some places, so I've been just sitting by myself, not even knowing who's around.

"But it would be nicer if people talked more about other things, like if they told me about some of the things they've done in their lives, or what they do every day."

Becky asked, "You said you don't mind 'most' of the questions people ask you about being blind. I'm just curious: Which ones *do* you mind?"

Barbara explained, "Well, there's just one that really bugs me, and that's 'Do you do your own cooking?' It only bugs me because every time I get asked it, I'm confused about what the person asking it really wants to know, so I'm never sure how to answer. Do they mean, 'Do you cook from scratch or eat microwave meals and takeaways?' Or do they mean, 'Does a carer or family member come in every day to do your cooking for you or do you do it yourself?' Or what? I don't know."

She put on a mock posh voice and said for fun, 'Do you have a gourmet chef coming in to make your meals for you every day or do you make your own?' "

Then she replied to herself, "The chance of getting all my cooking done for me would be a fine thing! I don't suppose they really ever wonder if a gourmet chef does it all for me though!

"I think from now on, I'm always going to try to remember to answer the question about whether I cook for myself by asking, 'As opposed to doing what?' Then they'll hopefully clarify what they really mean."

"As opposed to eating scraps off the floor!" said Becky for fun in a mock creepy voice.

Then she said, "They're probably just wondering how you do it yourself, given that knobs on cookers don't normally have braille on and nor does food packaging, and if you were to use saucepans on a stove it could be awkward not to see exactly where they were, because you might accidentally touch them when you were reaching for their handles and burn yourself."

Barbara replied, "Actually, you're probably right! Maybe I should explain to them how I get around those problems. Not that I'd want to be talking about that all the time.

"I went to this lunch at a church I started going to last year, and I didn't really enjoy it. Well, I did enjoy the food! What I mean is that I kept getting asked the same few questions about being blind by different people. ... Actually it would have been worse if the same person had kept on and on asking them, wouldn't it! Mind you, I think one or two people did ask them more than once! But anyway, I got fed up of having to answer the same questions.

"Then again, to be fair, it seems there are some people who actually like talking about their problems, for some reason, and people aren't to know I'm not one of them. At least not when I'm having a day out that I'm hoping to enjoy. You just end up thinking it wasn't fit for purpose."

Tony grinned and quipped, "I'm presuming you're not hoping to enjoy today then, or you wouldn't be talking about your problems now."

Barbara turned up her nose at the quip and replied, "I'm talking about social events that are especially intended for people to have a nice time at.

"Another thing I don't like at events like that is when people treat me as if I'm less capable than I really am. Sometimes I start taking my coat off, and without saying a word, someone gets hold of it and tries to take it off me, as if they assume I won't be able to do it myself. I'd prefer it if they at least asked if I needed help.

"And then there's something that bugs a lot of disabled people, and that's when people we're with get asked questions by strangers who should be asking us them instead, like, 'Does she want sauce?' 'Does she want another drink?' How are the people we're with supposed to know? Mind you, it doesn't bother me as much as it used to, because I can understand why they do it to blind people. Since they can't make eye contact with us, they probably think, 'How will she know she's the one I'm talking to if I speak directly to her?' That's fair enough, because maybe I won't. I don't understand why they do it to people with other disabilities though who can see perfectly well. I do wonder if it's because they wonder if they're mentally less capable as well as physically.

"Mind you, it's probably easy to get a mistaken impression of people's intentions, like thinking they're underestimating your abilities when they aren't meaning to. That was one thing I realised the day we had that church lunch, actually – that it's easy to be judgmental about people, as if it's an instant automatic reaction. Maybe everyone's like it; but sometimes, you can find out you're wrong.

"I was standing in the porch of the church just before we went home when someone came up behind me and touched me. I felt a bit irritated and thought, 'Must you feel the need to touch me just because I'm blind? I'm not a pet!'

"But then the person said, 'Excuse me, someone in a wheelchair wants to get past.' So I realised she was only touching me to alert my attention to the fact that she wanted to say something to me. I thought it was a funny coincidence that two disabled people were passing like that.

"On another day, a man sat next to me and started a conversation with me, and he was talking more loudly than he needed to; and I thought, 'Does this person think I need to be spoken to more loudly than most people do because I'm blind? That's a bit ignorant!'

"But then he told me he was a bit deaf, and wore hearing aids in both ears; and I thought, 'Oh! Maybe that's why he's talking louder than normal – because he maybe can't hear himself talk as loudly as most people can, so he raises his voice to the level where he can hear it as loudly as most people would hear their voices, not realising it's actually louder for most people than it needs to be.

"Actually it was funny: When he said he was a bit deaf, I decided to talk louder so he'd hear me better; but when I said the first thing that was louder than what I'd been saying before, he asked me to say it again because he hadn't heard it properly, when he'd heard everything I'd said before at a normal volume alright! Actually, I seem to remember someone saying hearing aids can distort sound when it's too loud, so maybe that's why he found it harder to hear me then."

Becky smiled and said, "It's a good thing you didn't voice your critical thoughts out loud to that man!"

Barbara grinned and said, "I know! Wouldn't he have thought I was rude!"

Tony smiled and quipped, "You are rude!"

Barbara, probably not realising it would sound as if she was confirming what he said, replied with a smile, "Shut up! You're a fine one to talk, having just told us about how you can be rude to strangers who are just checking to see if you're alright!"

Becky giggled at the irony of Barbara being rude in response to Tony accusing her of it. But she knew what she'd said hadn't been meant in a nasty way.

Barbara Talks About Rudeness, Blindness and Horrible Teachers

Then Barbara said, "Talking about being rude to people though, I remember at school I had a blind friend who was quite outspoken, and we were walking down the road arm in arm one day, using our white sticks. He was guiding me, because I didn't know the way and he did. Lots of people came up to us and asked him if we needed help. I'm not sure, but I think he might have felt as if it was hurting his pride or something, as if it meant they were thinking he wasn't as capable as he really was, because he kept being rude to them, giving them sarcastic replies about whether they really thought he couldn't manage! I was giggling away, all the way down the road, because every time he was rude to someone it sounded funny. I just couldn't seem to stop myself, even though I knew it wasn't fair of him or nice, and I felt a bit guilty for doing it.

"I knew I shouldn't have been laughing really, because they were only being caring and trying to help, and they might have had their feelings hurt by what he said. Actually I hope it didn't put them off helping other blind people, because sometimes we do need help.

"People often ask me if I need help while I'm walking to lectures and things, and I'm grateful. When I first came here, someone told me I might not get many offers of help because most people might wonder if I'd prefer to be independent; but actually, it's been nice because lots of people have asked me if I need help.

"Thankfully though, I was taught the way to my lectures not long after I came here, so ever since then, I've usually been alright and haven't needed help, apart from the occasions when

I've got lost in one particular place because I've accidentally gone a bit too far to the left or the right and ended up somewhere I didn't recognise, and then I haven't been able to tell whether it's because I've gone too far left or too far right, because the person who taught me didn't tell me what was on the left and the right of the path he taught me to use, probably because he didn't expect me to get lost. So I couldn't tell by the differences in the texture of the ground I was walking on or anything. Mind you, I've worked it out now.

"Anyway, my old friend who was rude to all the people who offered us help that day was nice most of the time. He used to tell me funny stories all the time. I wish I could remember more of them now. One day he told me he was talking to another blind person at our school when she said, 'Oh no, I've dropped sweets!' He got down on the floor and started feeling around, trying to help her find them. He couldn't find any sweets though, and a few minutes later, it turned out that it wasn't even really sweets that she'd dropped; she had this little teddy bear toy she carried around with her everywhere, and she told him that was called Sweets."

Becky asked, "Was he rude to her when she finally told him that?"

Barbara replied with a smile, "He didn't tell me. Another funny story he told me was about how he had a bit of an embarrassing incident one day after he heard a song on the radio from the late 1970s with a catchy tune, where the chorus says things like,

Hey fatty bum bum,
sweet sugar dumpling.

"I think the verses said things like,

It's not because you're so big and fat;
don't think I'm afraid of that.

"Anyway, he said he was walking down the road one day when he had a sudden urge to burst into song. He had that song on the brain, and he started singing it, when suddenly he felt this massive slap in the face, and a woman angrily said, 'Why do you have to be so rude to people?'

"She must have thought he was making fun of her. But he hadn't even realised someone was walking in front of him who might have mistakenly thought he was singing about them!"

The others found that amusing.

Then Barbara said, "Mind you, talking about rudeness, I think a couple of the teachers at the school Tony and me went to were ruder than any of the pupils ever were! Like this cookery teacher I've mentioned before, Mrs Cactus, or something not all that dissimilar – it's a decent nickname for her anyway.

"She would often insult me and other blind people, nit-picking what we did. She never had any positive suggestions about how we could change things for the better, it seems; she would just let us know we were doing things inefficiently, as far as she was concerned, saying things like, 'Normal people don't do it like that!', say if I was peeling a carrot and spent a little while feeling around it when I'd almost finished to find out if there were any bits of peel still on it that I needed to peel off, or if I was maybe holding the peeler in a different way from the way most people do because since I've never seen anyone do it, I didn't have anyone to imitate like a sighted person might. I was never quite sure exactly what she meant though, because she never explained precisely what the 'it' she was referring to was.

"The fact that I haven't starved to death since leaving her classes, though, seems to prove that I can survive perfectly well without her insults and criticism of my cookery efforts! She might be surprised to hear that, but still.

"She left to have a little baby Cactus a couple of years before I left school, and another cookery teacher came to take her place. I had a few lessons with her. She was nice. But that felt strange, as if she must be teaching the lesson all wrong, since cookery was surely supposed to be taught with insults and criticism – surely that was part of the job!"

The others grinned.

Barbara carried on, "Mind you, I've noticed I can get irritable myself sometimes when it's not fair. I remember once I went to this church, and the sermon was really long, and I thought it was boring. Afterwards, I was feeling grumpy and irritable because of that. They served tea and coffee after the service."

Her dad, Jeff, interrupted, saying, "You know, I could really do with some tea or coffee now! We've been here ages, and you haven't offered us any!"

Barbara apologised. She looked a bit embarrassed and said she'd make some soon. But she said, "Anyway, I'll just finish what I'm saying, since otherwise I'll forget what it was. I was just saying that this man offered to get me a cup of tea, and when he gave it to me, he said the handle of the cup was just next to my right hand. It turned out to be just next to my Left hand, and I said so, but because I was feeling grumpy and irritable because I was still recovering from this long boring sermon, I said it in a grumpy irritable voice; and I don't think he wanted to come near me after that. It was a pity really."

Becky asked, "Did you ever get irritable with your cookery teacher for saying insulting things to you when you were peeling and chopping carrots and things?"

Barbara replied, "No, I think I just put up with it. I wasn't one for getting into arguments with teachers. Maybe I would have ended up better off if I'd told her what I thought of her teaching methods, I'm not sure. Someone did feebly argue with her once, and just got sent outside the door."

The Little Group Becomes Light-Hearted

Becky grinned and remarked, "Well that would have been one way of getting out of doing her lesson!"

Then she said for fun, "The other day I was looking up the health benefits of some vegetables on the Internet, and I was reading a website that said, 'These vegetables are very good at fighting free radicals.' The first thought that popped into my mind was, 'Really? Surely we shouldn't be chopping them up then, since won't that stop them being able to fight? How can anything fight if it's all chopped up?' Then I realised that thought was daft, and they were talking about the nutrients in the vegetables.

"Imagine trying to swallow a vegetable whole, like a carrot or something, because you thought that if you did that, it would be able to go around starting fights with bad things in your body!"

Barbara grinned and said, "Trying to swallow a whole carrot would be bad enough, but imagine trying to get your mouth round a whole cauliflower or cabbage!"

They all giggled.

Then Barbara got up and made a pot of tea, and a bit later poured cups for the others. She had a little gadget called a liquid level indicator that she could hook over the side of the cup she was pouring liquid into and it would beeped when it got near the top of it. But she could never be bothered to use it, along with a lot of blind people, perhaps because it would always need to be washed up afterwards – not that it would ever take long at all. Or maybe it was simply that she was just in the habit of doing things in the way she always had before she was given it.

So instead, when she was making tea for herself, she would pour a bit of milk in first and check with her finger to find out if she'd poured in the amount she wanted, or whether she'd prefer a little bit more, and then she'd pour the tea, and would always put her finger about a centimetre into the cup, against the side of it to reduce the risk of accidentally pouring hot water over it, and take it out quickly when the hot water touched it, hoping she'd manage to take it out quickly enough that she wouldn't scald herself. Most of the time she succeeded.

When she was making tea for others, she'd just put what sounded like a decent-sized splash of milk in the bottom of the cup first, without checking to find out just how much there was, to eliminate the unhygienic look of her putting her finger in their tea twice.

She did prefer making tea from a teapot when she was making it for others, because it had cooled down a bit by the time she poured it, so she was less likely to scald herself than when she poured water straight from a kettle that had just boiled and it touched her finger. When she was just making it for herself, she poured the water into a big mug from the kettle, but she would turn it off a minute or so before it was due to boil so the water wouldn't be so hot. She never noticed a difference in the way it tasted.

She got each person she carried a cup of tea towards to talk while she was getting closer to them, so she could tell exactly where they were.

While they were drinking it, Jeff asked, "Barbara, why are there four dirty teaspoons next to your draining board? Don't you ever wash anything up? They must have been there since before Christmas!"

Barbara was embarrassed and replied, "Oh yeah. I forgot about those. But I think my room would be a whole lot messier than it is if I never washed up! I used them for something and then kept forgetting to put them in the washing-up, because I kept forgetting they were there. I wouldn't have forgotten if I could see, because I would have kept spotting them every time I went to the sink or looked at it, and that would have reminded me to do them, so I'd have washed them up by now."

Jeff teased, "Right! So can we take it that if you had a baby, you might keep forgetting it existed till it cried, because you wouldn't be able to see it was there?"

Barbara protested, "Oh Dad! Of course not! I can't imagine forgetting a baby, after such a life-changing event as having one!"

A bit later, Barbara said, "I had an embarrassing experience not long before Christmas. Someone lent me her cardigan because I was cold, and it was in a bit of a heap, so I wasn't sure which was the bottom and which was the top, and I felt both ends to try and find out, but they both felt the same! So it was a little while before I worked out which way up it went. I think she must have thought the situation was a bit awkward, because she called a friend of hers over to help, but thankfully I managed to work it out before anyone tried to intervene. She might have thought I was drunk, actually."

Tony teased, "And how much had you had to drink? Come on, admit it: You *were* drunk, weren't you!"

Barbara replied, "No, ... I'd only had One drink." Then she joked, "No alright, I'd sneaked round the back of the bar and nicked a whole barrel of beer, tipped my head back and opened my mouth – you've always said I've got a big mouth – and then I downed it in one! Then after I'd put the person's cardigan on, I put the barrel down over my head and walked back to my room with it there. I thought it would be useful if I bumped into anything; I wouldn't hurt myself so much; the barrel would kind of act as an extended crash helmet. Hey, maybe cyclists should all wear them. That way, if they fell off their bikes, they'd protect their upper bodies as well as their heads. ... Yeah OK, perhaps they could cut holes in them for their eyes first."

A couple of people in the room tittered. Tony said with a smile, "Hang on! If they had beer barrels over the top of them, surely they wouldn't be able to move their hands to use the controls on the bike, and then they'd actually be much more likely to fall off! So much for protection!"

Barbara replied with a grin, "True, good point!" They all laughed.

Tony Complains About Minor Mishaps and Other Such Things That Have Befallen Him, and Then More Humour Breaks Out

Then Tony grimaced and said seriously, "Actually, talking about food and drink and little mishaps, I went to a restaurant not long before Christmas with some people from my work, because they wanted us to go out together to celebrate. I had a suspicion I wouldn't enjoy it, but I went just in case it was better than I expected. It wasn't, so I'll know never to go again, especially since it was quite expensive!"

Becky asked, "Where do you work?"

Tony replied, "Oh, I don't do anything impressive. I work for the council, just doing stuff like forwarding emails that come into the main office to the relevant departments, and replying to ones about simple queries I know the answers to. Someone from a government department came to put speech software on the work computer I use, and thankfully it works with the program the council uses. Some blind people go for jobs but can't do them in the end because there isn't speech software that can work with the set of programs their workplace uses.

"But anyway, when I went out that evening, the first annoying thing happened before we even got to the restaurant! It was a cold windy night, and someone guided me there from the station – Becky probably knows about guiding already, so maybe I don't have to explain this, but you know, I mean with me holding their arm so I could tell where they were going and they could steer me past obstacles so I didn't crash into them; and they told me where kerbs and steps were, and whether the steps went up or down, so I didn't trip over them or fall down them.

"They did a good job of guiding me really – for some reason it was really crowded in town, and they guided me past all the people in our way and all the obstacles like lamp posts without banging me into a thing. That was good. I'm glad about that.

"The only thing was that since I couldn't anticipate which direction I was about to turn in each time we turned because I couldn't see where the people were in front of me, I found myself turning to the left and to the right suddenly every few seconds for over forty minutes. By the end of it I started to feel a bit dizzy and disorientated. So I asked the person guiding me if we were nearly there. They said we were, so I was reassured.

"But later I overheard someone we work with asking them if they'd had a good journey to the restaurant, and they said They'd been alright, but they thought I'd started feeling a bit feeble, since I'd started being a 'moany Tony', asking if we were nearly there. Flippin' cheek! I think they might have just said it for fun. I only asked once, and it wasn't a moan! I'd just started feeling a bit light-headed, and hoped it wouldn't get worse, so I'd asked in the hope of being reassured that we didn't have far to go, since I didn't have the advantage of being able to see how near the place we were, like they did. I didn't make any other complaints."

"That's unusual!" teased Barbara.

"You can talk! Come on, I'm not that bad!" responded Tony with a touch of irritation.

Then he continued, "Anyway, when I heard them accusing me of moaning, I thought, 'I'd love to be able to make you do the journey at a time when it's crowded with a blindfold on, being guided by someone else, so you can learn how it feels to do it without being able to see where you're going!'

"It hadn't helped that the wind was blowing a lot, blocking out some of the sounds from around me so I couldn't tell what was going on so much. That contributed to me feeling a bit disorientated. When you can't see where you're going and don't know how much longer you'll have to walk before you finally get to where you want to go, and you're not being stimulated by being able to see what's around you, and you can't even hear anything interesting, it can start to feel as if you're just hopelessly trudging down a monotonous road to ad infinitum! Actually, I've discovered it's nice when people tell me what's around me while I'm walking along."

Barbara grinned and teased, "So you didn't moan Then, but you want to have a good moan about it now? ... No, I'm only joking. Sometimes it's nice to get things off your chest, isn't it."

"Yes it is," said Tony. "It does irritate me when I get accused of moaning when all I've done is made some remark or asked a question! I suppose it's possible I do grumble more than the average person does on occasions, yeah. Maybe it's a bad habit of mine. But sometimes I'm just trying to find out information, and it gets mistaken for grumbling, like one day one of my work colleagues offered to guide me to the train station after work, which I thought would be nice, because I thought it would be quicker than if I just walked there myself, going quite slowly as I normally do to try to make sure I don't bash into any obstacles in the way, because my stick will hopefully hit them in time for me to realise they're there so I can sidestep them ... unless they're prickly bushes sticking out at chest height, and that kind of thing.

"Well, it turned out not to be quicker to go with them. Before we even left, it took longer than I expected. I'd put my coat on and was standing up to go when they asked me if I'd like them to walk with me. They said, 'Hang on, I'm just getting ready.'

"I assumed that must mean they were just putting their coat on. So I stayed standing up and waited, expecting to only be waiting for half a minute or so. But I didn't realise at the time that since it was winter, they put their gloves and a scarf on too, and they changed their shoes to walking ones. They fiddled around with a few things on their computer before shutting it down too. They didn't tell me they were doing all that at the time.

"Since it was taking quite a bit longer than I expected for them to get ready and I didn't know why, I asked them how long they were going to be, saying that if they were going to be a while I'd sit down again. Well, they didn't say anything helpful, like telling me how long they were likely to be or what they were actually doing. I found out what they'd been doing when I asked them later. At the time, they just said, 'Stop moaning!'

"I was annoyed, because someone who could see wouldn't have had to ask, if they were planning to walk to the station with someone else, but they'd just be able to see what the person was doing and make a silent judgment about whether they may as well sit down again, and they could have just done that without comment if they thought they may as well; so they might have been thinking worse thoughts about how long it was taking than me, but they wouldn't have got accused of moaning, and they would have understood what was going on and why things were taking so long!

"Anyway, on the way to the station, this person said, 'I'm just going to post a letter.' I said OK. I just assumed the post box must be right there. But they walked off. A couple of minutes later, when I found myself still waiting for them to come back, I realised the post box must actually be around the corner and on the next street! It's nicer to get more information about what's going to happen, instead of finding out the details after the event! You know, just that little bit more information would put your mind at ease! I think some people just don't think to tell you sometimes.

"Anyway, this person wanted to stop for a couple more reasons along the way, buying a few things, and I almost missed my train in the end! We had to do a bit of running at the last minute!

"They hadn't told me they were going to want to stop. It's fair enough if they needed to stop on the way; it's just that it would have been nicer if they'd told me they were going to want to when they offered to guide me, so I could have made a more accurate estimate of the time walking with them would take versus the time it would take me to walk on my own.

"I told them that the next day, but they just said, 'Well you caught your train, didn't you?' and told me to stop moaning again! It was annoying.

"Actually, some of my work colleagues went through this phase of wanting to get out in their lunch hour and get a bit of exercise ... only it turned out not to be exercise, and actually probably did them more harm than good, because they thought walking around the town would be good for them, but what with the pollution from the traffic, and the fact that they were walking too slowly for it to be exercise, I doubt it was."

Barbara smiled and said, "They wanted to walk instead of eat lunch? What were they on then, the no-food diet? Yeah, I bet you'd lose weight on that! You don't eat, but instead you walk; and then when you lose weight, you can tell everyone how healthy the walking must be for your waistline, and recommend they try it!"

The others chuckled.

Tony said, "Well, they weren't doing anything that drastic! They did really have a bit of food before they left. Or after they came back. Actually, if they were trying to get more healthy, they well-and-truly defeated the object sometimes, because there were days when they all decided to buy unhealthy food as a treat after their exercise. Sometimes they would skip the walk and just go for unhealthy food – not that I'm complaining!

"One day not long before Christmas, one of them invited us to their home after work, and they got chips for everyone, which was nice. But they gave them to us on plates with knives and forks, instead of still wrapped in the paper."

Barbara put on a mock posh tremulous voice and joked, "How shockingly bad-mannered some people are! Plates? It's like we're all suddenly regressing back to the Dark Ages! What is going to become of us?"

Tony grinned and said, "Shut up! I didn't say that was a bad thing. I think they just didn't buy enough packets for us to have one each, so it was a good way to share them. I was just going to say that I didn't realise they'd taken them out of the paper. They didn't say. One of them just put a plate in front of me and told me the chips were there and then spoke to someone else. Since I didn't know if the chips were still in the paper, but realised they must be on a plate because I'd heard it bang when they put it down, I put my hands over them all to find out, since I wouldn't have wanted to dig my fork in, only to pick it up with a ton of paper on it!"

Barbara joked sarcastically, "Oh, that would have been nice to eat! Salted paper! Yum!"

Tony smiled and said, "Well quite! Anyway, I think the others just thought I was being uncouth and bad-mannered. I got the impression that at least one or two of them, including the person who gave them to me, were a bit disgusted with my supposedly primitive manners! One said in this indignant tone of voice, 'Use your knife and fork!'

"I did after that. But then I disgraced myself again! I picked up what turned out to be a couple of really long chips on my fork, and felt around them with my knife to judge whether what I'd picked up was small enough to fit in my mouth. It was a bit big, but I thought it would probably just fit in it – yeah, don't say it, Barbara, I know I've got a big mouth. But it turned out that it didn't fit, and one chip wasn't firmly on my fork, so when I got it to my mouth, it fell off and bounced off the table onto my lap. There was a slight pause in the conversation. I got the impression people were disapproving, or feeling uncomfortable, wondering whether to say something, like asking if I'd like the chips cut up. I suppose they could have been quietly laughing at me though.

"Mind you, I've done things that would have looked worse than that! I remember at school, some of the meat they used to give us had horrible chunks of fat on it. But how were those of us who can't see at all supposed to know that any particular bit had a chunk of fat on it until we'd put it in our mouths? So when I discovered I had a big chunk of fat in my mouth, I would just take it out again and put it on the side of my plate ... or on the table next to it, because I wanted to make sure I didn't accidentally pick it up with my fork again and put it in my mouth again. But I suppose to anyone watching, it might have looked as if I was shockingly spitting my food out, and even dirtying the table with it! You know, it might not have occurred to them that they themselves could have easily just avoided putting it in their mouths in the first place, unlike those of us who couldn't see at all, so I was doing what I was doing for a good reason. If we'd had paper serviettes, I would have put the fatty stuff on one of those instead of on the table!"

Barbara laughed and joked, "Paper serviettes at school? What do you think it was, a posh cafe? Still, that would have been good, wouldn't it, spending our days in a cafe instead of at school.

"Actually though, I used to do the same thing with fatty meat. Maybe that's one reason why we were both on the bad manners table sometimes!"

"The bad manners table?" asked Becky.

Barbara replied, "Yes. It was a bit secluded from the other pupils. Anyone the staff thought had bad table manners and needed to be taught to have better ones, or perhaps just supervised by them in case we did something truly shocking, was told to sit there for a term or two. I don't think the manners of either me or Tony were ever improved by being there though.

"Mind you, at least neither of us did anything really naughty, like throwing an egg at the science teacher while she was on duty one evening supervising us all in the dining room, like someone did who was a couple of years older than me."

They giggled. Becky asked, "Why did they do that?"

Barbara replied, "I've got no idea! We all thought it was amusing though, ... well, except the science teacher, I expect."

Tony said, "It's funny how none of us ever came up with the idea of walking out of the dining room when the food was especially bad. Imagine a mass walk-out!"

Barbara giggled and said, "It probably wouldn't have been a good idea for us to have done that; we'd have just ended up going hungry!

"We didn't often have nice food at school, until the last couple of years I was there, when it massively improved, for some reason.

"I remember when I was about five at primary school, we were about to walk into the dining room for the evening meal one day when I got a bit of a tummy ache. I didn't say anything, because it was only mild, so I just wondered why it was there.

"It was going to be cheese salad for tea, which was by far my favourite one of the meals we had there, since I didn't really like most of them, and I was really looking forward to it, because we didn't have it very often. But I'd just sat down when I was unexpectedly sick in mine. They took me to the sick bay. I cried, mostly because I'd missed out on it, but I think they thought I was crying because I'd been sick. I was still crying a while later, because I was mourning the fact that I'd spoiled my favourite tea, and because I knew we were unlikely to have it again for ages, and I'd have to put up with food I wasn't keen on till then.

"A notoriously unsympathetic member of the care staff didn't ask why I was crying, but sternly told me off. There was a severely mentally handicapped girl at the school, and Miss Unsympathetic scolded me for crying for so long and tried to shame me by telling me that not even that girl would cry about what had happened for that long!

"That was ages ago now. It's funny what sticks in your mind."

Becky smiled and asked, "Did being sick in your food have anything to do with you being put on the bad manners table?"

Barbara replied, "No, I was on there at my secondary school.

"Actually, talking of manners, I once publicly disgraced myself when I was making an effort to behave with manners that were abnormally civilised for me. In our last year at school, a few of us were offered a bit of work experience, where we went out one afternoon a week to somewhere where we could help out a bit. ... Well, that was the idea.

"There were one or two weeks when I went to this day centre where old people would go and do activities and get the opportunity to chat to each other. There didn't seem to be anything for me to do where I could have been genuinely useful. Maybe befriending a lonely old person or two would have been something I could have done effectively, but I didn't get to do much of that, at least the first week I was there, when they were all due to watch a travel documentary not that long after I got there.

"They were going to have a couple of sandwiches and cakes afterwards. I was told to butter some scones and bread for them. Normally when I butter bread, I touch the end of the knife with the margarine on it briefly with my finger each time I take it out of the tub, just to check I've got the amount on there that I want. But I thought I'd better not do that in case they thought I looked uncouth and unhygienic. There were two staff members just standing at the table watching me. They could have buttered the bread and scones much more quickly and easily themselves, but they must have just thought they'd better give me something to do. So they asked me to do it. I felt self-conscious with them right there watching me all the time, as if they wanted to make sure I was doing it right.

"So I tried buttering the bread and scones without checking to see how much margarine was on the knife each time, just hoping for the best. Things seemed to be going well for a while, until ... there was one time when I accidentally got loads of margarine on the knife, and didn't realise till I put it down on a scone! I don't know why I didn't realise there was a lot more on the knife than there should have been as soon as I took it out of the tub, because I'd have thought the knife would have felt heavier than it should have been. But somehow it didn't, or else I didn't notice it because I didn't really have my mind fully on it any more because I was thinking about how I'd prefer it if the staff members weren't watching me so closely, and listening to their conversation; or maybe I was holding it for too short a time to really notice its weight before I put the margarine on the scone.

"Straight after I did that, the staff suggested I go and sit with the others and hear the documentary with them.

"I went to another day centre for a few weeks soon afterwards, for pretty severely mentally handicapped people. There wasn't much I could do there either, since the help was mostly focused on their practical needs and coping when they did unpredictable things.

"One day the boss told the staff in a meeting to give me things to do. Afterwards, someone went to the loo and made a horrible smell that wafted out into one of the other rooms in the building, and one of them gave me a can of air freshener and told me to spray it around. He could have done it easily himself, obviously, but it was just to give me something to do.

"You'd have thought it would have been one of the easiest things in the world to do; but I was reluctant to do it, because I was a bit worried that one of the mentally handicapped people or someone else might wander by at the very moment I was spraying it, and they might get a load in the face, or else I might accidentally spray it in the direction of where there was some food or electronic equipment, and a bit of it might go on it. It would have been different if I'd been in my own home."

Tony joked, "What, you mean you wouldn't have minded accidentally spraying it over Mum and Dad if they'd walked by at the wrong moment, or getting a bit on *their* electrical equipment?"

Barbara laughed and said, "Don't be daft! You know that's not what I mean! I mean I'd have felt more at ease doing it in a familiar environment where I knew where everything was, and things were more predictable."

Tony said, "Yeah, I knew what you meant really. Talking of unfamiliar environments, and things not being predictable, I'll tell you more about these walks my work colleagues did:

"They asked me if I'd like to go with them on them. I wasn't keen, but I thought I'd give it a go one day, to see if I felt better for stretching my legs. But I didn't like it at all! No one guided me into anything or forgot to tell me where kerbs were, so that was good, at least. And it was on flat ground most of the time so I wasn't stumbling over unexpected bumps in the road or anything. So it could have been a lot worse.

"But we went around places I'm unfamiliar with, and I didn't know what we were going past, or who was going past us. Perhaps I should have asked the person guiding me to tell me, but they wanted to talk about other stuff, which might have been nice if it was entertaining, but it wasn't. And then they started arguing with me about something, and because I didn't know where I was, I couldn't just walk away, because it would have been a struggle to find my way back to the office; so I just had to put up with it.

"I'd thought the walk was bad enough before the argument. I don't like walking in unfamiliar places with people for no good reason, especially when I don't know how long the walk's going to take, unless I'm being entertained while I'm doing it, or I'm walking fast enough that some adrenaline kicks in and I'm getting decent exercise so there seems to be a point to it, or if the person I'm with is at least telling me what we're going past. Otherwise, I can start feeling bored or even a bit disorientated after a while, because I don't know how long it'll be before we get back, and I don't really have much of a clue exactly where we are or what's around me.

"I suppose it might be like someone who can see trudging through a desolate desert, where the same bare landscape stretches as far as they can see; they walk for five minutes, and then they're discouraged, because the landscape hasn't changed at all, so they don't know if they're really any nearer their destination than they were when they started, or if they've been walking in circles, and that for all they know, they'll be doing that for the next half an hour.

"I'm not saying every blind person would feel the same way as me; I think some love walking, and if they were really chatty, they'd be so busy chatting, they wouldn't mind not knowing what they were going past or anything. I know I can be really chatty sometimes. But not with people I don't have so much in common with. And I don't like being like a captive audience for someone when they want to argue with me on a walk, because I can't realistically get away like a sighted person could!

"And I do like to at least feel as if I'm walking at a decent pace. Actually, I feel uncomfortable when I'm walking with someone who's going a bit slowly, like the person I was with was, partly because it's boring and I've got long legs so I like to stretch them, and partly because it makes me feel as if they can't be confident about guiding me if they're walking slowly, so I start feeling a bit uneasy, even though I know really that it might not mean they're not confident about doing it. Sometimes it might be because they assume I'd prefer to walk slowly. I suppose I might if I was worried they were going to bang me into things.

"Anyway, all that put me off going out walking with them again, so I said no from then on when they asked me if I wanted to go with them. The annoying thing was that I found out later that they'd started calling me lazy behind my back because I didn't want to go any more! They never asked me why I didn't want to go. They seem to have just assumed it was because I'm lazy, and they didn't say that to me, but bitched about me behind my back. That was irritating!"

Rita said, "That's a pity. But it's not all bad, is it. Don't give the impression that your life's just a heap of misery, and that people are always horrible to you. I mean, for one thing, when you're walking to work and to other places on your own, you do get a lot of people asking if you'd like their help, don't you, and you like that."

Tony replied, "Oh yes. It definitely isn't all bad. I don't really need help to walk to and from work, because I was taught the way there when I first started going there by someone who walked the route with me over and over again till I got it all into my memory; but it's still often nice to be asked if I need help, and I often accept, because it's more relaxing to be guided round all the obstacles like lamp posts and shop signs in my way, instead of having to concentrate all the time so I can discover them when I hit them with my white stick early enough to take evasive action. And actually, I do still get lost on occasions, say if I take a wrong turn accidentally or cross the road in the wrong place, not realising, and then discover I've done it when I start walking somewhere that doesn't seem familiar to me. It's sometimes hard for me to find my way back when that happens.

"But there are loads of nice helpful people out there! I must get asked if I need help an average of half a dozen times a day or more! People have even offered to carry heavy bags I've been carrying, even people who've sounded as if they were old and a bit frail. And people have walked with me sometimes for over ten minutes to help me get somewhere I needed to go. And I do work with some nice people who don't say bad things about me, as far as I know, and who've told me that if I need anything, they'll try to help. Thankfully, things are set up so I don't need any help most of the time, because I've got everything I use to hand, and I've got a computer to work on with an electronic voice on it like Barbara's. But yes, the world does seem to be full of nice helpful people. I'm not saying it's all bad at all."

Barbara smiled and joked, "Well, if you ever decide to give going for a walk with any of your work colleagues a go again, maybe you ought to try and think up entertaining things you can do when you're walking with them. I mean, maybe you could, say, put a load of mud in your shoes so your feet make squelching noises as you walk, and then you could say to the person guiding you, 'What are we walking on? It feels hard like concrete, but it sounds like mud! There must be mud on the ground that I can't feel, for some reason. Why do you keep walking me through mud? Is there mud all around here, or am I the only one walking through it? Actually, I can't hear You walking through it! I like the way you're making sure You walk on clean ground, while you're guiding Me through the mud! That's not very nice of you, is it!' "

They laughed. Tony said with a smile, "I don't think I'll try that one, thanks! I think walking around with mud in my shoes would be much worse than being guided around somewhere unfamiliar for no good reason without being entertained or told what's around me!"

Becky said, "Hey imagine if you were in a restaurant, and there was a waiter who couldn't speak English well, and some horrible mischievous person had told him that one English word for chicken was mud, so he came up to you and put a plate down in front of you, and told you he'd given you a mud pie or mud supreme. You'd think you were in for a worse time of it than you probably really had in that restaurant you started telling us about!"

Barbara said, "Hey imagine if two people were going out for a date in a restaurant, and they didn't know each other well, and the man was trying to make the woman like him more by saying things he hoped she'd like to hear, but he kept getting his words muddled up, for some reason; so he wanted to tell her he just loved the smell of freshly-cut grass, fresh home-made bread, and freshly washed and ironed sheets, but instead, he said, 'I just love the smell of fresh home-made grass, freshly washed and ironed bread, and freshly-cut sheets!' "

They laughed, and Becky said, "She'd probably think he was a loony! And imagine if he didn't even realise he'd said anything wrong, so he couldn't understand why she was shocked or surprised or puzzled by what he said, or why she laughed!"

Barbara Chuckled and said, "Or why she wouldn't go out with him on another date!"

Then the conversation began to turn more serious again for a little while, as Tony continued his tale of woe by saying, "I went out with a few of the work colleagues who liked to go for those horrible walks for a few hours one day before Christmas … not on a date, obviously, but just for a few pre-Christmas drinks and nibbles."

Barbara asked playfully, "Did you nibble any dates?"

The others sniggered.

But Tony carried on more seriously, "No. That could have been nice. But going there made me realise that I think a lot of sighted people tend to take a lot of things for granted. Actually, we probably all do that, including me. But I've got the impression that it just doesn't occur to some people who can see to think about what blind people are missing out on. ... Mind you, I think there are people who do the opposite and assume it's worse being blind than it really is, maybe because they wonder how they'd do anything at all if they were blind. Really, they'd probably be able to do more than they think they would after they got used to it, which might not take all that long.

"You know, at first, they might wonder, for example, how they were ever going to be able to even find their way around their own house if they couldn't see where they were going; but they'd soon learn to do it by just remembering where everything was, which wouldn't be hard, since they'd basically know where it was already. There might be quite a lot of things where they needed advice about how to find ways of tackling new problems; but there are people and organisations they can get advice from.

"But anyway, about people taking things for granted, I think that might have been partly what caused a misunderstanding I had with one of my work colleagues before Christmas. Like I said, she invited a few of us round to her flat for a few pre-Christmas drinks.

"We had a couple of drinks, and then she asked if anyone wanted coffee. We decided we'd have some, and everyone went in the kitchen with her while she made it and put a few cakes and things on plates for us.

"Well that was nice. But it was crowded, since it was a pretty tiny kitchen, with not much room for two people to walk past each other.

"I was standing in front of a worktop. I didn't dare feel around much to see what was around me, because when I put my hand out, I touched one of those glasses on thin stems that are easy to knock over, so I was worried that if I explored any more, there might be more things I could easily knock over. But I felt just enough to know that there were two big squarish objects in front of me on the floor under the work surface, which I assumed must be a fridge and a cooker. The kitchen was so small, there didn't seem to be room for anything else in there as big as that, so I assumed they were the only things under there. I wondered if maybe there was a gap in the work surface where the cooker stuck out the top.

"The work colleague whose home it was asked me to move so she could get to the fridge to get some milk. So that told me that the object directly in front of me was a fridge. I wasn't sure whether it would be best to step backwards and risk banging into the wall, or something that might be leaning up against it, for all I knew, or to move sideways and risk banging into someone else in there, since I wasn't sure I was quite far enough away from them to be able to step sideways without doing that, or whether there was enough room for me to step back far enough for her to be able to get to what she wanted without me banging into something. So I was a bit confused about what direction to go in. I decided to step sideways, since I thought that at least people could hopefully move quickly when they saw me coming, whereas walls can't.

"I didn't step on anyone, and she managed to get to the fridge.

"A few minutes later, I'd shuffled back to somewhere nearer where I'd been before. She asked if anyone would like ice cream. I was a bit surprised, because I assumed she couldn't have a freezer. But then I thought maybe she just had a small tub of ice cream in the freezer section of the fridge, and I wondered if she'd like me to move again so she could get to it.

But I thought it would have to be a Very small tub if it was going to fit in there with all the other things she might want to stuff in there if she didn't have a proper freezer, so I wondered if she was thinking of going out and buying some. So I asked her, 'Have you got some in the fridge?'

"She said, 'No, it's in the freezer.'

"I said, 'Do you mean the freezer section of the fridge?'

"She said, 'No, the freezer.'

"I said, 'Oh, so is your fridge a small one of those combination fridge freezers?'

"She said, 'No, it's just a fridge.'

"I said, 'Where's your freezer then?'

"She said, 'Under the work surface.'

"I said, 'I thought that was a fridge under there.'

"She said, 'There is a fridge under there.'

"I said, 'I thought you just said your freezer was under there.' There might have been a touch of impatience in my voice, since I couldn't understand how there could really be a fridge and a freezer and a cooker there, because the kitchen was so small.

"She got impatient herself, maybe because the note of impatience in my tone of voice irritated her, and she shouted, 'It is! If you'd open your ears, then you'd understand what I'm saying!'

"But the confusion was nothing to do with me not opening my ears. It turned out that there was both a fridge and a freezer under the worktop, separately, and the reason they could both fit under there was because she didn't have a cooker in the house, since she only ever used a microwave. Well I couldn't have known that. I just assumed there would be a cooker there, since most people have them.

"Anyway, I think ever since then, she's thought of me as being a bit nuts! ... Alright, don't say it, Barbara – I know what you're thinking – I Am a bit nuts."

The others sniggered.

Barbara giggled and said, "Maybe if you go round her house again, she'll give you some cakes that have all got nuts in, and that'll signify that she thinks they're especially appropriate because you're nuts."

Becky grinned and said, "Yeah, but it might just mean she likes nuts, and assumes you do. It would be awful if someone got into the way of thinking of reading too much into things, so, say, if she gave them a bit of fruitcake, they thought it must mean she thought they were crazy, so instead of thanking her, they got angry and stamped their foot and said, 'Are you suggesting I'm as nutty as a fruitcake?' "

Barbara giggled and said, "Yeah, or if she gave them a sausage roll and they said, 'Are you calling me a silly sausage, and hinting that you think I'm so lazy I can't be bothered to walk around much and just roll around everywhere all day? I've never been so insulted in all my life!' "

They laughed.

Becky, Barbara and Tony Joke About the Idea of an Eating and Drinking Course at University

Then Becky said, "Actually, thinking about being lazy and parties reminds me of something annoying my grandma said to me before Christmas. I know I shouldn't really criticise her behind her back, because I suppose it's not fair because she isn't here to defend herself ... that's if she Could actually say anything in her defence – and I do enjoy going round to Grandma and Grandpa's house a lot with my mum, and they do make us nice dinners.

"But I was with my best friends one evening one day before we broke up for Christmas, and we were having a few cakes together. My grandma wanted to talk to me, so she phoned my mum up and asked to speak to me, and my mum said I was out partying with my friends. When Grandma next saw me, she told me she'd phoned up when I was out, and she said, 'I'm not surprised you were out. I know all about you students, just doing nothing but partying all day! It must be a nice life!'

"I was annoyed! I'd spent most of my time for weeks slogging away reading psychology textbooks and writing essays, staying up way later at night than I suppose I should really! So it was annoying to think she thinks I don't do anything but partying!"

Barbara said, "She might have just been joking though."

Becky replied, beginning to grin as she went into joking mode, "I suppose so. After she said it though, I got to thinking: Imagine if there was a do-nothing course here, for people to prepare for times when they might be retired or unemployed and don't have much to do, so it was preparing them to do nothing all day in the most enjoyable way they could; so every day, they'd be encouraged to just relax and do nothing worthwhile, and then there would be do-nothing exams at the end of the course, where they'd get the highest marks for just lazily enjoying themselves, and anyone caught actually doing something worthwhile would be marked down.

"Mind you, it would be even better if it was a do-nothing and partying course, so anyone on it would spend every day lounging around and just feasting, learning how to do things like that in the most enjoyable way they could, and they had three years of practice just so they could learn how to party well, and then they would do partying exams, where they'd just stuff themselves with cakes and other party food for hours, just to make sure they knew how to do that with appropriate enthusiasm!"

Rita quipped, "Students would have to go on a weight loss course after that so they could try to get rid of all the excess weight they'd put on!"

Barbara grinned and said, "The party course would be good while it lasted though. Imagine it! A whole course that was just about partying! Maybe it would start each day in the early afternoon so people on it could sleep all morning, and first of all there would be wine tasting for two hours, then beer tasting for an hour, then savoury pastry tasting – you know, like sausage rolls and vol-au-vents and things, and then cake tasting for a few hours! And that would be the whole day filled up, and then you'd do just the same thing the next day! And the next day and the next!

"And maybe you'd taste things separately like that for the first week, and then you'd spend the rest of the three-year course practising enjoying all those things in the same session, and each session would last a whole day!"

Becky laughed and said, "As if people would need practice eating and drinking!"

Tony remarked, "You wouldn't want to just 'taste' those things; you'd want it to be a big-scale eating and drinking course."

Barbara grinned and replied, "Well, true, perhaps it could be a wine and beer-glugging course, for people who wanted to get better at drinking them faster than normal! The trouble is, if you were doing that all day, you'd probably be dead by the end of the first month! It would be more like a death course!"

They chuckled. Tony said, "Well alright then, maybe it could just be very enthusiastic tasting! The only problem would be that you might get so drunk from all the very enthusiastic wine and beer tasting that you might not really be able to taste the flavour of the cakes!"

Barbara said, "That's true! Mind you, it would mean they could put curry and chopped-up Brussels sprouts and vinegar and things like that in them, and you wouldn't mind!

"Imagine what your grandma would say, Becky, if she phoned you up in the evening when you'd spent the whole day wine and beer tasting and eating Brussels sprout and curry cakes, so you were raving drunk!"

Becky replied, "Yuck! I wouldn't fancy that! Hopefully the tutors wouldn't be so horrid as to put those kinds of ingredients in them! But if somehow I ended up on such a course and got drunk, if you were with me, maybe I'd hand the phone to you and tell you to pretend to be me!"

Tony said, "If Barbara was on the party course too, you might find it especially hard to get away with that, since she'd be drunk too! Imagine her saying, 'Yes, I Am Becky! I can't help it if you don't think I sound like Becky. All this partying I do on my party course must have made my voice suddenly go deeper. Tell you what: buy me more cakes! They might make my voice go back to the way it should be again, since I've just invented a theory that if you eat enough cakes, it makes your voice go deeper at first, but then if you eat more and more, there might come a point when they make it go back to normal again, like the way exercise can give you muscle pain at first so it feels as if it must be bad for you, but then if you keep it up over time, it makes you healthier. I reckon that must be the way it is with cakes. So I think I need more cakes to put it right.

Bring me more cakes! Then I might start sounding like the real Becky again!' "

Becky said, "Wow, imagine how fat I'd end up if I was eating cakes for hours every day on the party course, and then my grandma bought me a load more, because she was somehow taken in by that wrong-headed theory there! I really would end up having to go on a dieting course afterwards!"

Barbara joked, "Yes, that could be the equivalent of a higher degree course. You'd learn how to cut down on cakes gradually, till eventually you could do without them. So for the first year, you'd still be eating loads of cakes a day, since you'd be cutting down Really Really slowly."

They giggled again.

Becky said, "Yeah, and then imagine if instead of giving you cakes and other party food, the tutors started giving you pills that just tasted like those things, so they might give you a cake pill, and a cheese pill, and a chicken pill, and a sausage roll pill, and a vol-au-vent pill, and a trifle pill and so on, and you'd just suck each one for a while and swallow it, and it would contain any nutrients those foods contained, so you'd get all the benefit you'd get from eating those things for real, but none of the fat."

Barbara laughed and said, "Somehow I don't think you'd get many cake nutrients or sausage roll nutrients!"

They smiled.

Becky said, "Well there is that. But imagine if you could get pills for all kinds of other foods too, not to provide nutrients, but just for anyone who wanted to diet. So imagine if people could go to a posh restaurant and there would be a diet menu, and if you ordered from that, a waiter would just come and sprinkle a few pills on your plate, like a baked bean pill, and a pork pill, and a pudding pill, and a cake pill, and a rice pill, and a cucumber pill ... oh no you wouldn't need one of those, since they're so low-calorie anyway; but maybe there would be a vegetarian curry pill, and that kind of thing."

Barbara said, "I'm not sure they'd have baked beans in a posh restaurant. ... But just imagine if you wanted to eat more than one thing at once, and you accidentally ate the pudding pill with the pork pill, and the cake pill with the curry pill, and things like that!"

They laughed, and said things like, "Yuck!"

Becky said, "Imagine if someone invited a group of people out to a posh restaurant with them, and they all thought it might be nice, but what the person didn't tell them was that she thought they were all too fat, so she'd arranged for them to all have pills from the diet menu instead of food; so they got there, only to find the only menu on the table was the diet menu, and they had a choice of things like chicken pills and pudding pills and so on."

Barbara grinned and said, "It would be even worse if those pills didn't actually taste of the things they were pills of, but just had their nutrients in them, so you'd eat a pudding pill that tasted of nothing, and I suppose you'd just be meant to imagine you were eating something yummy while you were eating it, and it would give you whatever few nutrients a pudding might have!"

Tony Talks More About His Evening of Restaurant Mishaps

Becky smiled and said, "See, Tony, I bet that restaurant experience before Christmas you were telling us about could have been a whole lot worse than it was!"

Tony replied, "Yes, it probably could have been. I'm not saying it was that bad though. I just didn't enjoy it. If you want to know why, I'll tell you."

None of the others were sure they really did want to know why. But Barbara thought it might be worth the risk of encouraging him to tell them, just in case it was interesting, so she mumbled, "OK, go on then."

Tony said, "Well, the first thing that turned my restaurant experience slightly disconcerting was that I was cold when I got in there, but the person next to me was quite insistent that I should take my coat off, as if wearing a coat in a restaurant was an obscene indecency! Still, I'd only been sitting down for a few minutes when I decided I was brave enough to do that."

Barbara grinned and teased, "In an uncommonly heroic act of bravery, Tony takes his coat off! ... Actually, I know what you mean; I don't like the cold either."

Tony replied, "Yeah. Anyway, I thought I could always put my coat back on again if I got too cold. But the second I took it off – in fact, before I'd even finished taking it off, a waiter came and snaffled it – well I mean took it away and hung it up somewhere. I suppose it was a nice thought really, him hanging our coats up for us. But I was a bit taken aback, because he didn't tell me he was going to do that or ask if I wanted it done, and no one had told me he was taking coats, so the first thing I knew was that it was going sailing off to who knows where! I couldn't see where it had gone, and I was a bit concerned because I wasn't sure how to describe the colour of it for when I was asking someone to get it back for me later. I know roughly what colour it is, but I'm a bit vague about it. So I wasn't sure if I could describe it well enough for anyone to know which one it was.

"Thankfully the person who got it back for me when we left knew which one it was, so I didn't have the difficult task of trying to describe what it looked like when I've never seen it before.

"But when it got taken away, I hoped I wouldn't be cold. Thankfully I wasn't.

"Maybe it's just the norm in that restaurant for the waiter to take people's coats and hang them up somewhere, so he just assumed I'd expect it, and that's why he didn't explain what he was going to do, I don't know. But it was a bit of a surprise. And when I told the person next to me it had just been taken away and I wondered where it had gone, they ignored me at first! Perhaps they didn't quite hear me."

Barbara commented, "That reminds me of something that happened to me not long ago. I went to the doctor's for a blood test. Someone guided me to the surgery. At least that went smoothly. I sat down and took my coat off, and flopped the top of it backwards over the back of my chair, so the sleeves were hanging down just behind it on either side, and all I'd have to do when I wanted to put it on again was to slip my arms into them and then pull it up. I knew exactly where the sleeves were by memory, because it's something I've done lots of times before. But when I went to slip my arms into them, the person who'd guided me there pulled one side of it up, without saying a word to me, maybe assuming that would make it easier for me, since then the top of my coat would be nearer the top of me, where it would be if I had it on. But it meant the sleeve on one side was no longer where I'd expected it to be, and I spent several seconds feeling around for it.

"I think most disabled people prefer people to ask them if they want help, rather than assuming they're bound to and suddenly grabbing things of theirs. I know they mean well, but it would still be better for us if they asked first.

"I was at the doctor's another time with the same person to get a vaccine, and we were walking through the waiting room. I could tell there were loads of people there because lots of people were talking. The person I was with suddenly stopped, without explaining why, and grabbed hold of my white stick, trying to pull it out of my hand. I had no idea why she was doing it, and instinctively pulled it back. I asked her why she was doing it, and she said a nurse was there. That was only part of the explanation I needed. I asked the nurse if she'd come to do my vaccine, and she said yes. I was a bit surprised, since I hadn't expected the vaccines to be done in a crowded waiting room; I'd assumed everyone would go into a little room to have them done in private.

"I was being guided through a railway station with the same person not long afterwards to catch a train, and again, she suddenly stopped without explaining why. It turned out there was someone there who wanted to see our tickets. It would have been nice to have been told that at first. But perhaps she was so preoccupied with thinking about tickets that she didn't think to tell me, and it just takes a bit of practice to guide blind people properly.

"The same person was driving me to somewhere else once, and when we stopped to get out, she warned me there was a muddy grass verge outside my door that looked slippery. She came round to my side and opened my door. I got out, and was just beginning to propel myself forward when she put her hand on my arm – not hard – but it had the effect of counteracting my forward motion, suddenly stopping it in its tracks. That unsteadied me and I had to grab onto the car door for support so I didn't fall over. I asked her why she'd done it and she said she was worried I might slip. But putting her hand on my arm just at that moment had made it more likely that I would. I don't blame her; she obviously had good intentions. But again, it would have been nice if she'd asked me if I needed help rather than just assuming help was needed. Maybe it's that she looks after her little grandchildren a lot so she's used to doing little things for them."

Tony said, "It's a pity those things happened. Oh well, at least it's nice to know I'm not the only one those kinds of things happen to!

"In this restaurant, after the surprise with my coat, someone read me a few things on the menu, and I said I'd like a couple of things I thought might be nice ... or at least eatable for me, although I'd never had them before. But I don't know if she didn't read me the descriptions of what was on the menu, or whether it just didn't describe them well, but I ended up with something with fairly hot spice in when I don't like hot spices, although it was really nice apart from that. It was probably just as well I had a bit of alcohol to drink; I think that might have desensitised my pain sensors a bit so it helped me tolerate the hot spice.

"And for some reason, I was given my dinner on a little side plate; I don't understand why. Someone at the table kept refilling it for me. It would probably have made more sense if they'd just given me whatever it was they kept refilling it from to eat off, but perhaps that would have been shockingly bad manners, I don't know.

"But then when I'd eaten it, they told me I still had a bowl of rice to eat. I hadn't realised it was there. It would have been nicer if they'd told me about it earlier and mixed it in with the other stuff, or put some of the other stuff in the bowl, since the rice seemed pretty dry on its own. I asked if anyone had some meat they didn't want that could be mixed with it, and a couple of people put some in. My enjoyment was more important to me than the possibility of catching their germs at that point, possibly because of the alcohol.

"I'd just begun to eat it and enjoy it though when a twerp sitting near me started putting some stuff in my bowl and I didn't know what it was. Someone else asked him what he thought he was doing, and he said he was putting sauce in it. The other person said I might not like it, and the person sloshing it in merrily said, 'Oh he will!' Well it turned out that it completely ruined the rest of my dinner for me, and I didn't eat any more of it; it was this mega-sweet sauce that would have tasted sickly even on a pudding! If I'd been able to see what he was about to do, or if he'd told me, I could have stopped him before he did it! But I didn't get to do that.

"Then someone offered me some of his pudding, or the whole of it, to make up for me being put off my dinner. Not in the same bowl, of course, although I suppose it might have made the dinner taste a bit nicer by then if it had been. It was some kind of lemon sorbet. Thankfully it was less sweet than the sickly dinner sauce. I don't know how much of it if any he'd eaten before he gave it to me, but it was on this huge plate that was about six times the size of the one I got my dinner on! The pudding wasn't six times the size of it though. It could have been fun if it had been! It was quite small, but I don't know how much pudding was on there originally; maybe nearly enough to sink a ship. Perhaps he couldn't eat any more by then and was worried about not being able to fit through the door and get out of the restaurant if he tried, and that's why he gave it to me. But it was still nice of him.

"Either that, or maybe there's a weird custom in the more upmarket restaurants where it's considered classy, for some reason, if big dinners are put on little plates, and little puddings are put on massive ones!

"Still, I might have ended up pretty fat if the whole plate had been full up with pudding, especially because the day before, we'd had a bit of a do at work, being allowed an hour off at the end of the afternoon to eat sandwiches and cakes and have cups of tea and chat and things. It was quite nice, but the people who'd brought the plates in and had prepared the sandwiches and things and were going to do the clearing up and take their plates back home at the end had to catch trains so they didn't want us to sit around for too long, because they wanted to leave at the same time as normal and wash up before they left, so it was a bit rushed. So someone put some cakes in a bag for me to take home.

"That was nice. But they asked me which ones I wanted, and since I'd hardly had time to have any by then, I didn't know what was there, so I asked them. They were giving me a list of what was there, and I thought I'd wait till they'd finished before telling them what I wanted. Then they said there were mince pies. I said, 'Ooh, mince pies!' enthusiastically, thinking it was nice that they were back in the shops again. They must have misunderstood me and thought I just wanted mince pies and that was it, because they stopped telling me what else was there and said they'd give me some cakes, and just gave me several mince pies. I didn't realise what they were doing, since I couldn't see them, so I only found out when I got home. I enjoyed them, but it would have been nice to have had a variety of things. Some of the other cakes sounded nice."

Rita said, "Talking of food, shall we go and get some? Or maybe me and Dad could go and find some and bring some back here? I think I know where the burger bar is."

Barbara smiled and said, "Well if you realise you don't, just follow your nose!"

Becky joked, "The burglar bar. They sell roast burglar there. It's nice!"

They laughed.

Barbara and Tony asked for some chicken burgers and chips, and their parents treated Becky to some too.

When they'd gone, Tony said, "It'll be cosy eating dinner in here; we can carry on chatting easily. In this restaurant I've been telling you about, another reason I didn't enjoy myself was that I didn't get to have a decent conversation with anyone for the whole evening. The people on either side of me were turned towards other people having conversations with them I could only half hear, mostly because I couldn't hear what the people on the other sides of them were saying; and they must have been laughing at visual things that were happening a lot of the time, because what they were saying didn't even make sense to me sometimes! They seemed to be giggling away and referring to things I didn't even know were happening. Or perhaps they were just wildly drunk and talking nonsense!

"I could have started a conversation with someone next to me, but I thought I might be interrupting something, especially since I couldn't tell what they kept giggling about."

Barbara Admits to Having Behaved Badly One Evening

Barbara said, "I have that problem. Sometimes I'm with someone, but I don't know whether to strike up a conversation with them or whether I'd just be being a nuisance if I did that, because they might be reading something or playing a game on their phone, or occupied with something else. Or if they're eating, they might have just taken a big mouthful, for all I know. It can be a bit isolating really."

Then she cheered up and said, "But as for those people in the restaurant you went to, I wonder if they really were just talking rubbish. I think people Can talk nonsense when they're drunk, without realising it's nonsense. Well, I think I might have done that myself anyway. Of course, if everyone around you's drunk, you can be all talking nonsense with none of you realising you are, so you can all have a great time! It's just if there's a sober person there with you, They probably won't be enjoying themselves.

"But Saying daft things isn't as bad as Doing them! I can admit to this while Mum and Dad aren't here, although I'm not sure I should be admitting it in front of Becky."

"Go on!" Becky urged.

Barbara said, "Alright then. There's a priest here who takes Catholic church services every Sunday. He lives in a house about 20 minutes' walk from here. He has a party there every Sunday evening, where some people cook a nice meal for everyone, and people can drink as much alcohol as they like. Not long after I first came here, someone invited me there. I go there with some of my friends every week now, and the priest must have forgiven me for what happened, or else he doesn't know it was me, because he still lets me go there.

"I can't even remember what happened now, because I got so drunk it had blotted out my memories of the last part of the evening by the next day. But my friends insisted I was the one who'd done it. And I had a vague memory of having had a dream where I did something like it. But I can't understand how I could have done it; I wouldn't have thought I had the strength!"

Becky couldn't stand the suspense of not knowing what Barbara was supposed to have done any more. She grinned and said, "Come on, tell us what you did!"

Barbara replied, "Well alright. Hopefully I'd never do anything like it again! Goodness knows what I can have been thinking I was doing when I did it! Why on earth I thought it needed to be done, I've got no idea! And just How I did it, I can't work out to this day!"

Tony sniggered and said, "Come on, tell us what it was!"

Barbara said, "Alright. Well I've got no idea why, but I went to the loo at some point during the evening."

Tony sniggered again and joked, "You've got no idea why you went to the loo? What a shame you didn't do biology at school!"

Tony and Becky giggled. But Barbara grinned and said, "Ahem, if you actually want me to finish what I'm saying, as you keep saying you do, you'd better be quiet and listen!"

They went silent. Barbara said, "Well I do remember going to the loo, but I can't remember doing anything controversial in there. But maybe I did. It seems that for some strange reason, I decided to pretend I was doing woodwork, or demolishing something. I don't know. But maybe I banged the lid down again and again or something. It was only a thin lid. A few days later a couple of my friends told me they'd heard this banging coming from inside, and they'd asked me if I was alright, and I kept saying yes, and when I came out, they found out the lid of the loo was broken right in half! One bit of it had just fallen onto the floor!

"So either I broke it somehow, or one of *them* did and decided to convince me I'd done it, or else it was broken when I went in there, and they saw it when I came out and thought I must have done it. Maybe the banging was me knocking it onto the floor or something. I don't think *they'd* have done it though. Most people who go there are sensible and don't drink that much. I think I might try being sensible from now on!

"When I met my friends next and they told me I'd done it, I was embarrassed. But I thought a bit of bravado was called for, or maybe I just wanted a laugh, so the next time I went to the priest's house with them, I asked one of them to write, 'The Football Hooligans' Strategy Planning Headquarters' on a piece of paper and stick it up in the toilet.

"He did. But unfortunately the priest caught him doing it, and thought it must have been his idea! He must be a good friend to me, because he didn't say I'd told him to do it! Mind you, that might have made him look even worse, if the priest had asked him, 'Do you do Everything you're told to do?' But my friend just tried to quickly think of a way to convince the priest he'd just thought it would be a laugh to do it! I don't know what the priest thought in the end! But we still go there; he hasn't barred us from the house!"

Becky said, "Maybe there was already a big crack in the lid of the priest's loo from where some other hooligan had been banging it about for no good reason, and you just finished it off!"

They laughed.

Tony and Barbara Talk About Things They Can Find Awkward and Embarrassing on Social Occasions

But then Tony asked more seriously, “Do you genuinely enjoy going there, Barbara? I mean, I think social occasions can be awkward sometimes ... even if there Isn’t someone there who wants to break loo seats and things!”

The others giggled, and Barbara said she did like going there.

Tony said, “The thing is, when I was talking about what happened in the restaurant, I started wondering if Mum and Dad would say there are things I should probably have done differently to make the evening more enjoyable for me, like making more effort to start conversations. Maybe I could have done, although I explained why I didn’t; but it would be nice to think I could go out and relax, without having to worry about what I should and shouldn’t be doing to make sure I get something out of the evening.

“I prefer to talk to people one-to-one than to go out with people in a group or go to family gatherings at home, because if you’re talking to someone one-to-one, you get their full attention, so you don’t have to cope with feeling left out while people around you all talk to each other and you can’t hear what any of them are saying over the noise, or they talk about visual things like photos, or things you’re not interested in.”

Barbara replied, “Yeah, I know what you mean. I never have a problem like that at the priest’s house though. People are always coming up to me and talking to me, or some of us talk as a group, one person at a time. I’ve had some interesting conversations there.

"But I have had problems in other places. One of the most awkward things I find about some social occasions is that people come up to you and start chatting, or just say hello, and you might only have met them once before, or there might be several people there who sound alike, and you don't know which of them's saying hello, because you've only got their disembodied voices to go on when it comes to trying to work out who they are – disembodied because you can't see them – and they all seem to expect you to know who they are, and you feel a bit foolish and embarrassed about asking them, especially if you worry they might say, 'I was speaking to you only half an hour ago; don't you remember?' So it's a lot nicer if people I haven't met many times say their names when they come up to me so I know who they are."

Tony said, "Yeah, the same thing happens to me. The other day I was a bit embarrassed when someone I must have spoken to before but not for some time came up and said hello. I was embarrassed to ask her who she was, so I asked her how she was, thinking that if she told me more about herself, it would help me remember who she was. She started telling me about some problems she had, and I still couldn't remember who she was – I'd probably only ever spoken to her briefly before – but then I started feeling even more embarrassed about the idea of asking who she was; I mean, can you imagine telling someone about your problems, and then them saying, 'Actually, who are you?' It wouldn't sound very sensitive, would it!"

The others chuckled.

Then Barbara said, "It's just as bad when someone says something to you, but they're not close enough to you for you to be able to be pretty sure they're talking to *you*, so you don't know if they're talking to you or someone else! If you answer, they might say, 'I wasn't talking to you'. Actually that happened to me once! But if you don't answer and they *are* talking to you, they might wonder why you're not answering them! So it's nice if people can say your name when they come up and start a conversation, if they know it, so you know they're talking to *you*.

"I did once hear a blind woman say that when she was younger, she felt awkward when people did that, because she thought it must mean they were remembering she was blind every time they did that, and it made her feel self-conscious, because she just wanted to fit in inconspicuously with ordinary people; but as she got older, she started just wanting what would make her life easiest, so she preferred it when people did do that.

"It's also nice if people say goodbye when they get up and go. Sometimes I've said something, and there's been no answer, and it turns out the person's gone away without saying they were going. Or sometimes there's been a pause in the conversation and then I've been embarrassed to say anything else, in case they've gone and I discover I'm talking to thin air!

"I tell people who can see that it can help if people who don't know what my name is stand fairly close to me when they say hello so I'll be pretty sure I'm the one they're talking to, or if they think there'll be any confusion for some reason, that they touch me very briefly and gently on the shoulder when they begin to talk to me so I know it's me they're talking to, preferably with the flat of their hand. Some people poke me when they start talking to me, and I don't like that. It can sometimes make me jump a bit, since I can't see them coming. And it's uncomfortable.

"I've had people overdoing the touching in another way too. I went to this church for a while, and afterwards quite a few people who were probably just trying to be friendly would come up to me every week and squeeze my arm hard, or grab my hand and squeeze it in a painful grip when they said hello. I always found it a bit startling because I couldn't see them coming, so I couldn't brace myself for what they were about to do or predict it or move away, so I'd be thinking my own thoughts, when suddenly, Squidge! My arm or hand was being squashed! I was normally grumpy with them after they'd done that. They'd ask me how I was, and I'd think, 'I was fine till you came along and gave me a fright!' I didn't feel much like talking to them after they'd done that.

"Still, at least they were trying to be friendly. I've been to parties with family members, and they've gone off chatting to other relatives or friends of theirs, and I've found it awkward, because I've just been sitting there with no one to talk to, and no one's come up to me to say hello, and I don't want to move in case I knock something over, or in case I bang into someone and that makes them spill a drink they're holding or something; and I can't just get up and leave the place, because I don't know the way home from there. And I can't see where the family members I came with are, so I can't just go over and talk to them, even if I do risk getting up and walking around.

"Or even if I can hear them and I know they're close by, but I can't hear what they're saying because lots of people are talking at once, so no one conversation sounds distinct enough for me to hear, I normally still don't want to risk getting up and going over to them so I can hear theirs, especially if there are so many people talking I'd have to raise my voice and embarrass myself by feeling as if I was making a bit of a scene, saying I'd like help getting over to them without banging into anyone, which I especially don't like doing if I can hear kids playing in the place where I'd have to walk, who might have to interrupt their game and move themselves and their toys to let me past if they don't want to risk being stepped on, because I can't see to step over whatever's in the way.

"I'd hate to knock into someone holding a drink, or step on a child's precious toy that might be there for all I know, or bash one of my knees on a coffee table, or kick a glass over or something, while I'm going over to talk to someone I can hear; and even if I don't think there are many things in the way between me and them, I still won't know if there'll be any spare seats near them when I get to them, or whether I'll have to stand near them and end up being in people's way, because I'm in a place some people want to walk in to get somewhere!

"So I tend to stay where I am. But then I can feel as if I'm isolated and just stuck somewhere when I don't want to be.

"Sometimes people I know stand near me talking to each other, but they've got their backs turned to me so I can't hear what they're saying above the noise. And although I wouldn't have to go far to be near enough to them to join in their conversation, I tend to just stay sitting where I am, at least if I've got a drink and a flimsy paper plate of food, since if I stood up with those things and bumped into someone at some point during the conversation or while I was walking up to them, everything could go on the floor.

"Besides that, holding a flimsy plate in one hand, a drink in the other and attempting to eat at the same time seems like quite a challenge. I don't know what the others do. I won't be able to see if there's a table or some other space I could put my drink on near the people whose conversation I'd like to join in with, so things could be awkward if there isn't one.

"And I wouldn't want to leave my drink under my chair and come back for it later, since it could be a bit of a faff to find it again, at least if I'm not familiar with the layout of the house the gathering's in; and besides, someone might have kicked it over by then! So I tend to think I'd better make a choice between eating and drinking and socialising.

"And of course, I can't entertain myself by looking at what's going on around me, such as kids playing with toys. So I often end up feeling bored and under-stimulated for hours. I'd rather be in my room by myself where I can at least do my own thing, like listening to comedy or browsing threads on Internet forums. Having food improves things a bit while I'm with the others; but it would be a lot nicer if I had someone to chat to as well. Ironically, if I do spend time by myself instead of going to these family gatherings, I get accused of being antisocial!

"Sometimes instead of chatting, they put the telly on, and watch a film that normally isn't to my tastes, and even if it was, I wouldn't be able to follow it well, because I can't see what's going on, so I don't know what's happening during bits where there's no talking. For instance, if there's a shoot-out between a gang and the police, I won't know who's being shot. I could ask someone to explain what's going on, but since I don't normally like the films, I don't really see the point, and it might spoil their enjoyment of them anyway. But sitting through them can make me feel bored as well.

"Sometimes when I'm with the family when one of those gatherings is about to start and some of them are chatting, I go near enough to them to find out what they're talking about and whether it's something I might like to join in with, and they're oohing and ahhing over photos I can't see, or talking about people I don't know, and I just hang around in the background to see if the conversation will get interesting enough for me to want to listen to soon. I've got to find some way of entertaining myself! I've tended not to actually go up to them because I haven't known whether I'd start finding the conversation interesting enough to stay for or not, or whether there might be objects between me and them I'd bang into, or even whether there's a spare seat near them it would be easy for me to get to.

"It never occurred to me that it might be a problem for anyone before, but not long ago I discovered some of them were being horrible about me behind my back, accusing me of spying when I did that, as if I somehow haven't got the right to listen in on family conversations that are going on in public for all to hear! So I'm going to avoid those extended family gatherings where I can from now on.

"And at the end of an afternoon or evening at one of them, where I've mostly been sitting on my own feeling left out, I've had my family members coming back and asking me if I enjoyed myself! And chances are they'll think I must have some kind of attitude problem if I don't sound enthusiastic! They might say, 'You're hard to please, aren't you!', as if they imagine my experience of the party's been just the same as theirs, so they can't understand how I can't have enjoyed it! But it seems they don't give me much of a thought while those things are actually going on.

"A nice thing happened when I was somewhere different though. I was on a holiday that was organised for blind and partially-sighted people, where there were volunteers who'd come to help, and I was sitting somewhere where I couldn't quite hear any conversation that was going on one evening, and someone who was experienced at helping blind people came up and offered to guide me to where there was a spare seat in the middle of people who were chatting. It was a lot nicer once I was there.

"It's interesting though: I've never had a problem like that here. And I've never been to a party here where they've played really loud music either, although there Are parties like that here, for people who like them. I know some blind people like that, but maybe just when they're dancing. It can be like being deaf as well as blind when the music's really loud and you're just sitting there, even though you can hear it blaring, because it drowns out almost all other sounds, so you can neither see nor hear what's going on around you or where your friends are, and you can't enjoy a conversation. So there can be a crowd of people in the room, but you can just be sitting on your own – or feeling like you are – just feeling isolated."

The Mood Improves as The Little Group Gets Something to Eat, and They Start Making Jokes

Becky said, "This conversation's getting depressing! Shall we ..."

She didn't finish her sentence, because just then there was a knock on the door, and Barbara and Tony's parents came back in with some nice food for dinner. The group immediately cheered up, and They all started eating it happily.

Barbara said, "Hey imagine if you could get lion burgers and tiger burgers! How would you like to eat those?"

Tony replied, "I'd love it! The more lion burgers and tiger burgers they made the better! I can't understand for the life of me why anyone wants to preserve creatures that eat people! Do they look pretty or something? It would be nice to eat them instead! The sooner they get rid of them all from the world the better, in my opinion! ... Mind you, I wouldn't fancy being the one to have to catch them!"

They chuckled, and Barbara said, "No one would have to catch them; people would just shoot them! ... Or at least I hope they would! Imagine someone trying to herd a whole load of lions into a huge lorry to take to the slaughterhouse! And then imagine them getting them all out near your house, if you lived near it!

"But anyway, if companies started making lion burgers out of them, and they were popular, lions wouldn't disappear; the companies would start breeding them intensively to kill them for food, and before long there would be loads and loads of them!"

Tony replied, "I suppose you're right. Yikes! But imagine if farmers tried to turn lions and tigers vegetarian by making them all eat grass, in the hope that they wouldn't have to hunt animals to feed them on, and they could keep them safely near human habitations!"

They giggled, and Becky said, "I'm pretty sure that wouldn't change their instinct for eating flesh; and scientists would have to genetically engineer super-long, ultra-fast-growing grass if they were going to be able to eat enough to fill themselves up!"

Barbara joined in, "Yeah. And then just imagine if the leader of a group of ramblers said to the group one day when they were out, 'We're coming up to a field of lions now, and we're going to go through it; but don't worry; look at all that long grass; they're obviously being well-fed. And I'm confident you're all fast runners anyway, because of how fast you all ran when I accidentally led you into a field that turned out to have a bull in it that time!'

"Imagine what it would be like trying to run through really really long grass; I suppose it might be like trying to wade through the sea!

"And just imagine if people thought the long grass looked beautiful and started growing it in their gardens! When a husband and wife were getting ready to go downstairs in the morning, the wife might say, 'Can you cut the grass today, darling? It's blocking out the light from all the rooms in the house! I opened the curtains just now, and the room didn't get much lighter than it was before!'

"And the husband might say, 'I don't think I'm going to be able to cut the grass, sorry. That's partly because I can't find the lawn mower! Last time I cut the grass, I left it in the garden, and later that day I went out, and I couldn't see it anywhere! The grass had grown up so tall so quickly around it that it completely obscured the view of it, and I couldn't work out where it was! I've been out looking for it several times since, but I've never been able to find it!'

"And just imagine if a mum one day said to her children, 'Would you like to go out and have a picnic on the grass?'

"One of them might say, 'Do you really mean *on* the grass? Just supposing we somehow managed to climb up to the roof and then stepped Onto the grass, we'd very quickly fall Into it, and within seconds we'd be underneath most of it!' "

They chuckled .

Then Barbara said, "You know, isn't it funny how the words hyacinth and hyena are quite similar. Imagine if hyenas were bred to be put in burgers too, and they were considered to be a bit of a delicacy, as burgers go; and one Valentine's Day, a man said to his wife, 'I think it would be nice to get something a bit special like some hyenas for when we have a romantic meal on Valentine's Day', and his wife was sure he must mean hyacinths, so she said, 'What a lovely idea! I'll get a nice vase out the cupboard to put them in, and then we can put them on the table.' And he said, 'A vase? How would they ever fit in a vase? And why would you ever want to put them in one? I'm hoping to be able to fit them in the freezer!'

"And his wife would say, 'Why would you put hyacinths in the freezer? Surely you'll want them out on the table where everyone will see them!' "

Tony chuckled and said, "Well that would be better than if the hyenas were still alive, and the husband expected his wife to kill them and prepare them for dinner herself, so one Valentine's Day he suddenly let a pack of them into the house!"

They all giggled, and Rita said good-naturedly, "You're mad, you lot!"

Becky Tells the Others About Something Interesting She Heard About a Scientist Who Discovered He Had the Brain of a Psychopath

Then Becky said seriously, "That reminds me of something I heard on the radio. There was this neuroscientist who said he'd discovered he had a lot of the same genes that psychopaths have. He looked at his ancestry, and discovered there were famous psychopaths in it. He'd been adopted by a different family. He said he thought the reason he hadn't turned into a violent psychopath himself might have been because he'd had a very loving upbringing, and that people are more likely to turn into violent psychopaths if they've experienced cruelty themselves.

"But he said there had always been things wrong with him all through his life that his family had told him about. He said he'd had problems with getting more angry about things than he should have done, and also, he didn't have any sense of danger, so he sometimes did reckless things that were actually stupid, but it didn't occur to him at the time that they would be. He said once he'd taken his children for a walk in a forest where there were lions! He'd just thought it would be fun. It was only afterwards when his wife got upset with him that he realised he shouldn't have put them in danger like that."

The others thought that was interesting and surprising, and they became thoughtful and quiet.

There was a pause in the conversation for a little while, while they thought about that and then finished enjoying their food.

Tony and Barbara Complain and Joke About More Mishaps at Parties, and Unwanted Christmas Presents

When Tony had finished, he said to his mum and dad, "You know, while you were getting the food, me and Barbara and Becky were talking."

Barbara was worried for a few seconds, wondering if he was about to tell them what she'd said about how she'd mysteriously broken the lid of the priest's loo in half. But he didn't.

Their mum quipped, "Knowing what you're like, I'd be very surprised if you hadn't been talking!"

Tony replied, "True, I suppose. We were just talking about how some situations can be more awkward when you're blind. I was just thinking that I'm glad you got our food for us instead of us having to worry about doing it ourselves. Thanks."

His mum said that was OK, and then she and their dad decided to go off and explore the university for a while. They asked Tony if he'd like to go with them, but he said he'd prefer to stay and chat to the others. He quipped, "Sight-seeing isn't much fun when you're blind."

His mum protested that she could tell him what was around, but he said he'd still prefer to stay with the others, so the parents went out on their own.

After they'd gone, Tony unwittingly dampened the mood again by saying, "I've got food-related awkward situations on my mind at the moment, after we were talking about them before. Another one at those buffet-type parties, which I bet you've had too, Barbara, is when someone asks us what food we want, and we don't know because we can't see what's there, and they don't know either because they can't see it well either till they go up to the table it's on, so they can't tell us. We're most likely to get what we really want if we go up there with them, so they can tell us exactly what's there and we can say yes or no to each thing as we're going along; but both we and they sometimes aren't keen on the idea, because if they guide us there, get our food, and then have to guide us to a seat past all the people standing there holding food who we might worry about banging into, while they're carrying our plate and their plate as well, it can be a bit awkward, although maybe not as awkward as they might think.

"I mean, they might not realise we'd only have to hold their arm on the way back, so they could still hold two plates and guide us at the same time; or if the space between people and things is narrow for a while, if they put their elbow behind them a little way, it's a well-known signal to a blind person someone's guiding to walk behind them. I'm not sure if you know about that, Becky?

"Anyway, another thing I think a lot of people don't know is that when they get to their places, it won't have to take that much effort to show the blind person where their chair is; a good technique is to put the plates down and then put the blind person's hand on the back of their chair so they'll know where it is – or they'll at least know where the back is and be able to imagine where the rest must be!

"I told someone that the other day after they guided me somewhere and told me there was a chair there but didn't say exactly where. It turned out it was in front of me, but I assumed it was behind me, because I could feel something solid behind my knees, and they'd guided me to chairs that were just behind me before; so I just sat down, and I ended up accidentally sitting on a low table! I suppose it's a good thing there wasn't a plate of cakes on it or something! I wouldn't have fancied going around for the rest of the day with squashed cake all over my backside; and I don't suppose they'd have wanted to eat cakes after I'd sat on them either. But thankfully that didn't happen!

"The technique of putting a blind person's hand on the back of a chair so they know where it is is similar to another one, where if a sighted person guides a blind person to a car they want to get in, if they put the blind person's hand on the open car door, or the door handle if the car door's closed, they'll know both where it is and what way round the car's facing, so they'll know which way round the seat is that they're expected to sit on after they get in, and what kind of distance it must be from where they're standing.

"I'm not sure if you already know this, Becky, but another thing is that if there are steps, someone who's blind but can walk well and is being guided by someone else will cope with them alright, as long as the person guiding them tells them when they're just in front of them, and also lets them know whether they go up or down. I've been guided by quite a few people who told me there was a step just in front of me, but didn't say whether it went up or down, and I had to ask them quickly before we took the next step!"

He said in a bit of a tongue-in-cheek way, "I hope you don't make that mistake when you're guiding Barbara. Still, I haven't heard her complaining, and knowing how much she likes to complain, I expect I would have done if you'd caused her to get an injury."

Barbara responded, "Cheek! And this coming from the person who's been doing most of the complaining in the room today! You moany Tony!"

Tony said, "Oy, don't call me that! Right, just for that, I'm going to do a bit more complaining. ... Actually I feel like doing it anyway. I think it's because we've just had Christmas so this stuff about social occasions has been bugging me just recently. I know some of it's pretty trivial really. It's just a niggly thing that's been on my mind. I just feel like saying that I'm being put off social occasions, and one of the reasons is this thing about getting food. If someone guides you up to where the food is at a party, so they can tell you what there is so you can choose what you want yourself, it might sometimes seem like a bit of a hassle, as I said. It is nice in some ways when they do that.

"But one problem I've discovered is that if someone does kindly offer to tell you everything that's there so you can choose what you want yourself, if you wait for them to list everything before you say what you'd like, you might well have forgotten some things you'd like by the end of it; but if you tell them what sounds nice enough to have as they're going along, your plate might be full while there's still a lot of food on the buffet table, so they might not tell you about the rest, and the food that you haven't found out is there yet might actually turn out to have been nicer than the food you've said you want, for all you know! If you'd known about the other food, you might not have said you wanted what you said you wanted.

"One option would be for them to tell you everything that's there first, and then go through it again for you to say what you'd like; but that'll inconvenience people if there's a queue behind you.

"It's really good if someone manages to list everything there is there by memory while you're sitting down, and then gets what you want for you. But I don't think that's normally easy. And it can't really be easy for people to guide you with your food through a crowd either, carrying both your likely flimsy plate and theirs. But if they just get your own food while they're guiding you, and go back to get theirs when they've guided you back to your place, they might end up at the back of the queue again, and that won't be fair on them!

"There was one time when someone tried to solve the problem by sitting me right near the food. But the people I knew there were sitting somewhere else, and no one came up to chat to me for the whole afternoon, so I was bored.

"I did once hear about a blind man who thought he'd been ignored the whole time at some church event, but someone later told him people had been nodding or waving to him in greeting as they walked by. They must have somehow all forgotten he wouldn't be able to see them. Collective selective amnesia! So I don't know if anything like that was going on when I was sitting by myself all afternoon.

"Sometimes people's solution to the food problem is to just go up by themselves and get you a selection of what's there, asking you what you don't like so they can avoid it. But often you still end up with stuff you don't like much, and you find out later you missed out on stuff you love that you didn't know was there till it had gone."

Becky said, "That's a shame. I'm not sure what the best thing would be to do about it. Still, it would all pale into insignificance if you were being guided back one day and a Lion started chasing you!"

Tony grinned and joked, "Well there is that! You never know what those naughty vicars are going to get up to nowadays: 'Let's have a little get-together in the church hall!' they might say, not telling you they're planning to invite the lion from the local zoo!"

They all laughed.

But then Tony got serious again and said, "The thing is though, yeah, this thing about parties isn't a big problem. It's still a bit of a pain though!

"It's not always much better if you tell people what food you like and don't like and they go and get it for you, because you can still end up with things you don't like, because you didn't expect them to be on offer there so you didn't mention them; or the person getting food for you can be over-cautious and you miss out on things you like, say if you tell them you don't like tomatoes, and they go up there and see some pizza, but don't get you that because they think you won't like it because it's got tomato somewhere in it, but really you love pizza. You have to be so precise if you want to try and avoid that kind of thing happening, like saying, 'I don't like those big globby slimy seedy bits in the middle of a tomato, unless they're thoroughly mashed up and mixed with lots of other ingredients, say in a pizza, or if there are just a few slivers of them hanging onto the less tangy outer bit of the tomato in an otherwise nice mild cheese sandwich.'

"The trouble is, the other person's never likely to remember all that!"

Barbara grinned and said, "Yeah, plus it would take so long to say all that, the food might have run out by the time you'd finished!"

Tony replied, "That's true. Anyway, I suppose getting things you wouldn't have chosen if you could see what was there is a lot better than getting nothing at all. It wouldn't be nice to be forgotten altogether!

"Well, I say that, but I can't always be sure. On one social occasion I went to, the person in charge asked me if I wanted some food, and I said yes, and they didn't tell me what there was so I could choose or anything, but they just got me some stuff and plonked it on my lap, and then just turned to go away, without even telling me what they'd got me! I asked them, but they sounded a bit irritated to have to turn back and tell me."

Barbara grinned and joked, "I hope they actually put a plate underneath what they gave you! You don't mean they just plonked the food straight on your lap, do you? So there might have been cream cakes, and potato salad and stuff, going squelch, right onto your lap, getting all mixed together! Yum!"

They all laughed. Tony said, "No, thankfully they didn't do that! Alright, thinking about it, it could have been a lot worse than it was! They did at least give me a plate.

"Mind you, it was still a bit weird. They didn't really give me a very good description of what they'd given me when I asked them what they'd got me. They told me a sandwich they gave me was cheese, but when I took a mouthful, I discovered that yes, it was cheese, but it was also some kind of unidentifiable paste, and lots of sweetcorn. I've never had sweetcorn in a sandwich before! Thankfully, it was nice though.

"I didn't realise there was any stuff there that I would have liked better, so they asked me if I wanted some more when I'd finished what I had, and I said yes, thinking they'd probably get me the same kind of things, most of which were at least fairly nice. I liked the idea of another sweetcorn and cheese sandwich! But I didn't get another one. Instead, the sandwiches turned out to be different! Again, the person just plonked the food on my lap, ... well, the plateful of food anyway, and just walked away without telling me what they'd got me.

"One of the sandwiches they got me was a bit of a strange mystery! It seemed to be a mixture of sweet and savoury stuff. Nothing to do with sweetcorn though this time. Maybe cheese, but something else that I thought at first might be chutney, because I think that can be a mix of sweet and savoury things sometimes; but then as I took more and more mouthfuls, I began to wonder if it might be too sweet for that, so maybe the sandwich was some kind of weird concoction of cheese, and maybe even cake icing that someone in a semi-drunken state might have just decided to fling in it on a whim while they were preparing it! Maybe not, but goodness knows what it really was! I didn't enjoy it anyway!"

They chuckled, and Becky said, grinning, "Yuck! Hopefully people don't invent weird concoctions like that on the spur of the moment while they're a bit drunk at too many parties!"

Barbara grinned and joked, "Cake icing and cheese sandwich! No wonder they didn't admit to what they'd got you!"

Tony said, "Well, I don't know what it really was! I certainly wouldn't have had it if they'd given me the option of having it or not, instead of just giving it to me!

"Actually, one thing that puts me off these social occasions is that if someone gives you a plate full of savoury stuff, and you don't like some of it, but you think you ought to eat it out of politeness, or some of it's alright, but it isn't really any nicer than the kind of thing you eat routinely, you can end up feeling quite full after you've eaten it, so if later you discover there are things there that you really like the idea of having, you can realise you feel too full to eat them! It's annoying!

"Even if you're sitting right next to the food so you're close enough to hear the person who's getting you some telling you what there is as they're going along, you can still end up with things you don't want, because they might not describe them that well, say if they tell you there's pizza and you're really pleased, but you don't find out till you've bitten it that it's got that spicy pepperoni on it or something, which you don't like. That kind of thing happens to me sometimes.

"I went to this get-together for people in my office recently, and someone came up to me and said, 'One of each?' I thought, 'One of each what?' She said she meant sandwiches. Well I didn't know what was there, so I asked if she'd go and see and then tell me, so I could decide what to have. She said she would, but she came back with a plate of one of each after all. She opened each one and gave me an idea of what was in it. I wouldn't have had two of the ones there if I'd been given the choice before she brought them, but since she had, I thought I may as well give them a go.

"Well to my surprise, one had pickle in it. She didn't tell me that, so I didn't know till I bit it; and then, the unwelcome spectre of my old schooldays suddenly intruded itself into my mind! I don't like pickle and wouldn't normally have it. The last time I did was at school when we used to have sandwiches on

Sunday evenings to give us a break from the normal pigswill rejects they gave us. Actually I don't know if Becky knows, but me and Barbara went to special boarding schools for blind and partially-sighted people, where they taught us in braille and we did our work in it and so on. I don't know how many of those will be left soon, since blind people often get sent to mainstream schools now.

"Anyway, I was immediately reminded of my yucky school-days when I bit that ham and pickle sandwich at the party. Schoolday memory sandwich! Ugh!

"And then I tasted another sandwich, some kind of prawn thing, and it tasted as if it had been scraped off a toxic waste dump! I still ate it though. Actually I ate both sandwiches quickly. People probably thought that meant I really liked them, but actually it meant I was trying to get the experience of eating them over with as soon as possible. I mean, it took a bit of bravery to eat them, and I knew my bravery was only going to hold out for so long!"

He grinned, and continued, "Also it was partly in the hope that someone would see I didn't have much food left and put something nicer on my plate. I know I didn't have to eat them, but also it seemed a shame to waste them, even if one of them Was toxic waste, because some people might have liked them if I hadn't had them, so they might have been unhappy to see them wasted. You know, some people might like sandwiches that taste as if they've been scraped off a toxic waste dump!"

Unfortunately for Tony, his parents had come back in during the last of what he was saying. He knew they must have done because he'd heard the door open, but he'd wanted to finish what he was saying before greeting them, and they hadn't wanted to interrupt. But then His unamused mum said, "You are rotten sometimes! I'm sure people do their best!

"I know it's not very nice when things don't go to your liking, but don't forget that far more things are going right in your life than are going wrong: You've got warmth, shelter, a talking computer so you can browse the Internet and work on things, nice music to listen to, people to chat to, nice food ... most of the time, enough to drink, and people who are willing to help you, even if they don't get it quite right all the time! I bet things go right for you a lot more than they go wrong."

Tony went slightly red in the face and said, "Oh I know! I know there are a lot of things I ought to be grateful for. And I'm not really criticising anyone. I just don't like the way I'm at a disadvantage sometimes, at least compared to the people around me; and every so often it's nice to get things off my chest. I'm just getting more and more disillusioned about going to events like the ones I've been talking about the more this kind of thing happens, so I think I might stop going to them.

"I remember going to Christmas parties when I was little that I enjoyed. I think they were run by an organisation for blind people, but I can't remember who they were. But those parties were nice. I think all the food was already on our tables when we sat down for tea, and a sighted person was at each table to help us and tell us what there was, and they gave us things a few at a time, so we didn't have to get everything at once. Either that or people came round with plates of each type of food every so often and offered us things. So we didn't have problems like missing out on food we like because we went up to a food table with someone to get our food and our plates were full by the time we discovered there were things we really liked there. And we always had people to talk to while we were eating, because it was prearranged that we would all sit in little groups at the tables.

"Anyway, I really liked the other sandwiches I had at the event I was talking about when you came in. It would have been nice to have had more of those instead of the schoolday delight and mercury magic ones, or whatever they were."

Risking being rebuked by her mum herself, Barbara said, "I remember at school we had a meal that we all hated; we were sure it was just made of old leftovers; we called it dustbin delight, or YMCA flan – YMCA standing for yesterday's muck cooked again. Things would have been even worse if another meal was bad enough to have been nicknamed toxic waste dump sandwich!"

Tony and Becky chuckled. Tony said, "The get-together where I had that was even worse, because I got a cold a couple of days after it, and I'm pretty sure it came from a germ I caught from either the person who went and got the sandwiches for me, who I did hear sniffing once or twice, or the person who made them! Or I suppose someone could have sneezed over all the food on the table before anyone got any and given us all colds!"

Barbara put on a posh solicitous voice and said for fun, "Would you like a germ sandwich, sir?"

They giggled.

Rita and Jeff then explained that they'd come back so soon because they'd seen some books in one of the departments they'd become interested in browsing, but they were in such small print they needed to come back to get their glasses before they could. They got them and went out again.

Then, feeling freer to speak his mind, Tony complained, "I had another problem at that work event I was talking about when Mum and Dad came in. There's a tradition in my office where everyone gives each other Christmas presents. I wouldn't be surprised if most people think it's a pain, but it just carries on because no one wants to look like a meany by saying they'd rather not do it.

"I got some presents, which might have been nice, but it wasn't. Well actually I did get a couple of really nice little boxes of chocolates. But I got another one where they tasted sweet at first but they had this after-taste that made me wonder if someone had just come across them on a riverbed somewhere. But I just felt as if I had to keep eating them, because every time I got this horrible after-taste in my mouth I had to eat something to get rid of it. Too bad that had a horrible after-taste as well so I had to eat another one to get rid of that, and so on, till I'd finished the box. ... Well, OK, I didn't really eat the whole lot at once; but I did eat a few in one go whenever I dared eat any, wanting to get rid of the after-taste each time."

They laughed.

Then Tony continued, "Someone else gave me some other chocolate things, and they turned out to be an assortment of dark chocolate and milk chocolate. Well I didn't know that at first because I just got told they were chocolates. I don't like dark chocolate; it must be too strong for a delicate little lad like me. I would have given the dark chocolate ones away instead of eating them if I'd known."

He smiled and the others sniggered at his description of himself as delicate. Then he carried on, "All the chocolates felt the same so I couldn't guess which were the plain ones and which were the milk ones after I discovered that some were plain. But I hoped there were mostly milk ones. Every time I ate one that turned out to be a dark one, I had to eat another one, hoping it would be a milk one that would take the taste away. If it was another dark one, I had to eat yet another one, hoping it would be a milk one that would take the taste away. If it turned out to be yet another dark one, I had to eat yet another one, hoping that would be a milk one that would take the taste away, and so on. I suppose I could have gone and got something completely different to eat instead, but I was feeling too lazy to get up! And also there was always the possibility that the next chocolate would be a really nice one!"

The others laughed, and Becky quipped, "You want to watch that habit! It looks as if all those chocolates and unwanted sandwiches and things are still being stored around your waist even now, in the form of juicy flab!"

Tony said, "I know! I wouldn't mind so much if all the flab had come from eating things I like! Another present I got was this fudge, in a few little packets. I was just expecting it to be ordinary fudge, which I really like, because someone just told me it was fudge. But I was literally startled when I put a bit in my mouth and it turned out to be this really strong-flavoured thing – some kind of mixture of butterscotch and cough candy or something! I thought, 'What's the point of it being made of fudge if it doesn't taste remotely like fudge? It may as well just be ordinary toffee!' People who can see would have been able to read the label and be warned about that, but I was all unsuspecting!

"It's funny, because the year before, the person who gave me that had given me some biscuits that hardly had any flavour at all. They weren't as nice as the biscuits I buy regularly myself from the shops. If only the biscuits and the fudge could have been somehow merged to create a strength of flavour somewhere in the middle!

"I tried opening another one of the packets of this so-called fudge, hoping that would be ordinary fudge, but again, I was startled when I ate the first bit; it was this really intense strong sweet orange flavour. I didn't like those ones any more than the others.

"But even though I didn't like the bits of fudge much, they set off this sugar craving in me, so I felt as if I just had to eat them to satisfy it!

"So yes, Becky, if you were wondering why I'm covered in a load of ugly flab, that's the kind of thing it's made of!"

The others chuckled. He wasn't really all that fat.

He continued, "Now I'm going to have to spend a good few months non-stop on my exercise bike trying to get rid of it! It's going to be a real pain!"

Barbara sniggered and joked, "If you go on your exercise bike non-stop for a few months, you'll have more than a pain! You'll have died of exhaustion and hunger long before you meant to finish!"

Tony grinned and said, "Come on, you know what I mean! I'm thinking I'd better do some exercise every day. Mind you, I suppose that's good for people, so it's worth doing anyway."

Barbara responded, mostly in jest, "Yes, I knew what you meant really. How about getting some recordings of radio comedies and listening to them while you exercise, to make it more fun so you stay motivated to carry on? Then you might not mind getting fat and having to slim down so much, because it'll be an excuse to listen to comedy. The fatter you are, the more you'll have an excuse to listen to it instead of doing serious things with your time, so you might even start encouraging people to get you Christmas presents that make you too fat. Of course, the downside is that you'll have to exercise while you're listening to it."

Tony laughed and retorted, "If I actually wanted to get fat, I could think of a much more enjoyable way of doing it."

Barbara said seriously, "Really though, I know what you mean about being given Christmas presents you're not keen on. Someone likes to get me a fruit and nut mix every year; but I must have had muesli for breakfast hundreds of times over the past few years, and I often snack on nuts and put dried fruit in porridge, so I know it doesn't sound nice to say it, but receiving a fruit and nut mix is a bit like getting a quarter of a box of cereal for Christmas. I mean, I know it's not their fault, and it does tend to be more fancy than the muesli; but it doesn't feel special. They started getting them a few years ago when I actually asked for one. But nowadays I'd prefer something like fancy chocolates."

Tony grinned and said for fun, "How would you like it if someone got you a loaf of bread one year? You know, I bet the man who invented the Jehovah's Witnesses just did it because he was fed up of people getting him disappointing Christmas presents. You know, maybe one year one person got him a bag of Brussels Sprouts, someone else got him a big onion, and another person got him a bundle of straw for his horse, and he thought, 'Those things are good and practical, but at Christmas you want something a bit special. Every year this kind of thing happens! I'm fed up! Right! That's the last straw! I'm going to start a new organisation where I'm going to find an excuse to ban Christmas, and then I'll never have to put up with disappointing Christmas presents ever again!' "

They giggled.

Then Becky said, "I read that a charity's estimated that nearly sixty million unwanted Christmas presents get given every year! I don't know how accurate that is. But it was based on a poll where over half of the people asked said they received at least one unwanted gift every Christmas, and nearly half said they found it hard to think of what to buy people, which is probably one reason why they end up getting people things they turn out not to want.

"And I read on another website that over a quarter of presents get returned to the shop they came from!

"How about telling people who give you Christmas presents you're not keen on that from now on, you'd like them to give the money they'd normally spend on getting you a present to a local charity, and say you'll do the same with the money you'd normally spend on getting them a present if they're happy with that? Or you can buy cards from charities with writing on them that says the money that was spent to buy them's the equivalent of some kind of item or service they provide that's going to help someone. If you go online, I think there are websites that review charity gifts like that, so they can probably be used to find good ones.

"If people agree to give you cards like that instead of ordinary presents, you'll have the satisfaction of knowing their money's hopefully being spent on something decent, instead of on something that might disappoint you."

Barbara said, "That's a good idea actually! I'll think about that!

"People could do that instead of giving me Christmas cards as well, actually. Some people get me cards that they must have put some thought into finding, because they've got raised pictures on them so I can feel them; but I can never work out what they actually are! So much of the detail's still visual – you know, like how could you represent snowy ground in a form where a blind person could guess what it was? It is touching that they put thought into at least trying to find a card with a picture that's more accessible to me than normal.

"But unfortunately, a few of these cards have a lot of bits where the cardboard tapers off to sharp points, so the person who got it can guide my hand around it to tell me what everything is, or I can feel around it myself, and the edges feel prickly. I'm sure 'ouch' wasn't the reaction they were hoping for when they went to the trouble of finding it for me!

"I hope they don't go away thinking I'm ungrateful. Or worse, maybe they could be disappointed. Mind you, I don't think I've ever said 'ouch' all that loud; the cards aren't that bad.

"But talking of charity, I went to a Christmas party at our local society for blind people the Christmas before last. ... Well, they call it a society for blind people, but I think me and Tony are actually the only blind people in it. Most members are partially-sighted; they're much much older than us, and they're slowly losing their sight, or a bit of it, because of age-related medical conditions. But I think most of them can still see quite a lot.

"Anyway, we had this Christmas party. I didn't expect to like it much, because I knew it would be for people much older than me. But I thought I'd go and see.

"It wasn't really my thing, because they spent a lot of the time singing along to songs that were out about fifty or sixty years before my time – you know, the songs of their youth. There aren't many activities going on for young blind people where I live. I don't understand the appeal of sing-alongs anyway, but then, maybe that's just me. Or maybe songs that were around when they were much younger bring back good memories of some enjoyable times they had in those days, or remind them of the way they used to entertain themselves before they had televisions and the fun they had doing that or something. I don't know. But maybe that's why they like them. I think a lot of the people who went enjoyed it anyway, so that's the main thing.

"But something funny happened when we were all given a Christmas present at the end. I don't know if we were all given the same thing or whether people got a variety of things. Mine was pretty small, but I was hoping it might be a little box of chocolates. But it was funny what it turned out to be! Well, at least, it made *me* laugh! It was a little packet of tissues! Maybe the people who decided to give us or me them thought, 'We all know how much colds and other infections are passed around at this time of year, and we'd hate to think of you needing tissues and not having enough; so since we're pretty sure you'll end up with a cold at some point during the winter, here are some tissues to make things easier for you!' "

They laughed, and Becky responded sarcastically, "What a cheery Christmas thought that would have been!"

Barbara said, "I asked one of my relatives a few days later whether they really were just tissues. She said they really were, but they had little pictures of Christmas trees on them. That was a bit of a strange thing for blind people and other people who can't see much to get, if anyone besides me got them, but still! A lot of the society's members can see quite a lot, I think, so maybe most of them could see the pictures, if they got them too. Maybe the people who bought them for us or me were thinking, 'Colds are normally so bad at this time of year that you'll probably use this packet up in no time; so don't worry that they'll look inappropriate if you're still using them in April when the spring flowers are out because you've forgotten they've got Christmas pictures on them by then; you'll probably have used them up long before. Happy Christmas!'

"I don't know – maybe they were thinking it would be nice to get us something that was practical, cheap and Christmasy at the same time. At least it was something useful, so really, it was probably a better idea than getting me something edible that I might not have liked.

"Mind you, if they want to be practical, they could improve on that if they put their minds to it. They send their letters out in very large print, like the ones inviting people to their Christmas parties. I have to get someone who can see to read them to me. It seems a funny thing for a society for blind people to do, but then, almost all their members can see quite a lot, so it'll be useful for *them*. If they sent all mine by email, my computer's electronic voice would read them to me. I have told them that, but they still send most of them out in print. The same thing goes for other organisations, like the health service.

"Actually it was funny, because one of my relatives read me the letter inviting me to the party that year and told me it was in giant print, and she laughed and said it reminded her of stories you hear about tourists going abroad, and when they speak to people who don't understand their language, they talk louder, as if they think that'll make them understand it better. She joked that it's as if people at the society for blind people think that if they write their letters in big enough print, even a blind person will be able to read them. Mind you, like I said, it will help most of their members, who can see quite a lot."

The others giggled.

But then Barbara said, "Maybe I shouldn't be joking about these things really. If Mum was here when I'd told the story about the tissues, she'd probably have told me I should be grateful instead of having a laugh about it, because some people in the poorest parts of the world might think of having tissues as a luxury, and would have been really glad to get them, even if they couldn't see the pictures on them, so being able to joke about it just shows how well-off I am. I suppose that's true really.

"Actually, About what you were saying before, Becky, I do like the idea of recommending to some people that they give the money they would have spent on Christmas presents for me to a charity instead. It would probably be far better spent sometimes, given that one or two people often spend a fair bit of money on presents for me that I'm not keen on. I feel a bit bad when they do that, because it seems like a waste of money.

"I've never mentioned it before, but there's someone who seems to manage to get me inappropriate presents every year, for some reason, despite their probable best intentions. I don't know why they do it, but it seems they make a decision based on what looks attractive in the shop. Well it doesn't matter how attractive it looks – its beauty will be totally lost on me! I mean, there might be blind people who'd like things that look physically beautiful, maybe so they can show them off to other people or take pride in having them or something, but I'd prefer something that was of practical use or that I could enjoy using ... or eating.

"I mean, last year they got me something that seemed to me to be some kind of pretty table decoration. It had a bit of dried fruit on it; but you get loads more of that in just an ordinary plain packet, which is probably a lot cheaper than that was. The rest of it was this kind of stand, which might have looked very pretty in the middle of a table with fancy dried fruit on it for visitors to pick from, but any beauty it had was lost on me, and I would have thought they would know that! It might have looked nice in the shop, but it would be nicer if they went for something they knew would be appealing to me personally. Maybe they want to get something that'll look nice to the people watching me open it. Or maybe they don't know what to get me and just pick up something that catches their eye to get the job done. Or maybe they assume that if it looks attractive to *them*, I'll find it attractive too. I don't know.

"But I remember I told them once I wanted them to get me a nail file, and they got me this weird elaborate set of implements for manicuring – goodness knows what people use them all for – but I don't understand why they did that, since they know full well I'm not some obsessive beauty fanatic who takes elaborate care over doing my nails. If they thought a nail file wouldn't be much on its own, they could have got me a nail file plus a box of chocolates or something.

"I think at least part of the problem is that people don't know what to get me because there are a limited number of things I can enjoy because I'm blind. I feel a bit left out when I'm with the family and Christmas presents are being handed round, because I can't see what anyone else is getting, and I can hear people laughing when they get novelty or funny gifts where the pleasure people get from them is visual, but I don't know what they're laughing at, and I most often end up with some kind of fattening confectionary I'm not keen on. I have got a couple of relatives – a husband and wife – who used to get me imaginative thoughtful presents every year till recently. But we hardly ever see them now.

"It's nice to get presents when you're a kid, and it's nice to give presents to children. But when you're an adult making an effort to get presents for other adults without knowing what they'd really like, or receiving things you don't really want, Christmas just seems like a pointless hassle, at least to me."

Becky asked, "As bad as that? Is this something you've been thinking for a while, or do you only feel this way when you're in a bad mood?"

Barbara replied, "I've only been thinking it for a couple of years, but it's not an opinion that comes and goes depending on what mood I'm in. None of my opinions do that! I used to like Christmas a fair bit more when I was a kid and got nice toys and games to play with."

Becky joked, "It's a pity you don't still like playing with toys now then. Imagine what fun you could have!

"You know, this is an abnormally grumpy conversation for you! It's not what I expected when I came in here. What is it, the national day of complaining?"

Barbara joked back, "Yes, and it's illegal not to complain today, so you'll have to do your share soon."

Becky Talks About How People Need to Think Carefully When They Buy Things

Then Becky said with a bit more sympathy, "Actually, I can understand what you mean, since I've had a few gripes about presents myself. But what you said about wondering if someone gets presents for you that look visually attractive rather than things that would be most suited to you personally reminds me of a programme on telly where they were saying that some manufacturers often entice people to buy their products, such as foods, by making them look nice, so a lot of customers might be missing out on things they'd like better, because they go for what looks good rather than what looks just average, because it looks appealing so they assume it is, and because it'll likely catch their eye first; so they're less likely to notice things they might actually like better, and which might be healthier and better value.

"The programme presenters tested that out. They made this cottage pie thing that sounded as if it should have been called Yucky School Dinner Stew because of its ingredients, but they gave it a nice name, and put a nice picture on the box of a cosy family scene by a log fire in a cottage, or something like that, to see if those things would help it sell more than other products around it. It did sell more.

"It reminded me of things I'd learned on my psychology course about how people can go for what looks good, when they might find something better if they just investigate a bit more. Like sometimes in supermarkets they have special offers on that look good, when on the bottom shelf under what's on offer, they've got things that are very similar that aren't on offer, but they're actually cheaper. I read that supermarkets can put the more expensive things at eye level so they'll be what people see first.

"I've heard that people can make mistakes like that when they're buying much more expensive things too, like houses, especially because salesmen can act and talk as if things are more impressive than they really are, to appeal to people's emotions like enthusiasm, to try to sell them things they might not be so keen on if they spent more time thinking about what they're really like, such as by writing down – or just thinking about – the pros and cons of them, thinking through logically whether it really would be a good thing to buy them."

Becky Tries to Criticise Certain People For Not Thinking Things Through Carefully, But it Leads to Some Laughter and Joking

Tony said, "That's bad. But I wonder whether if it was normal for humans to take time thinking everything through logically, humanity wouldn't have even progressed beyond the Stone Age, because everyone would have been so logical about things, spending so much time mulling over the pros and cons of things like the idea of marrying or getting together with whoever they were thinking of marrying or mating with, that they would have always found enough things about them that they didn't like that they were put off the whole idea, so humanity would have died out. Maybe it's a good thing that humans don't put as much thought into things as they probably should all the time.

"Well, really, there should probably be some kind of happy medium between not thinking enough about whether the person you feel like getting together with is really suitable for you so you might end up unhappy, and thinking about that kind of thing so much it puts you off everyone!"

The others thought that maybe what Tony was saying made sense.

But then Barbara teased, "How would you feel if we spent so long thinking about what you just said about humanity dying out if everyone always thought everything through carefully we found enough things wrong with it that we came to the conclusion that it wasn't a logical point of view?"

Tony teased back, "You can try that if you like, but if you think about it for that long, maybe we'll have moved on to talking about something totally different; so if you want to tell us what's wrong with the idea, we'll be talking about, say, whether tomato sauce on cheeseburgers makes them taste nicer, and you'll say something like, 'Actually, I think some women would still want men if they thought about it logically, so humanity wouldn't really have died out if everyone did that.' "

They chuckled.

Then Becky said seriously, "It *is* good to think things through logically a lot of the time though. People are more likely to make bad decisions when they don't do that, like when they don't think through the pros and cons of doing a thing. I heard part of a radio programme not long ago, but turned off not that long after I started listening, because I was annoyed that the presenter didn't challenge what his interviewee was saying. I suppose he might have done after I switched off, but I'd lost hope that he would by then.

"I got interested in it in the first place because I volunteer to help you, Barbara; it was about how some blind people who are educated in ordinary schools say they miss out on having friends, and end up with other difficulties too, because they've got an adult who can see helping them during lessons who tends to stay with them during their breaks too, which might put other kids off coming up and talking to them. "

Barbara asked, "You thought of listening to the programme in the first place because you volunteer to help me?"

Becky replied, "Well, that just made me think it might be worth listening to it, to find out more about what it's like for blind people in ordinary schools, to help me get more of an understanding of what problems they can have, and to see how it compares with your experiences of going to a specialist school for blind and partially-sighted people. But during the time I was listening, it didn't say much."

Barbara quipped, "I'm sure it would have said more if you'd listened for longer. You couldn't expect to have heard that much of it when you switched it off after a few minutes!"

Becky replied, "Well it didn't sound as if it was going to get better! It was putting forward the point of view that blind people get more help than is good for them in ordinary schools, partly because they're less likely to make friends if an adult's always with them, and partly because they get help with things they could really find ways of doing themselves, which would make them more independent. But it was as if the programme was taking it as a given that that's the case, instead of querying it to determine whether it really is. There weren't many interviewees talking about their experiences, from what I heard. Actually I think I just heard one, complaining about other kids probably being put off making friends with him because an adult was with him during his breaks.

"But there must be a reason why things are the way they are, whether it's good or not. What if they're the way they are because there's no better alternative? What if the interviewee *had* been left alone during his breaks, and then on the programme, instead of complaining that he didn't get to make friends, he'd complained that some bullies had taken the opportunity to sneak up to him and steal from him, knowing he couldn't see what they were doing, and he'd sometimes been suddenly slapped in the face by a bully who knew he wouldn't be able to see who'd done it, or to see them coming so he could duck or defend himself, and he wouldn't be able to run after them afterwards to retaliate; or what if he'd sometimes wanted to go to the loo during his breaks but found it hard to navigate the crowds of kids in the corridor so he could get there, and some mean-spirited ones had often laughed at him trying to get through and deliberately put things in his way?

"And there's no guarantee the other kids would have wanted to come up and make friends with him if his helper hadn't been with him during his breaks. Being left all alone feeling isolated every day at those times would have been even worse.

"I mean, maybe a better system could have been created, such as if a rota was arranged where trusted members of the class who volunteered were given the responsibility of making sure he was alright during his breaks instead of an adult. Then he might have made friends, because the classmates who volunteered to help him would have probably introduced him to their own friends, and then some of them might have become his too. But from what I heard, he was just criticising the system, and there was no discussion of whether there were possible solutions or whether it was the best system it was possible to come up with because other ones would be even less satisfactory.

"And as well as that, although there seemed to be only one or two interviewees talking on this programme, it gave me the impression that its makers assumed they were speaking for all blind children in mainstream schools. But that wasn't necessarily the case, so they should have actually found out the views of lots of people if they wanted to represent the views of lots of them, since how could anyone tell if the opinions of the ones talking were the opinions of lots of other people too without them doing that? I mean, how could we tell if they were problems worth being concerned about if for all we know, only a small minority of blind kids who go to ordinary schools have those problems and feel the way the people being interviewed on the programme do, because better systems are already put in place in a lot of schools, or else some of the adults who are there to assist blind children actually help them make friends by introducing them to other kids? Or maybe some of them enjoy talking to the adults so much they don't care about making friends."

Tony smiled and asked for fun, "If you feel that strongly about it, why don't you write to the programme makers and tell them all that? ... Mind you, they might not take what you say that seriously if you say, 'I've got loads of complaints about your programme, but I only listened to a few minutes of it, so I don't know if it actually deserves them.' "

Barbara giggled. But Becky said, "I think you've as good as answered your own question there! I'm not going to write to them if I'm not absolutely sure I'm right about what the programme was like, am I! But tell you what: If you think I still should, why don't You do a similar thing, writing to them and saying, 'I loved everything about your programme ... but actually I didn't hear any of it!' "

Barbara grinned and joked, "Maybe I could get him to do that as a dare! Go on, Tony, I dare you!"

Tony joked back, "Well, maybe I will, ... as long as you accept a dare I give You, Barbara: Write to them yourself, and say you think you could do a better job of presenting shows than all the presenters on their station, so you demand that the management sack them all immediately and employ you to present the shows that every single one of them used to do instead! Tell them you're convinced you could stay awake 24 hours a day every day so you could do the work easily!"

They all laughed.

Barbara grinned and said, "I wonder what they'd do if someone did that!"

Becky said, "Probably file their letter in the bin!

"Another thing I didn't like about that radio programme I admittedly didn't hear much of was that the interviewee was complaining that when he went to university, he couldn't discipline himself to get down to work; it was a course where students had to work a lot on their own, learning course material and writing essays on it. He said at school, he'd always had an adult assisting him with his work during the lessons he was supposed to use to do personal study, probably doing things like reading study material to him that he couldn't access himself because it was in print. He said that meant he'd never got into the habit of disciplining himself to get down to work on his own. That sounded as if it was just an excuse to me, as if he was blaming the system unfairly, but the presenter just accepted it. He should have asked him whether there were any other reasons why he found it hard to get down to work. That might have been quite revealing. Easy access to parties, maybe?

"I wouldn't have thought disciplining himself could have been that hard! I mean, he would have to have done at least some of his homework on his own before, I expect; and everyone's got to transition from being told what to do to taking the initiative and organising themselves at some point, so why should it have been worse for him? If he was older than most people when he started having to, that should actually have made it easier.

"The programme was giving the impression that what he was saying was one of the criticisms of the system of helping blind kids in schools in general; but it might really not have had much to do with it. It should have either made it clear that his experience wasn't necessarily representative of the experiences of blind people in mainstream schools in general, or else a lot of other blind people should have been questioned before the programme, so there could have been a report on the views of several blind people, to see if they were all similar, so people could have made a better judgment about whether there really is a problem that needs to be fixed."

Becky suddenly grew a bit more light-hearted and teased, "If you'd been to a mainstream school instead of a specialist one, Barbara, I can't imagine you blaming that system for all the times when you don't do your work."

Barbara joked, "No I wouldn't; I'd blame *you*. I'd say, 'It's that Becky again! She said she was going to read part of a book I need to study for my course to me, but she read me a novel instead, and I was enjoying it so much I just couldn't bring myself to ask her to stop! It's all Her fault!' "

Becky said for fun, "If you ever start accusing me of things like that, whenever I hand in an essay late or finish a project late from then on, I'm going to say, 'Sorry, it's that Barbara's fault! She's such a tyrant, she locks me in her room and makes me stay up till four in the morning helping her! And even after that I can't get to sleep, because she falls asleep on me and uses my head as a pillow!' "

Barbara grinned and joked, "Credit me with a bit of sense! I mean, your head would be a bit hard for a pillow, wouldn't it! I'd at least want to make you lie down and use your stomach for one!"

They giggled.

Then Tony said, "Imagine if you were interviewed on the radio yourself, Becky, and used that as an excuse for not working hard! It would cause newspaper headlines, wouldn't it, like, 'Scandalous Blind Student Uses Child as Pillow After Making Her help her for Half the Night!' "

Barbara grinned and said, "I wouldn't be very pleased with her if she did that! ... I wouldn't mind you using other excuses on the radio to give us all a laugh though, Becky, like, 'Someone bought me some chocolate-scented perfume, and I loved it so much I wanted to sniff it for hours on end non-stop, so I ended up just not having the time to get down to doing any work. It's all the fault of the person who gave me the perfume!'

"Or you could say, 'I joined an exercise class, and I was so dedicated to it I wanted to practise the exercises all the time, and I did try to work while I was doing them, but writing essays turned out to be just impossible while I was flinging myself around the room exercising, so I just couldn't do any work! It's all the fault of the people who started the exercise classes, for not giving us exercises that were gentle enough that I could work at the same time as doing them. I mean, even if they'd asked us to do vigorous things with only our arms it would have been alright, because I could have typed and done all my other work with my feet or my nose ... or at least I could have tried. I'm sure I'd have still been alright if they'd just given us gentle exercises to do with our feet and noses at the same time as we did the vigorous exercises with our arms, because I'm pretty sure I could have typed and read while I was exercising my nose and feet only gently.' "

Becky grinned and said, "I know someone who came here after getting kicked out of a better university because he didn't bother doing much work. He doesn't blame anyone else; he just says it was his fault for spending too much time having fun instead of working. He joined lots of different activity groups at his old university, like canoeing, hang-gliding, the film society, and quite a few other ones.

"Just imagine if he said things like, 'It was the university's fault for having so many spare-time activities and letting me do them! I mean, when they saw me walking towards the swimming pool, they should have closed it immediately before I got there so I couldn't use it! They should have banned hang-gliding, or else they should have locked all the gliders up quickly when they saw me coming! Whenever they saw me walking towards the place where they put films on, they should have quickly swapped the one they'd been going to put on with a film of grass growing or paint drying or someone slowly ripping up paper or something – you know, something I'd have found so boring I would have walked out ... because of course, if I had, I would have immediately gone back to my room and got on with my work. Naturally.' "

The others laughed.

Barbara asked, "Do *you* make excuses for things? What do you tell your tutor when you hand in an essay late?"

Becky grinned and joked, "I say, 'Barbara made me hand it in late. She confused me about what day it was, after she'd made me stay up for so many nights helping her I couldn't think straight, so I still thought I had several years before I had to hand it in.' "

They chuckled, and Tony queried, "Several Years?"

Becky joked, "Yes, I say Barbara confused me so much I couldn't even remember if they gave us days or weeks or years to do our essays!"

They laughed, and Barbara joked, "If you really do say anything like that, I'll put daft things in my essays from now on, and tell my tutor you put them in without me realising, like, 'Queen Victoria was forced to spend long hours every day digging up the roads, and driving lorries full of air to put in the holes she'd dug, so there wouldn't be a frightening vacuum in them that would suck everything around them into it, like black holes do.

But lots of car drivers got really fed up of her digging holes in all their roads, so one day, one of them angrily got out of his car and threatened to push her into one of them. Actually he tried, but she'd filled it with so much air there wasn't room for her in it, so she just floated over the top of it. Then she called the police on her mobile phone to report the incident.'

"And I'll say, 'The Second World War started when a giant seagull flew in a leisurely manner into the grounds of Buckingham Palace, and stole an equally giant goldfish from a giant pond there, and started flying off with it. The Queen's youngest daughter spotted the seagull, and noticed that it had a tag that said, "Made in Germany" affixed to its leg. So the Royal Family called the German Ambassador and demanded compensation for the giant goldfish. But he said he couldn't possibly give them any, because the seagulls he worked for hadn't paid him in months.' "

Becky grinned and said, "If you put things like that in your essays, your tutor might invite you to his office for a private chat and say, 'If your knowledge of history's that bad, you probably shouldn't be on this course!' "

They chuckled, and Barbara joked, "Yes, but I'll say I only put that stuff in my essay because you told me to."

Tony grinned and said for fun, "Would you really put something in an essay just because Becky told you to?"

Becky smirked mischievously and said, "Alright, if you would, put this in the next essay you write: 'Coffee first came to this country after it was invented by a Frenchmen, while he was experimenting with burning paper dipped in various chemicals to see how brightly he could make it burn. When he burned paper dipped in ink, he thought it had such a pleasing odour that he'd enjoy eating the ashes, although the fumes made him cough, so he called his new creation coffee. Then he thought it might be nice to drink it in hot water instead of eating it, after he tried a bit and it made him cough even more because the texture was so dry. Then it occurred to him that if he enjoyed it so much, other people might as well, so he started mass-producing it and selling it, and it's been popular ever since. But what most people don't know is that it's a mixture of shreds of burned paper and ink. Its manufacturers pretend it comes from a plant because they know people would be put off buying it if they knew how it's really made.' "

Barbara said with a grin, "If I wrote that in an essay, the tutor would think I'd gone nuts, or else that I must have been drunk when I wrote it ... partly because there hasn't ever even been a mention of studying coffee on my course!"

They giggled.

Then Becky said more seriously, "I told one of my tutors he was being daft once!"

Barbara laughed and said, "Typical you!"

But then she said seriously, "Honestly Becky! Outspokenness like that might get you into real trouble one day! Why did you call him daft?"

Becky smiled and replied, "Well it was soon after I first got here. It was a media studies tutor. We were all talking at the beginning of a lesson, and he came in and said he was going to play us a recording of something. He said, 'Be quiet and listen! You'll love this! It's really good fun!'

"So we were all quiet and listened, and it turned out not to be much fun at all! So I told him I didn't think it had been much fun, and asked him why he told us it was going to be a lot of fun when it wasn't. He said, 'Well, saying that got your attention, didn't it!'

"I told him it wasn't a very clever tactic to use really, because the next time he told us something was going to be fun, he might really mean it, but we wouldn't believe him, because we wouldn't trust him so much, so we might not be so quick to pay attention. I told him I didn't think it was fair of him to stir up people's emotions like eagerness for fun on false pretences."

Barbara asked, "What did he say?"

Becky replied, "He said that maybe I was right, and that I might make a good student if I became good at noticing when emotions were being stirred up without a good reason, since part of the course would be about how some publications in the media sometimes try to stir up emotions to attract attention and newspaper sales or sway opinions."

Becky, Barbara and Tony Laugh and Joke About a Line Tony Misheard in a Song

Tony smiled and said, "Talking about emotions, you know how sometimes people and songs use phrases as if they mean they think the heart is what controls caring and loving emotions? The other day I was doing something, and the radio was on in the other room, and there was a song on with a chorus that was going, 'One mind, two hearts' over and over again. I don't know who the song was by or what it really meant – maybe the singer was singing about going out with a total moron who he was saying didn't have a mind, so his was the only mind in the relationship; or maybe he meant he and his girlfriend were always of one mind, which I can't imagine really being possible.

"But anyway, I probably misheard, but one time, it sounded as if it said, 'One mind, three hearts'! What would that have to mean?"

They laughed. Becky said, "Maybe it would mean he was saying his girlfriend had no mind and two hearts, while he had the mind and the other heart. ... Or maybe it would mean she had an entire three hearts, and he had no heart but one mind. ... Or maybe it would be talking about just one person, who had three hearts and one mind. I wonder whereabouts in the body the extra hearts would be."

Tony grinned and said, "I expect it's talking about emotions really though instead of real hearts. I don't know why people ever got to think the heart's got anything to do with emotion. But if that's what the song was about, just imagine what it would be like if someone had three times the normal amount of loving emotion; what would they be like? Maybe they'd be walking down the street, stopping to hug everyone in their path, arriving at work really late every day because they'd spent so much time on the way hugging people, like getting a later train than they should have done because they spent so much time on the station platform hugging everyone there, and then hugging the station staff on the way out of the station."

Becky grinned and said, "Yeah. And then imagine if their boss shouted at them and said he was firing them, saying, 'You're an absolutely useless worker! You never turn up on time, and when you do turn up, you just want to hug people instead of doing any work!' If they had all those extra metaphorical hearts but no mind, the boss might carry on the lecture by saying, 'When you do actually do a bit of work, you make mistake after mistake! If you only had a mind, you might actually achieve something worthwhile, you worthless no-good idler!'

"Then as soon as the boss said that, the person might jump up and hug him, saying, 'Oh, you're so sweet! I just love the way you're always so honest with me! Thank you for sharing that with me; you're a beautiful person and I love you very much!' "

Tony laughed and said, "Imagine if an ordinary person did that to a boss after he'd just heaped a pile of criticism on them! The boss might think they'd gone stark raving bonkers, or else that they were trying to be manipulative and get into his good books!"

They giggled.

Then Barbara said, "But imagine if that song really did say, 'One mind, three hearts', and it said it over and over again! I wonder what people who heard it would think!"

Becky said, "Or imagine if it kept saying, 'One mind, four hearts'! Or 'One mind, six hearts'! Or 'One mind, nine hearts'! Or imagine if it said a different thing each time, so it started off saying something like, 'Three hearts, one mind', and then it said, 'Five hearts, two minds', and then, 'Fifteen hearts, ten minds', and it kept going up and up like that till the end of the song!"

They chuckled, and Tony said, "Or what about if it said there were more minds than hearts, so it kept saying things like, 'One heart, five minds'?"

Barbara laughed and said, "If a person had five minds, I wonder where they'd all be! Perhaps besides having one in the normal place, they'd have one in each leg, and one in their stomach, and one in one of their hands or something!"

Becky grinned and said, "Yikes! Imagine if someone like that had a leg amputated. The mind in the leg might make it go hopping all around the operating theatre, scaring all the doctors and nurses! And just imagine if the person ate some food, and the mind in their stomach objected to it because it was junk food, so it got angry, and it made the stomach start growling! Or imagine if they picked some junk food up, but the mind in their hand objected to putting it in their mouth because it was so unhealthy, so their hand put it down again. But what if the mind in their head still wanted to eat it. Maybe the minds would have a quarrel. Or maybe the person would just put their head down so they could reach it with their mouth and eat it that way. Imagine if they were out in public at the time! ... And imagine it was only after they'd done it that they remembered that they could have just used their other hand that didn't have a mind in it to pick the food up.

"Or imagine if the hand with the mind in it flung the food across the cafe they were in, and then the person went and got it back so they could eat it!"

They giggled. Then Barbara said, "Or imagine if that song was about other things besides minds and hearts, so it said things like, 'One hand, fifty-two fingers; one face, forty-three noses; one head, ninety-seven ears; two feet, eighty-nine toes; three stomachs, seven legs; three heads, one hairbrush!' "

Becky queried, "One hairbrush? Would that be a part of their body then, maybe growing out of one of their three heads?"

They all laughed.

Then Tony said, "Imagine a person like that going to the doctor! They'd look like some scary spooky monster, wouldn't they! I wonder what the doctor would diagnose them with! ... Or maybe he'd just run out of the room screaming!"

They giggled again, and Barbara said, "Or imagine if they looked normal, but inside them they had about ninety-three hearts. So that would have to mean they had, maybe, two in each leg, five in each arm, one in their stomach, one in their head, and goodness knows where else they'd be! Imagine if they told the doctor they were feeling ill, and the doctor did some tests on them and found all the hearts! I wonder what they'd do!"

Tony chuckled and said, "I dunno, send them off to a museum or something, maybe."

They grinned.

Becky, Barbara and Tony Find Something Else to Laugh About

Soon after that, the conversation became serious again for a little while, as Becky vented some annoyance about having been recently accused by someone on her course of trying to win an argument about whether people should eat meat by stirring up people's emotions such as horror and sympathy for animals being killed in slaughterhouses to put them off it. She hadn't really been doing that. She'd just wanted to explain that there was research that had found that it would be healthier, better for the planet because it would reduce carbon dioxide emissions a lot, and kinder to animals if people in the Western world reduced their consumption of meat a lot.

When some people had objected to what she was saying because they were rather fond of eating meat, she'd described gruesome practices in slaughterhouses to back up her argument that eating meat caused a lot of animal suffering; and doing that could stir up people's emotions no matter how matter-of-fact the description was. She'd spent some time explaining to the people she was arguing with that there were other reasons for her point of view too, so she resented the accusation that she wasn't trying to win the argument by using logic and reason but just by stirring up feelings.

Barbara put her head in her hands after Becky vented her irritation about that and joked, "I'm beginning to get a headache! I think I need another cup of tea! I reckon I might be getting a new disease called the listening to Becky complaining disease, and the cure for it's about ten cups of tea and about five cakes in a row!"

Tony sniggered and said, "That would be quite a nice disease to have then really, wouldn't it. Imagine calling in sick to work after you got a job, saying you couldn't come in because you had a bad case of the listening to Becky complaining disease, and you were just going to have to spend the entire day drinking cups of tea and eating cake."

Barbara and Tony laughed.

But Becky protested, "What's wrong with listening to me complaining? Don't forget you said it's illegal not to complain today earlier, Barbara. All I was saying was that some people criticise other people for saying things that are bound to stir up people's feelings, but that there's nothing wrong with stirring them up if you're giving them good reasons why what you're saying makes sense as well, so you're not just stirring up emotions like anger or enthusiasm and so on to get support for opinions you haven't got good evidence for.

"It's only bad logic to use arguments that stir up emotions if you're not giving people any good evidence for your beliefs ... although some politicians, salesmen and advertisers would say stirring up emotions like cravings or enthusiasm for something, and like fear of what might happen if people don't get to have it, works for them, so it makes perfect logical sense for them to do it, because it gets people to do what they want them to, such as buying certain things or voting for them – you know, like if advertisers tell people they'll really enjoy eating more chocolate to stir up their cravings for it, not mentioning that they won't enjoy getting fatter afterwards, or how some salesmen might warn people they could be at risk of having their house broken into if they don't buy their new burglar alarm, to stir up their fears of not having enough security, not mentioning that in the area where they live, the risk of crime isn't that high.

"Or imagine if a politician made a party political broadcast that was just full of claims like, 'Our party is the party of progress! Voting for us will herald an exciting new dawn for the country! We will turn this country into a hive of productivity! The well-being of our people will increase exponentially!'

"If he went on and on like that, it might stir up enthusiasm and excitement in a lot of people and encourage them to vote for his party, regardless of the fact that he wasn't giving any details about just how they were intending to achieve all that, so people could judge how possible it was really going to be. I mean, naturally there wouldn't be time for him to explain that much detail in just a short party political broadcast; but if he didn't give any at all, and if his party was always vague about the details of how they intended to achieve what they claimed they would, it would be reasonable for people to wonder if they really had any workable plans.

"But perhaps a lot of people who were stirred up with enthusiasm by the exciting rhetoric wouldn't stop to think about that, just hoping for the best, especially if they hated the other party.

"So perhaps from the point of view of people like that, bad logic is sometimes good logic. ... Well, actually, you wouldn't be making any logical argument at all if all you were doing was trying to entice people to do things or to think certain things by stirring up emotions in them like craving or fear or enthusiasm, so I suppose they might say that if it gets them what they want, sometimes non-existent logic is good logic, ... or something."

Barbara tittered and said, "Careful Becky, you're beginning to sound as if you might soon start tying yourself in knots."

Tony grinned and joked, "Hey, that sounds like a fun game! Let's tie Becky in knots! ... Actually, that wouldn't be easy, would it. Imagine if it was really possible to bend your arms around so you could tie them in knots, and there was a craze where people thought it was fun to really tie themselves in knots. What if you tied the knots so tightly you couldn't untie them again? Imagine having to walk around all day with knots in all your fingers and your arms. How do you think you'd cope?"

Barbara replied, "Maybe there would be quite a lot of people whose jobs it would be to travel around and untie people who were daft enough to have tied their fingers and arms in knots and couldn't undo them."

Tony said, "Imagine how embarrassing it would be if a parent tied themselves in knots they couldn't undo sometimes, and they had to get their child to undo them, and the child was really good at it."

They giggled.

Becky said, "Or imagine if you were in a restaurant taking someone classy who you really wanted to impress out for a really posh meal, and you were a bit nervous because you were really hoping things would go well, and whenever you were nervous you would twiddle your fingers around, and sometimes that tied them in knots you couldn't undo, and you accidentally tied them in knots that evening, and you were really embarrassed, but you couldn't think of anything else to do but to ask the waiter if he could try to untie them for you, in front of your posh guest.

"Or imagine if you thought you'd just Have to ask your guest to untie them for you, because you couldn't think of anyone else to ask. And imagine if they couldn't untie your fingers, so you had to eat this really posh food you were supposed to eat using a knife and fork with the tips of your fingers instead! And imagine if when you tried, some of the food got lodged between the bits of your fingers that were tied together, so you decided the only thing you could do was to put your face down right into your plate and munch your food up like an animal, and you got it all over your face, and accidentally got your hair all in it, so when you lifted your face up, the food dripped down you."

Tony Finishes Telling the Others About His Recent Restaurant Mishaps

They laughed. Then Tony said, "That idea makes my restaurant adventures last month look pretty trivial! Well, they were really. They just made me a bit uneasy at the time.

"I didn't finish telling you the story, Did I – the one where my coat suddenly sailed off into the ether as soon as I took it off. ... Actually, I discovered later it had sailed off into the hall to be hung up. ... I think I started that restaurant story a few years ago now, didn't I, and somehow never got to finish it."

The others smiled.

Then Tony became more serious, as he said, "Actually, it's a pain not being able to see sometimes. Maybe I'm just being a whingebag, but I'm not going to go out with those people again.

"At the end of the evening, one of the people in the group I was with offered to drive the ones of us who'd come by train back to the station so we didn't have to walk back to it in the cold. It meant she would have to make a few journeys, so it was nice of her to offer. It was a lot nicer going back in her car to the station than it had been walking from there to the restaurant in the cold wind earlier!

"The only thing was that I was left sitting in the hall of the restaurant for a while while most people got up to go and she took other people back first, and it started feeling a bit colder. I asked her if she could get my coat, and she must have assumed I was asking because I thought she was driving me to the station right then, because she told me she wasn't going to give me a lift till she'd taken other people there, and walked off. I said I just wanted it because I'd begun to feel a bit chilly, but she must have been out of earshot by then, because she didn't respond. So I was just sitting there not knowing how to get to my coat and not knowing where anyone was who I could ask to get it for me. The others who were waiting had gone out to have a smoke, but I didn't want to do that, since I don't smoke, and it was cold out there. If I could see, I could have just got up and gone and got my coat – it wouldn't have been a problem.

"Thankfully though, I might have just felt chilly because there was a draft when the door was opened, because I felt alright most of the time while I was waiting.

"I suppose I should be grateful really that the woman driving us back knew which coat mine actually was! If she hadn't, I suppose I'd have had to feel everyone's coat that was hanging up till I felt one like mine; ... and imagine if someone had come out while I was doing that and said with annoyance and disapproval and surprise, 'What are you doing feeling my coat, young man! Have you got some kind of coat fetish, or are you trying to find something to steal? If you are, I'll have to report you to the police immediately!' "

The others giggled at the thought.

Then Barbara said, "Actually, that story reminds me of something one of my blind friends told me about how she went out for a meal in a pub once with some people from a new church she'd just joined. I think it was supposed to be a welcome meal for new members. She'd never been to the pub they went to before.

"She was given these chunky salmon sandwiches, and she really didn't like the texture of the salmon, and it made her feel a bit queasy. She doesn't know if it was that or something else that caused the problem, but after a while, the sick feeling got a bit worse. She hoped it would just go away at first, so she didn't say anything, but it didn't go.

"Then everyone decided they were going to leave soon. They went off to get ready or say last goodbyes or something, and she was left all alone for a while. Then the sick feeling got bad enough that she felt as if she was actually going to be sick. She obviously couldn't see where the loos were, and she hadn't been to them so she had no idea where they were, so she couldn't have just jumped up and gone there to be sick.

"She would have been sick in a pint glass. She'd had an empty one in front of her earlier she could have used, but it had been taken away, and she felt around the table but couldn't find another container she could use. Everyone was well out of earshot, so she couldn't ask anyone to guide her to the loo. Well, she could have shouted across the room to someone, but she's a bit shy about doing things like that. So she was sick on the floor."

"She wasn't so shy about doing that then?" quipped Becky.

Barbara replied, "Well, she had to be sick whether she wanted to be or not! By the time she realised she wasn't going to be able to hold it in till someone came back to her, it was too late. Being sick got people's attention though! The organiser of the event cleaned it up for her. Then she guided her to the loo so she could wash her face and so on. She felt better for having been sick.

"A few days later, she heard someone else who'd been at the event telling the organiser she'd have made her clean it up herself. The organiser said, 'That could have been messy!'

"My friend didn't think it was fair of the person who'd said she'd have made her clean it up herself to be so judgmental. She sounded as if she was thinking it must have been her fault she was sick on the floor, as if it just hadn't occurred to her to think about whether it was fair to judge someone who couldn't see anything and was in an unfamiliar environment in the same way she'd judge someone who had all the advantages of being able to see, and could have just got up without making a fuss and found the loos."

Tony said, "Well I'm glad I at least didn't throw up at the restaurant! That would have made the evening even worse!

"The person driving us back to the station gave me my coat in the end, and she guided me out of the restaurant. When I got in her car, she put the seatbelt on for me. I don't know why people do that; the seatbelts and seatbelt holder things are always in the same place, so it's not as if I'm going to have to feel around for ages before I find them; I can pretty much put my hands on them immediately because I'm familiar with where they always are. I suppose someone who's just beginning to go blind and isn't used to doing that might need help. But since I've been blind all my life, I'm used to putting my hand out to where I'm pretty sure they're going to be and finding them.

"But anyway, my coat had flopped open, and it was dangling over the seatbelt holder, making it awkward for her to get to, because my pocket was full of gloves and things, so it had turned into a big bulgy thing flopping right over the seatbelt holder; but I didn't realise my coat was dangling right over it till she started trying to fit the seatbelt into the holder and found it difficult, and I felt it move and realised it must be in the way. Maybe she couldn't see so well because it was dark, because she was leaning right over me, fiddling around for what seemed like ages before she managed to get the seatbelt into its holder. Most of the time, sighted people can do things more quickly than blind people; but I would have been able to put it in much more quickly than her; I would have just pulled my coat up out of the way when I felt for the seatbelt holder and found part of my coat flopping over it."

Barbara said, "Some people put my seatbelt on for me too. I prefer to do it myself as well. Oh well, it's better to get a bit of extra help you don't need than not to get enough. There's someone who's been in the car when I've been given a lift to some places, and when the car stops, she normally says to me in an impatient tone of voice, 'Get out then!' She seems to think I should be able to just fling the door open and jump out, no matter how many times I explain that I'm not going to do that when I don't know if there's a car parked right next to us or some other obstacle in the way that I might bash the door into if I just fling it open, or whether I'd be opening the door and getting out right into a busy road. I prefer to ask someone to confirm that nothing's in the way before I open the door, or else to wait till someone else gets out and comes round and opens it, so I know it's OK to get out.

"Another thing this person keeps doing is to make comments when I'm dropped off near my home like, 'You should be familiar with where you are now. You can get out and walk the rest of the way yourself.' Somehow it never occurs to them that although I know we're very near my home, I won't know which side of it we've parked on, which side of the road we're on, how far away we are from it, or whether the front of the car's facing it or facing away from it. Those things make a big difference to knowing what direction to walk in when I get out, and how far I'll have to walk before I get there!

"Thankfully she's the only one I've ever known to make comments like that. Most people who've given me lifts are understanding and happy to help me as much as I need."

Tony said, "That's good. At least the person driving me back to the station didn't make ignorant comments! We got to the station safely, and I caught the train to my local station and then got a taxi home, so I was soon back in the warm.

"But the next day, the person whose idea it was for us to go to the restaurant in the first place asked me if I'd enjoyed it! I thought she might not appreciate it if I told her what I'd really thought of it."

Barbara asked for fun, "What did you say, 'No it was horrible; never do anything like this again!'?"

Tony laughed and said, "That would have caused a bit of controversy!"

Becky Tells the Others Funny Stories About Mistakes Made in Restaurants and Elsewhere, and Then They Tell Stories of Their Own

Becky grinned and said, "Well I've heard about much stranger and worse things than that going on in restaurants. One of my friends was telling me some funny stories not long ago about things that went wrong while people were trying to eat meals in them, that she read about on the Internet.

"There was one story about a man who got a job as a waiter in a posh restaurant, and one day he was carrying a tray with four glasses of water on it, intending to put them down on a table where a family was sitting. When he stopped at the table, perhaps he was carrying the tray at a slightly tilted angle without realising, or else he stopped abruptly, because the glasses kept on going, and they all zoomed onto the table and spilled all their water on it. The family tried to get away before it deluged over the edge, but the table was in a corner so it was a bit difficult to get out, so they didn't manage it in time, and got drenched.

"He worried about what they would say, but the dad burst out laughing, and then the rest of them did. They said it was a good story for them to tell people about their holiday. The waiter was relieved and told the management what he'd done, and they gave the family free puddings.

"Another man got a job in a posh restaurant, and was opening a bottle of champagne for a couple celebrating an anniversary one day, when for some reason, when he tried to get the cork out, the bottle shot backwards and went on the floor, and the champagne shot up and went all over him, in his hair and through his clothes, and it went on a couple of people nearby too.

"I read about a mishap that happened in someone's friend's home, not in a restaurant. He was only about ten at the time, and he fancied a snack while his friend was doing something else. He looked in the fridge and found a jar that said it had vanilla butter cream icing for cakes in it. He liked the sound of that and took a great big mouthful, only to get an unpleasant surprise! It turned out that the family were storing lard in the jar, so he'd taken a great big mouthful of lard. The family must have decided to reuse the jar after the icing mixture had run out."

Barbara giggled and said, "At least it's not only blind people who make mistakes like that then. Actually I know it isn't. I remember going on a trip to Wales with some people from my school when I was about ten. Some of the staff took us mountain climbing for several days, for some reason. The PE teacher guided me, with me linking arms with her so I could follow her, and she would tell me what the ground was like just in front of me so I knew when to step up and so on.

"Anyway, I don't know which staff member was responsible for making cups of tea, but for days, they put salt in it instead of sugar. No one could work out why it tasted weird for a while.

"And another time, I was out with a relative who can see, and we went in a cafe, and for some reason she put sugar on my chips! I'm not sure if she just didn't read the labels on things, or what.

"Mind you, talking of spilling things, one day we had a picnic at school. It was for the guides – they had a pack of guides there. ... Are guides in packs? Anyway, they did guides at our school, and I was in it for a while; I told you it was a boarding school because there were blind people from all over the country there, who couldn't get home that often because it was too far away, didn't I. The maths teacher ran a little group of guides in the school, and we went out one day at the weekend and had a picnic. The only thing I remember about it is that I must have started holding my drink at a slightly crooked angle, and it must have dripped a few drops onto something without me realising. The maths teacher told me the drink was spilling, and said to me crossly, 'It's alright to spill things, but not alright to not know you're spilling them!'

"It sounded as if she meant, 'It's alright to spill things deliberately, just not if you don't realise they're spilling.' "

They laughed.

Tony said, "That story about someone eating lard by mistake reminds me of something I did once. Years ago, I wanted to make a cup of tea one day, and either Mum or Dad had poured gravy into a milk bottle to keep for another meal, and I didn't know and poured it in my tea, thinking it was milk. I didn't realise till I tasted it!"

Everyone in the room smiled.

Tony Complains Some More About Some Little Difficulties Being Blind Can Lead To, and Mentions a Few Things That Make Life Easier

Tony continued, "I've made a few mistakes that were caused by being blind since I've been living on my own. Mind you, I've never done anything that bad. I know someone who accidentally put pears on his dinner, mistaking the tin of pears for a tin of peas or other vegetables. And I know someone who put a tin of cherry tomatoes on their pudding, expecting to have opened a tin of cherries. I often sniff things I open to try to avoid making mistakes like that, and sometimes to reassure myself they don't seem to have gone off. But it's not always easy to open exactly what you were hoping to when tins or tubs and jars of things feel exactly the same as each other.

"I've got a system where I put different tins in different places; so as long as I remember what I've put where, and someone's told me what they are in the first place, I'm alright. Like I put tins of chicken chunks on the top shelf of the cupboard, tins of beans on the left-hand side of the bottom shelf, and tins of fruit cocktail on the right-hand side of the bottom shelf.

"If I've just bought two tins but I don't know which is which, I shake them, and sometimes the sound they make helps me work it out, since tins of soup or vegetables in water sometimes sound quite loud, but tins of chicken don't make much noise.

"It might be a bit awkward if someone moved my food around so I got a tin of one thing out the cupboard, expecting it to be something else; but thankfully that's never happened.

"I have had people sometimes move a few of my things, not meaning any harm. It's never been a big deal for me, because it's only been minor things, but it's nice if people remember where they were before and put them in the same place after they use them, say if they're visitors. It's just a bit of a pain having to feel around for them if they're not where I expect. I know they don't do it deliberately though.

"A similar thing's happened when I've given people cups of tea, and then they've put the cup down somewhere, and

I've forgotten to ask them where they've put it, and they haven't told me, so when I next want the cup, I've been feeling around the place looking for it, although it's normally either near the chair they were sitting on or on the work surface in the kitchen, or on the draining board.

"Sometimes they've washed it up for me, which is nice, but they put the washing-up liquid back on a different part of the draining board from usual, just not thinking about it, and when I've wanted to use it next, I've put my hand in the normal place, and then wondered where it could have got to when I can't find it, so I feel around for it, and it might take a bit of time to find it, even if it isn't that far from its normal place, if I feel around in the wrong direction first.

"Mind you, I've put things down myself and then forgotten exactly where I've put them, so I've had to feel around for them, like if I put something near one end of a big work surface and later misremember it being near the other end, so I start feeling for it there first. Maybe an impatient person would scold me, saying, 'You should know where that is; you put it down yourself!' But I haven't got a photographic memory.

"Another thing I don't like is when I drop something on the floor, and I know someone who can see could just see it at a glance and pick it up with no problem."

Becky interrupted, "Well unless they've got arthritis or a back problem, or another condition that makes it difficult for them to bend down."

Tony responded, "That's true, there is that! There might be more people who've got problems easily picking things up than I think. I was just thinking about times when it's been a pain to feel around for things till I find them, especially since I know one person who used to sometimes say things impatiently like,

'You were touching it just now!' Well I might have been touching it with my elbow or something, but you can't feel the detail of things with your elbow, or even with the back of your hand, like you can with your fingertips, so you can't necessarily distinguish what you're feeling for from other things. I mean, for one thing, you can feel more parts of something at once if you're feeling it with more than one finger at once, which makes it easier to tell what shape it is, so you've got more chance of determining what it is."

Barbara said, "Yes, I don't like it when people sound all scornful like that. Thankfully most people I've met seem to be understanding. But sometimes I've had that kind of problem, like not long ago I was trying to find something on a table, which was chock-full of stuff so I was a bit worried about accidentally knocking something over, so I was feeling for it very slowly from the right of the table to the left. Then a sighted person came in and I asked them whereabouts it was, thinking it would be nice to just be able to find it immediately. They told me it was right at the front of the table, in a tone of voice that made it sound as if they thought I was silly for not knowing something they thought was obvious, or for not checking there first. But another reason I missed it was that it was in the closed box it had first come in, which I hadn't expected, so I wouldn't have recognised what it was even if I had touched it.

"And a couple of days afterwards, I was talking to the same person, and I went out of the room to get them something, and when I came back, unbeknownst to me, they'd moved. I started walking back to where they'd been before, and they laughed and told me I'd gone past them, as if they thought that was a silly thing to do. But since they hadn't told me they'd moved, I'd hardly say it was my fault.

"One thing that happens occasionally at home in our big sitting room is that if I'm doing something in a different part of the room from the one I'm in most of the time, or if I'm in the same part but in a different position from usual, I can head off towards the door, but if I accidentally start off walking in just a slightly different direction from the one I'm supposed to be going in, I can be walking at a different angle from the one I should be without realising for a little while, and end up somewhere different than where I'd intended to be, sometimes banging into something. It doesn't happen often. But I can just imagine someone impatiently saying, 'How long have you lived here? You should know the way round by now!' "

Just then, Jeff and Rita came back in. They told the others what they'd been doing, and said they wanted to go home soon. They were persuaded to have a cup of tea first. They ended up staying a bit longer than they'd intended to.

Tony explained to them that he, Barbara and Becky had just been talking about making mistakes.

When they'd got a cup of tea, Barbara continued the theme, saying, "I remember I was walking somewhere unfamiliar once, and someone told me I needed to turn left. I assumed they meant sharp left, so I did, and they had a go at me, saying, 'I said left!' Well I had gone left. It turned out they'd meant I should just bear left a bit."

Tony said, "I've had comments like that. Another thing that bugs me is that sometimes when I drop something on the floor, I don't want to risk getting my hands all dirty by feeling around on the floor for it, so I feel around gently and carefully with my feet. But sometimes when I've found it, someone's been watching, and they've thought I've just trodden on it, and they've said, 'You're stepping on it now!' in a tone of voice that gives the impression that they're thinking, 'You clumsy idiot!'

"I'm not saying that every time I tread on something I've dropped I'll be doing it because I've been trying to find it with my feet; it's just that sometimes I won't really be treading on it, as such, when it might look as if I am."

Rita said, "People who tell you you're stepping on something might not necessarily be thinking you're just being clumsy though. They might just want to alert you to the fact."

Tony replied, "Maybe. It's just the impression I can get from their tone of voice.

"Mind you, I know I've complained about a few things, but actually, most people I've met have been nice and understanding.

"And also, lots of things are getting better for blind people. I had this blister on my foot recently, and it got a bit infected; and the doctor prescribed some cream and antibiotics for it, and there was braille on both the boxes, saying what they were! It's brilliant that they do that kind of thing nowadays! Someone even bought me a sponge cake that had braille on the box recently that said what it was! I kept the box as a souvenir because I was so pleased!"

Barbara said, "Wow, that's good! it would be good if all boxes and other containers of food had braille on, especially bags of frozen vegetables, since the vegetables often stick together in the freezer so they feel like a big lump, so it's hard or impossible for a blind person to tell what they are by feeling the shape of them through the packaging like we normally would. I don't know how they stop them sticking together in the shop!

"I do like the fact that a lot of medication's got braille on it. Unfortunately, sometimes they stick print labels over the braille.

It's still possible to feel the braille through them. It's just more difficult. I remember I had to have a few kinds of eyedrops once that were given to me in an eye hospital, and print labels were stuck over the braille on all the boxes of them! I could still feel what it said, but it became a lot easier when I mentioned it to someone and they tore the print label off the one I showed them.

"Still, it's a lot better to have braille labels on boxes that are covered up with print ones than not to have braille ones at all. Actually it could be essential to have braille labels on medication. A while ago the doctor told me I was anaemic and had a vitamin D deficiency. He prescribed me some vitamin D and iron tablets, and the boxes had braille on them that said what they were, so that was nice. But when I'd finished them I decided to buy more from the supermarket to keep myself topped up, so my levels didn't get low again. The supplements I got from there weren't high doses, just the recommended daily ones. I was still a bit anaemic, so the doctor advised me to take three of the iron tablets a day for a few weeks.

"Neither of the bottles of tablets from the supermarket had braille on. Maybe there's a law that says prescription medications have to have it on but supplements that can just be bought over the counter don't, I don't know. But both bottles felt exactly the same, and the tablets felt the same too, and I got them mixed up. For a while I thought I was taking iron tablets when they were really vitamin D tablets, which was a pity, considering I was supposed to take an iron tablet three times a day and the vitamin D one once a day. Still, I bet I'm not vitamin D deficient any more!

"After a while I wondered if I could have got them mixed up, so I asked a sighted person which was which, and then I discovered I had. I put a bit of wrinkly Sellotape on the lid of the iron tablet bottle after that so I'd be able to distinguish it from the other one. I just hope I don't forget which bottle I put it on!"

Tony said, "That's awkward! It's just as well you found a sighted person you could ask about it! I've heard that some people have recently developed technology that'll mean blind people can hold a gadget in their hand and move it over a piece of shopping or a letter or something else with print on it, and it'll have an electronic voice that'll read out what it says. That'll be brilliant, as long as it's affordable!

"Shopping's easier for me than it used to be though, because a lot of supermarkets let you order things online now and deliver them. I've got a computer with an electronic voice like Barbara's, Becky, and it reads things that are on the Internet and documents on my computer to me, so I can order things online myself. So that's how I get most of my shopping nowadays. It's really nice to get it delivered.

"Another thing that makes things easier is that a lot of the pages that display products on the website of the supermarket I get my shopping from have got cooking instructions on them, so I can read and remember them, or go back and check them when I want to cook the food they're referring to, so I no longer have to find a sighted person to ask what the cooking instructions on them are after I've got them. ... Well, not normally. Occasionally a page tells you to put the food in the oven and heat it up, which you'd hope people would know to do anyway, but it doesn't tell you how long for or what temperature to put it on, so I still have to ask. But most of the time things work well.

"That's apart from the fact that I do have one little bugbear, which is that I always seem to have a bit of a problem cooking things like sausage rolls and pasties, because when I cook them for the length of time the instructions say they're meant to be cooked for, they often aren't crisp enough for my liking, and I won't know whether they are or not till they've cooled down enough for me to taste them, and I've always turned the oven off by then so it's cooled down itself. If I could see I could check what they looked like as soon as I got them out the oven and then just put them back for a while longer if they didn't look cooked enough for my liking, like if puff pastry things didn't seem to have risen.

"But since I can't, I have to use a process of trial and error to determine how long to cook them for before I manage to cook them the way I like them. Too long and bits start spurting out onto the baking tray.

"I once cooked some sausage rolls when a sighted person was there, and when I'd cooked them for the length of time the instructions said we should, he told me they still weren't brown. So I cooked them for a few minutes longer, and he said they still weren't brown! I think that happened a couple more times before he said they looked properly cooked!

"The instructions do say they're just guidelines and individual cookers might vary. So maybe that's part of the cause of the problem.

"Still, at least I've never got food poisoning."

Becky joked, "I suppose you could always live on chocolate. Then you wouldn't have that problem."

Tony grinned and replied, "No, but I might end up with much worse ones!"

Becky and Barbara chuckled.

Then Tony said, "I do have a few other little problems when it comes to food, like when I buy some new things and then realise after the delivery driver's gone that I can't identify which thing is what, say if I buy a tin of soup and a tin of pears and they both feel exactly the same, or a box of chicken pies and a box of choc ices and both boxes feel the same. Before Christmas one day, a delivery driver asked me if I needed any help, and I said no, only to discover when he'd gone that I couldn't identify quite a few things, because I didn't normally buy them, so they were in unfamiliar-shaped boxes.

"Sometimes I open boxes to feel what's inside to identify it, but that's not ideal, because I think some things go off more quickly once they've been opened. I especially wouldn't want to do that with tins of things that are supposed to be eaten soon after they're opened ... or things that are intended to be Christmas presents for other people!

"I'm lucky really, because I have got friendly helpful neighbours who'll tell me what things are and read cooking instructions on boxes of food for me if I take them round to them. I should probably be more grateful; it's just that it does sometimes feel irksome to have to go trundling my way around with a bag of groceries to see if a neighbour's in so they can tell me what's what, when I know someone who can see just wouldn't have to do that; they'd be able to tell at a glance what was what.

"Still, at least I've never made a bad mistake, thinking something was one thing when it was another and only realising when it was too late. Well, I have sometimes bought two things that felt exactly the same, like packets of soup or yoghurts with different flavours, and ended up not knowing which was which, so I just resigned myself to not being choosy about which I had when, and just opened the first one I touched when I felt like eating one.

"I do the same thing if I buy a variety pack of crisps, you know, if there are packets of cheese an onion, ready salted and other flavours in it. I think it would be good if there were raised markings on the packets, different-shaped ones for different flavours. Then blind people would get to know which was which after we'd tried them, so after that we could always choose which one we wanted.

"One thing that bugs me is when I find I've bought a few things that feel the same, like microwave meals with similar ingredients, and one tastes really nice and I'd like to buy it again, but I don't know which of the ones I bought it is, and I've thrown the cardboard outer packaging in the bin by then and it'll be all covered in gunk, because I threw it away as soon as I took it off, so I can't trundle around with it till I find someone to ask to tell me what it is. Or something worse is when I unexpectedly really don't like something, but I'm not sure which of the ones I bought it is, and I've thrown the container it came in away by the time I've eaten it, so I can't ask someone what it is so as to make sure I don't buy that one again. That hasn't happened very often though."

Jeff said in a cajoling tone, "Come on, grumpy guts. I don't think this is really the time to complain about your problems."

Tony quipped, "Alright, I'll complain about someone else's. I know one blind person who accidentally put a box of mince pies she'd had delivered in the freezer, thinking it must be a box of battered fish portions or something. I don't know what they were like to eat after that! I'm not sure how she got them mixed up, because frozen food always feels pretty cold when it gets delivered, and things that are meant to go in your cupboard don't. But maybe the box of mince pies was a bit cold because it was just before Christmas so it was really cold outside when the driver was bringing it in, although he can't have been out there for that long. Maybe the mince pies had been next to the frozen food in the van; or maybe she'd temporarily forgotten she'd ordered mince pies so she wasn't expecting them; I don't know.

"The other day I bought a cauliflower cheese ready meal. The driver who delivered my shopping said, 'The cauliflower looks very green.' I wondered if cauliflower's supposed to be green, since I had a vague memory of hearing that it was some other colour like purple. But the driver's tone of voice made it sound as if he meant it looked fresh, so I just took it to mean that. But later I checked online out of curiosity, and found that cauliflower normally is purple, although there's a strain of it that is green. Anyway, it tasted decent enough, so maybe it was that kind.

"Not that I've really got any understanding of the difference between green and purple, not having ever been able to see them. I just know that green can be a healthy sign of freshness, but that it's also the colour of some kinds of mould, I think. Hopefully the driver wouldn't have sounded so cheerful if he was telling me the cauliflower looked mouldy though! I'm pretty sure he wasn't though, since as I said, it tasted decent."

Barbara Brings Up One Problem Blind People Can Have, and Then Tony Tells More Little Stories About His Mishaps

Barbara said, "I've had the same kinds of problems as you sometimes with not being sure what's what. And one problem is that if you can't do something that most people find really easy and just take for granted that people can do, I reckon some people might think you must be incapable of doing things you find easy as well. You know, like if you were at a job interview and you weren't familiar with the layout of the room so you asked the interviewer to guide you to a chair, they might think, 'Well if she can't even walk the few steps to find the chair on her own, is she going to be able to do anything in our workplace?' But in reality you might not have a problem walking around an environment when you get familiar with it, and you might be really good at sitting at a desk all day where you've got everything you need to hand, doing your work."

Jeff sniggered and teased, " 'You might be really good at sitting at a desk all day'! That would be a nice job for a lazy person, wouldn't it! I might fancy that one myself every now and then! But imagine how much telling an employer that would impress them! Imagine if someone said something like that on an application form, because they thought the employers would appreciate honesty. Imagine if they said, 'I love spending days lying around on the grass in the sun', or, 'I do have a tendency to flop around over my desk having naps all day', or, 'My dream would be to stuff my face in the works cafe all day'!"

Barbara smiled and said, "Oh Dad! You know what I mean! I meant a blind person might be really good at sitting at a desk all day Doing their Work!"

They all giggled.

Tony said, "I agree with what you're saying about job interviews, actually. I remember a job interview I went to once that went wrong. I got most of the way to it by train. That was easy; I don't know if Becky knows, but most of the time, train travel's not difficult for a blind person, because as long as we can find or get guided to a station staff member to start with, they'll guide us to the train we need, and phone through to the station we want to get off at to say we're coming, so someone will come and meet us off the train and guide us to the one we want next, or out of the station if that's what we want. ... Well, normally they do. So as long as there's an announcement at every station saying which one it is, we'll know when we need to get off.

"I did once try to get into London by train, only to end up coming all the way back again without having got off once, because there were no announcements about which station was which, and when it stopped for a long time at the terminus station I was actually supposed to get off at, I wondered if we were there or whether we'd just stopped for quite a while at a red signal. Five minutes before we'd got there we'd stopped for quite a while too, and I didn't hear the doors open, so I thought we must just have stopped at a red signal, and that they must sometimes stop for quite a long time at those. I didn't hear anything from outside that would have given me a clue about where we were, and there was no one in the carriage for me to ask. So I just stayed on the train at what turned out to have been the terminus station. I was supposed to get assistance onto my next train, but no one opened the door and asked if I needed help, so maybe no one turned up, or they did but went away again when they didn't see a blind person get out.

"Then the train started again, and I still stayed on it, hoping to hear an announcement about where we were, until I realised I must have come all the way back again when I finally heard an announcement at the station we'd just stopped at, saying we were in the place I'd started from! Thankfully it wasn't a really long journey! I wouldn't fancy going all the way up to Scotland and then just coming all the way back again! Mind you, you'd eventually get an idea that something was wrong if you started going all the way up there and then coming back again, because of the amount of time it was taking.

"But I think things have started getting better; thankfully on most trains, they've started announcing what station they're at, even at the little ones, so we've got a good chance of knowing which one's ours.

"I think they might have even started doing that on buses in some places, which is good. I've always asked the bus driver as soon as I've got on the bus if he can tell me when we get to the stop I need to get off at. Most of the time they remember, so it works well. There've just been one or two times when I've had problems, like one day when I was going to work, and the bus driver forgot to tell me when we got to my stop. I realised we must have gone past it several minutes later when I got pretty sure I'd been on the bus for longer than usual. So I got off at the next stop, hoping someone would help me find my way back to the one I was supposed to get off at. Thankfully an old lady got off with me, and she guided me across the road to a bus stop on the other side where the buses were going the other way, and told me when the one I needed came along, so I got on it and managed to get off at the stop I was supposed to have got off at before.

"As for that job interview I mentioned, I didn't have any problems with transport there. After I'd got off the train, I took a taxi the rest of the way to where the interview was, because I wasn't familiar with the area so I didn't want to have to risk wandering around lost when I was supposed to be being interviewed; I've found before that you can be close to a place but still wander around for some time trying to find it, if you can't see road signs, buildings, whether you're on the right side of the road or the wrong one, or anything else. There are often lots of helpful people around who'll guide you to a place if you ask, and I've had lots of offers of help before; but there aren't always people around everywhere, so I wouldn't want to just assume there'll be people there and wander happily out into the unknown till they turn up."

Barbara said, "I know what you mean! It's funny how it can be easier for a blind person to get right up to the other end of the country than it can be to get around their own neighbourhood, at least if they're not used to walking around it. It's nice to let the train or some other transport do most of the work.

"I've got lost in places I thought I knew quite well sometimes. There was one time when I was walking home from the station after I'd been somewhere, and I thought I knew the way quite well, but I think I must have accidentally walked past a crossing I was supposed to cross the road at. I can't have been walking close enough to the kerb to find the little bobbly bits they put on the ground to let blind people know a crossing's there. I found a crossing after a while, and assumed it was the one I wanted, but it must have been the wrong one, since I crossed over the road and kept on walking on the other side, but ended up somewhere totally different from where I'd expected to be. I went round a corner and found myself on this really quiet road with a pavement that got narrower and narrower, and realised I was lost. I couldn't hear anyone around to ask for help. But after a while, someone did come up to me and ask if I needed help, and they guided me back to a place I knew the way home from.

"I actually got lost in a garden once – well, it was mostly like a concrete patio, so I don't personally think it was worthy of the name garden, although people who could see the plants in it always said it was nice; but it was the back garden of the family of an old school friend of mine, who used to invite me around to her house for the weekend sometimes, and it had flowers and other plants around the edges. I wasn't all that familiar with the layout of it, but I did know how to get from the back door to some chairs they had there.

"I thought it would be nice to sit in the sun for a while one afternoon when they had some friends around and they were indoors showing each other photos, and I was getting a bit bored. My friend was helping with some washing up, but I didn't want to go in the kitchen in case the person who was putting the things away thought I was in the way of wherever she might want to put them and got annoyed. I've had complaints like that from one or two people before. So I told the people who were looking at photos I was going to go and sit in the sun, and went out and sat on a chair. I was using my white stick to help me go out, because there were obstacles in the way I didn't want to bang into.

"Then the sun disappeared. I'd been enjoying the warmth of it, so I wanted to sit in it again. I didn't know whether it had just gone behind a cloud, or if it had just moved a bit, since it was around the time in the afternoon when it would start disappearing off to the other side of the garden.

"I waited for a bit, thinking it might come out again if it had gone behind a cloud, but it didn't. So I wondered if it had just shifted over. If I can't feel the warmth of it on me, it could be even just ten centimetres or so away and I wouldn't know. I got up and walked a little way, but I didn't feel the warmth of it, so I thought I'd go across to the other side of the garden to find out if it was there, especially since I thought there was a chair there I'd be able to sit on in the sun if it hadn't been taken away.

"So I went across the patio to the other side of the garden, trying to find the chair. But I couldn't. I didn't know if it was still there, or whether someone had moved it or taken it out of the garden. I didn't want to wave my stick around to find out if it would hit something that sounded like a chair, because I was a bit worried there might be plants in the way and other things I might accidentally vandalise with it. So after a few timid little pokes around with it without success at finding a chair, and still no sunshine, I decided to just go back indoors.

"But that turned out not to be as easy as I'd thought it would be! I went to where I thought the door was, but I didn't find it. I thought there might be more flowers around the edges of the garden there, and again, I didn't want to wave my stick around trying to hit something that sounded like a door so I'd know I'd found it, because I was worried about knocking flower heads off, or vandalising something else! So I just gently poked about with it for a while, not being able to find the door. I found a window ledge; but since I didn't know whether it was on the right or the left of the door, and how far away from it it was, it didn't give me a clue as to what direction to go in to find it.

"I decided to go over to the other side of the patio again and then try walking back over, to see if I could find the chair I'd been looking for or the door. So I did. I walked in a slightly different direction on the way back over, and found the chair that time. I think it was in pretty much the same place as it had been in before, but I just hadn't found it the first time I tried. I knew what direction I needed to go in from there to find the door. So I managed to get back indoors.

"But goodness knows who might have been watching me trying to find my way back in! Maybe they just thought I looked like a daft weird idiot, flapping my stick around aimlessly or something. No one said anything. But who knows what they might have thought!

"Anyway, I can imagine it would have been a whole lot worse if I'd been wandering around outside an office block where I was soon due to be interviewed for a job, wondering if the interviewer was watching!"

Tony said, "Exactly! I wouldn't have enjoyed that when I went for this interview I started telling you about. Not that it would have made much difference, as it turned out!

"The taxi driver who drove me to where the interview was going to be guided me into the building where it was going to happen, and showed me to a seat before he left.

"I'd said on my application form that I'm blind, so the interviewer must have known, unless she didn't read it properly. But when she called me and I asked if she could guide me to the room the interview was going to be held in, somehow I got the impression she wasn't impressed, as if she was thinking, 'Is someone going to have to take time out from their work to lead him around by the arm whenever he gets up? And if he needs help with something as basic as this, what else will he keep asking us for help with?' Well I don't know; she might not have been thinking that at all. I was just worried she might be.

"Of course, in reality, as soon as I'd learned my way around a place, or the part of it I was working in, which might not have taken long at all, I wouldn't need to be guided any more, unless it was really noisy so I couldn't hear what was going on around me above the din, so I wouldn't be able to do things like hear people coming and know to avoid them, or hear acoustic clues to whereabouts I was like little echoes that come off walls that enable me to judge how close to them I am, or the differences there are in the acoustics that let me know there's an open doorway right near me. It can be a bit disorientating to walk around a noisy environment because I can't hear those. I'd still have my white stick to help with problems like that though.

"The other thing that could sometimes be a problem is if it was risky to move around without being able to see because there was dangerous equipment around there, but there wouldn't have been any there. There might have been people leaving their chairs out and putting boxes in the middle of the floor, and that kind of thing; but my white cane would help me deal with those hazards.

"Anyway, there was a funny side to what happened, because we had to go upstairs to get to the interview room, and after the interview, the interviewer guided me to the stairs and started going down in front of me. But we'd just started walking down when a worrying thought must have suddenly struck her! She asked me, 'How often do you fall down the stairs?' Well as soon as I'm able to remember where the stairs are in a building, which is normally after I've been shown where they are for the first time, I'm usually no more likely to fall down them than anyone else is. But I made a silly sarcastic comment like, 'Hardly ever normally; but I suppose I might fall down them often if someone kept putting banana skins on them.'

"Maybe an image came into her mind of me slipping, hurtling down the stairs, knocking her flying and landing on her at the bottom, squashing her flat, because then she announced, 'I want you to go in front of me now.' So I did.

"I never heard from her again after that day. Maybe she thought she'd better not give me the job because she was worried I'd keep walking down the stairs behind people and slipping, falling and knocking them flying till one by one they were all dead; or maybe she thought they'd all end up suing the company for having employed this horribly destructive maniacal clumsy blind person who kept falling and knocking them down the stairs all the time! You just don't know what goes on in people's minds, do you!"

They all laughed. Barbara said while giggling, "Of course, she might not have given you the job for a different reason entirely!"

Barbara Talks About Some of Her Experiences, Including Sometimes Hearing Echoes Coming Off Objects as She Walks Around so She Knows Where They Are

But then she said seriously, "Mind you, I think one of my tutors decided I was incapable of getting a good job after university, or else she's always thought that about blind people. She's just made a few comments about not knowing if there's really any point in me being here, since I'm unlikely to get a good job afterwards. Well, I know there will be a lot of limits on the kinds of jobs I can do, and more on the kinds of jobs I could do as quickly and efficiently as a sighted person could, which will obviously make a lot of employers prefer to employ someone who can see; but it might still be possible for me to get something decent.

"My tutor started making those comments after she'd helped me walk from one of the buildings I have lectures in to the other one day. Her attitude made me start thinking blind people ought to be careful sometimes about accepting offers of help from some people in situations where we can do without it, because then the people helping us might start to think we accepted their help because we couldn't do without it, and that we're incapable of doing more things than we really are, when we might really have accepted their offer of help just because help would make it easier for us. Well, hopefully only a small minority of people would ever think that. I don't know though.

"Anyway, like I said, I have my lectures in two separate buildings. The route between them isn't very long at all, but it twists and turns quite a bit in little ways, just because you have to keep going left and right to avoid objects in the way – I think they're raised flower-beds – I'm not quite sure – but they're about waist height, I think, at least judging by the way they make the acoustics sound. People might assume I'd have a problem finding my way from one building to the other because you have to keep changing direction slightly to get there – unless you're a rampant vandal, I suppose, who really wants to go in a straight line so he just clambers up and tramps straight over the top of the flowers!"

Barbara grinned when she made that joke. Then she continued, "But anyway, I've never had a problem getting there, ever since someone taught me the way there and I practised with them a few times till I remembered what direction to go in when. One thing that makes it easy is that I can hear the slight echoes coming off the objects in my way – they're solid and big enough to make the echoes strong enough to hear. Most blind people can tell a certain amount about what kind of place they're in, and sometimes whether there are big things in their way, by clues, such as a food smell outside a cafe, but also by the acoustics. You can tell whether a room's big or small by whether the acoustics make it sound enclosed or open; and if you're walking along by the side of a big wall, you can tell if you're going past a wide open doorway, at least if you're making a bit of noise, say with a white stick sliding along the ground, because the echoes that come back from the sound you're making will make the acoustics suddenly sound less enclosed, like Tony mentioned.

"Often I've been walking across a quiet road, and I've been able to hear that there's a car parked by the kerb, because I've heard the way it changes the acoustics slightly; I think it's the echoes that come off it when my stick makes a noise when I move it along the ground and the sound waves from it hit the car or something – I'm not entirely sure how it works.

"But if you click your fingers when you're near a wall or a car and listen carefully, you might hear a quiet little echo coming back from it, or something similar. I think the reason most people who can see can't usually hear those kinds of things is because they're mostly concentrating on what they can see, so they're not listening out for them, whereas blind people are paying more attention to what their ears are picking up than would be normal for a sighted person. But someone who can see told me he'd noticed the echoes once after he listened out for them out of curiosity after I'd told him I could hear them.

"I think there's a small minority of blind people who can't hear them, probably especially people who haven't been blind for long, and people with hearing problems of course. Actually, it's surprising how much good hearing, or at least hearing that's equally good in both ears, can help blind people walk in a straight line. I had an ear infection once that made me deaf in one ear, and I found I kept walking at a diagonal by accident. I'm not sure why that kind of thing happens.

"But even if your hearing's good, you won't hear the echoes all the time; I once accidentally bent the end of my old white stick right up, because I didn't realise a parked car was by the kerb when I was crossing a road, because I didn't hear any echoes coming off it; and the bottom of my stick went underneath it, just as I was stepping forward holding the top, and the middle of it hit the underneath of the car, and obviously couldn't go any further forward, so it bent a lot. I couldn't use my stick after that, because it wouldn't even reach the ground when I was holding it! Thankfully a strong person saw what happened and came up to me and asked if I needed help, and managed to bend it back for me.

"Actually it's funny: The other day I was imagining what it might have been like if someone had been trying to teach me to listen out for echoes coming off objects, and they were a bit like my old cookery teacher, and criticised me and insulted me when I made mistakes like that time when I bent my white stick, and they would always say, 'You're not very good at this, are you!'

"Imagine if eventually they said, 'I think someone ought to put, "You're not very good at this, are you!" on your grave!', meaning it was so appropriate for me it ought to be the thing I was remembered for.

"I'd have thought, 'Yeah! It would look as if it meant, "You're not very good at being dead, are you!"' I might have told them that and said to them, 'Maybe it'll be true. You'd better watch it! Maybe I just won't be able to get the knack of being dead, so I'll keep rising to life again and haunting you!'

"That's if people who aren't properly dead Can be described as haunting people. I'd be like a zombie, popping up and appearing to the person at the most inconvenient moments! And maybe I'd do it really well, so I'd have finally found the thing they couldn't tell me I wasn't good at!"

The others giggled. Becky said, "Yeah, and just imagine if it really Was your old cookery teacher who kept saying that before you died, and you sometimes popped up and appeared to her in her cookery lessons when you'd turned into a zombie. Someone might make a little mistake, and she might be just about to criticise them and insult them for it as usual, when you'd appear to her and she'd scream instead!

"They'd think she was demented, not being able to see you themselves! The one who'd made the mistake might say soothingly, 'There there, Mrs Cactus-Monster or whatever your name is! All I did was accidentally put a spoon in the fork section of the cutlery drawer; it's not that bad! See, I'll just put it back in the spoon section now. All done! See, it was easily remedied, wasn't it!' "

The others laughed.

Then Rita said, "Tell us more about the way you can hear echoes coming off some things, Barbara. You've never told me about that before."

Barbara replied, "Alright. Sometimes when I know I'm near an open doorway but I'm not quite sure where it is, if I haven't got my white stick with me to find it with, then as long as there isn't too much noise around to hear very faint sounds, I click my fingers, sometimes a few times, and then I can often tell where the doorway is, because I can hear where the acoustic that sounds more open is.

"Sometimes I click my fingers when I'm sure I'm near a doorway and want to find it, or when I know roughly where the doorway is but don't know if I'm heading for the middle of it so I'll be able to walk straight through it without banging into the door frame on either side, or whether I'm too far to one side or the other so I might. Or if it's a double door that sometimes just has one of the doors open, but sometimes they're both open or both closed, if I click my fingers, I can tell whether one of the doors is open, and which one, and roughly where the sides of the opening are.

"That kind of thing works best with echoes that are on a level with your ears, or not too far below them. You can often hear things a bit lower down though if they're pretty solid, like a wall or the back of a bench. The bigger they are and the closer to one of your ears they are, the more chance you've got of hearing them. With smaller things, you have to use other methods of finding them.

"I remember at this holiday camp for disabled people I mentioned earlier, several of us slept in dormitories that had an ensuite loo and shower each. Unfortunately in mine, the loo stuck right out into the middle of the bathroom, instead of being in a corner. I sometimes used to accidentally bash my knee on it when I went in there. One day I went in there to wash my hands or something, so I didn't shut the door, and one of the volunteers who'd come to help us and slept in our dormitory came in after me and told me to wait because there was water on the floor and she'd just mop it up. I bashed my knee on the loo again, and she said, 'You keep forgetting that's there, don't you.' But it wasn't that I forgot. It was just that it wasn't easy to judge exactly where it was without seeing it. If you knew roughly how many steps you had to take to get to it but went even half a centimetre too close to it, you'd hit it.

"But then I discovered a way round the problem. I found out that if instead of walking straight forward to get to the loo when I went in the door, I turned sharp left and walked a few steps, I'd get to the washbasin, and I could reach out my hand from there and touch the loo, and then I could walk towards it with my hand on it, so I knew exactly how close to it I was getting. It didn't matter if I accidentally gently banged into the basin, since I'd be hitting that with my stomach, which has got a fair bit of padding on it, so it didn't hurt, unlike bashing my knee. Most of the time I held out my hands a bit in front of me so I found it with those though. It was high enough that I could do that comfortably.

"Anyway though, with bigger objects that are higher up, it's easier to hear where they are if you're close to them. I used to walk down a path that had a bench about halfway down on the grass next to it, and I could often tell where it was, because as I walked by, sliding my white stick along the ground in front of me, which would make a noise, I could hear an echo or different acoustic coming off the back of the bench, with whichever ear was nearest, just for a second or so as I passed.

"I don't mean the echoes make it sound noticeably echoey around me. They're just like tiny changes in the acoustics."

Becky remarked, "That's interesting!"

Then Tony smiled and said, "Talking of benches, I remember going for a rare day out with our school; I think it was to some botanical gardens. Anyway, the only thing I remember about it is that when we first got there, we sat down for a rest."

He grinned and joked, "If we needed a rest by then, it must have been because it was tiring, all sitting in the back of the minibus or whatever we went there in while someone else did the driving."

The others tittered.

Then he carried on, "Anyway, when we sat down for this rest or chat, some of my classmates sat on a bench, while me and one of the care staff who'd come to help us sat behind it on the grass. I was just lounging around when I found a baby's dummy on the grass; goodness knows how long it had been there. But for some reason, I decided it would be fun to fling it, thinking it would be a laugh if it went over the heads of my classmates on the bench and landed on the lap of one of them and gave them a surprise!

"So I flung it, and I didn't think I'd thrown it that hard, but it flew right over the bench and hit this man who was walking along the path in front of it. I found out when the care staff member next to me told me. I did laugh, because she told me the man had looked at *her*, as if he thought She was the one who'd thrown it; and he might have thought she'd aimed it at him deliberately!"

Barbara said, "That reminds me of when I accidentally threw a book at a teacher once. We were all waiting for her to come in and start the class. She was a bit late. I found this little book on the floor, and I don't know why I threw it at the doorway; I think I was just a bit bored, and thought it would be a slightly amusing way of killing a second or two of time. But she came in at the very second I threw it, and it hit her! Thankfully, I think she accepted that it was an accident."

The others giggled.

Barbara Tells the Others About What She Believes to Have Been a Misguided Favour That Led to Her Getting a Bad Name Among Some Staff at the University

When the laughter died down, Becky asked, "Barbara, were you thinking of telling us something else about that tutor with the bad attitude you mentioned earlier?"

Barbara replied, "Oh yeah. There *is* more to that story. As I said, when I'm walking from one of the buildings I have my classes in to the other, I can hear the echoes coming off the objects in my way when I move my white stick and it makes a noise sliding along the ground, and also I'm familiar enough with the direction I'm supposed to be going in to know when to turn left and when to turn right whenever it sounds as if an object's looming up in front of me; and I can hear them whenever they're on both sides of me at once so I know I'm going in the right direction, because I know the acoustics are supposed to sound a little bit enclosed like that at that point along the way.

"I was walking along listening to the echoes coming off the objects to help me find my way one day when that tutor – who's actually the head tutor in the department – came up and asked me if I wanted help to get over to the other building.

"I accepted the help, because being guided by someone is easier than using a cane, partly because it's more relaxing, because when you're using a white stick, you have to concentrate every second you're walking along, so you can move out of the way the second it hits an obstacle so you don't hit it yourself, and also because you've got to rely on your memory to make sure you keep going in the right direction, because you can't see what you're heading for, or anything else for that matter, so you've got to concentrate all the time to make sure you go where your memory tells you you're supposed to be going. And you might be busy listening out for things like echoes that are coming off things too.

"But I think accepting help might have made the tutor assume I was accepting it because I was finding it hard to find the way. And I think that might have given her the impression that I'm not really capable of finding the way, despite me having been here for a while; and I think that might have made her think I'm incapable of doing more important things like getting a good job after I leave here. But then like I said, she might have thought that kind of thing before that ever happened anyway.

"But something worse than that happened. I don't know if it had anything to do with her watching me finding my way between the buildings, but not long after she guided me from one to the other that day, I was told the tutors had got the university to pay to get workman to lay a path with a distinctive kind of surface on it between the two buildings to help blind people find their way, and they were going to invite me to a meeting to ask me my opinion on it. I assumed they meant they were going to ask me what I thought of the idea before it happened. So I was planning to tell them I didn't think there was any need to do it, because I could get from one place to the other with no problem, and I thought most other blind people who ever needed to do the same thing would probably be able to do that too once they'd been taught how to get there, which wouldn't take long, since it only takes a couple of minutes to get there.

"But instead of doing that, they spent thousands of pounds putting this new path in, and Then called the meeting and asked me what I thought of it! That was just recently. They must have been expecting me to be really pleased with them and to think they must be really caring for doing it. So imagine how unhappy they were with me when I was annoyed instead, because I didn't like it and hadn't been asked what I thought about the idea before they made the decision to put it there! I'd like to have had the chance to suggest they do things differently or not at all before they spent all that money on it.

"The path they laid was covered in big bobbly bits of concrete that aren't comfortable to walk on, and instead of curving round at the end to lead onto the ramp up to the building we need to go to, it stops dead against the wall of it! So any blind person trusting it to lead them there and following along it, not using their white stick well enough, so they get too close to the wall to stop in time when their white stick hits it, will end up going smack bang into it!

"Also, instead of sauntering along on a gentle curve between all the obstacles like I used to, the path stops dead against each one and then makes sharp turns round it, so following it would mean breaking my stride every time my stick hits one of them so I can make whatever sharp turn around it I'm supposed to be making.

"I was a bit upset that they'd wasted so much money making a path that would just be in danger of leading blind people smack bang into the wall and that was uncomfortable to walk on, and I was annoyed that I hadn't been asked for my opinion of the idea before they'd done it so I never got the opportunity to tell them it was easy to manage without it before they bothered putting it in. But they must have been disappointed that I was unhappy, so I think they've just thought of me as stroppy and ungrateful and difficult ever since."

Tony said with a grin, "Well they've got the right idea about you there then! ... No, I don't really mean that. It's a shame really. They should never have put the path in without asking you for your opinion of the idea first!"

Barbara replied, "No. And there's this man on the university staff who uses a wheelchair, who's been disabled ever since he broke his neck in an accident; he's employed as a disability rights advocate or something – I can't quite seem to remember his official title at the moment; people always just use his name. But I don't really like him, and he doesn't like me now!

I think he was probably consulted about putting this new pathway in, and he probably thought it was a good idea and expected me to be happy. But he's been complaining about me since I got annoyed at the meeting about not being asked what I thought Before they made up their minds to put this path in. Whether they consulted any blind people at all, I don't know. But if they didn't, but just thought consulting someone with a completely different kind of disability would be a good idea, well it actually seems as if it was a Bad idea, even if he does think he's qualified to be a spokesman for disability rights in general!"

The Conversation Turns More Light-Hearted, as Tony and Barbara Start Joking and Telling Embarrassing Stories

Tony said, "Still, it would have been worse if they'd put the path in and then asked you to contribute to paying for it. At least they didn't do that!"

He joked, "Actually, imagine if they'd made all the bobbles on it out of dried dog food. A blind person with a guide dog would get to where they wanted to go alright, without even learning the way there, because the dog would just follow the bobbles directly to where they wanted to go, eating as they went!"

Barbara giggled and said, "Yes, but it might take a long long time to get there, since the guide dog might take half an hour to eat them all! And then what would happen if another blind person came along! There might be none left, and just a very full, very sick guide dog at the end who'd eaten way too much and hadn't recovered by then!

"And just imagine if the university staff had somehow thought it would be a good idea to use tinned dog food instead of the dried stuff. The blind person might find themselves walking through a load of squelchy half-eaten dog food on the way to the end of the path!"

Tony grinned and said, "That's true. You know, I was talking to a blind person with a guide dog the other day, and she reckons it's easier for blind people with guide dogs to walk around than it is for blind people who are just using white sticks a lot of the time, since the dogs get to learn what certain words mean, like door and chair and find, so if you say, 'Find the door!', chances are it will, so you don't have to faff around trying to come across it yourself, or follow bobbly bits of ground that lead you into walls, if you don't know where it is. ... Well, that's the idea. I wonder how many people with guide dogs have been taken to the wrong door, and only realised that after they ended up in the boss's office by mistake, or when men ended up in the ladies' loo or something."

Barbara laughed.

She said, "I know a blind woman who's got four grown-up sons. She told me some funny stories about embarrassing things that have happened to her. She said before her sons were born, her best friend once came to see her with her guide dog who was called Unity. They chatted late into the night. For some reason, the guide dog managed to run away. Neither of them could see to go and find it, so they asked the man who was this woman's husband at the time to go. He went to look for it, and couldn't find it at first, so he was walking around the streets calling its name. So he spent some time in the middle of the night walking up and down the streets calling, 'Unity! Unity!' He must have sounded like an insane hippy who somehow thought it was a good idea to call on everyone to have more peace and harmony with their neighbours in the middle of the night!

"And she said that when one of her sons was a teenager, she needed to go shopping with him to buy him a new school uniform. He didn't like going shopping, so she didn't trust him to get something decent-looking; she thought he might just take the first thing he tried on, even if it didn't fit him that well, to get the shopping over with. So she decided to feel what he'd put on while he was wearing it to see if it at least felt as if it fitted him well. She heard someone coming out of a changing room and thought it was him. She started feeling their trouser legs, saying, 'Oh good, you've made a good choice; they don't feel too baggy; they're a nice fit.' A man answered, and she realised it wasn't her son at all. She apologised, and he said it was alright and that she'd made his morning.

"And she loves to go sailing. I don't know why. But she goes to a sailing club for people with disabilities, and they let her go out in a little boat on her own. I don't know how she does it; they go on a lake, and maybe they think there aren't many things around, so there isn't much chance of her bumping into anything, and maybe the people in charge radio her to give her directions back in when it's time to go in, or someone sails up to her and directs her in; I don't know. But she said one day, she was merrily sailing along, and she didn't realise, but there was another sailing club there where they were all having a race. Some of them were just reaching the finishing line when she sailed across it the other way, and they had to scatter so she didn't collide with them. So she ruined their race. But she said she doesn't get embarrassed easily, so it didn't bother her too much, even though it must have bothered the people who'd been racing."

Tony Talks About the Radio Show He Does on a Little Internet Station, and Tells Some Funny Stories About What He's Done, and Also Some He's Told on it

Tony said, "Those are good stories! Do you think she'd mind if I use them on my radio show?"

"Radio show?" asked Becky.

Tony replied, "Yes. I present a radio show – only on a little Internet radio station that started recently. It doesn't have many listeners, but it's fun to present it. I play music and tell funny stories I've heard or found on the Internet and printed out in braille to read on it."

Becky asked, "Don't you have problems using the studio equipment?"

Tony replied, "Not many. We broadcast from our own homes, and I play music that's on my computer. I've got some software that's designed for putting radio shows together on that plays the music I want it to play and records my voice. My shows are prerecorded. I think most of the people who do shows on that station prerecord them. I send them to the radio station manager when I've finished them and he broadcasts them at the times when they're scheduled to go out. I've got a good microphone connected to my computer so I can record my voice between the songs. The electronic voice on my computer tells me what each track is, so I can be reminded which one of my songs is going to play when, so I'll know to announce the right one when I'm about to play it. It's set up so what my speech software says isn't broadcast over the microphone.

"I did have a few problems when I was first trying to use the software I use to broadcast with, because my speech software didn't tell me everything I needed to know, like exactly how much time there was to go before it would be time to finish my show, or before each song finished; but those problems have been fixed now. The speech software's got a function where people who know what they're doing can write scripts for it, which are like instructions to get it to say things it wouldn't do otherwise in programs that weren't designed to work with it; and someone wrote some of those for it, so it gives me and other blind people who use it to present radio shows more information about which words are coming up on the computer screen while we're using it now than it did before, and he invented new keyboard commands for it to help us access various bits of useful information when we want it, such as how many seconds a song's got to go before it ends. So the radio software's easier for us to use now."

Becky said, "Tell us some of the funny stories you've told on your shows. And tell us about some of the things that go on at the radio station."

Tony replied, "Well it's only a little local station, just one of the little community ones. I had a little bit of trouble getting onto it in the first place. I asked whether I could do a show on there, and one of the presenters, who used to work on a popular local commercial radio station, emailed me to ask me if I'd like to meet him for coffee to talk about how I'd do shows. Actually I don't like coffee, so one of my friends joked, 'It's going to go down well when you reply to him by telling him that, isn't it!'

"Anyway, it didn't happen in the end. I was fairly new to the area and didn't know the way to many places. So I asked him if he'd be happy to have coffee in a community centre not far around the corner from me, and he said he would. But then

I asked if he'd call for me and guide me there. I wasn't quite sure where the doorway was and didn't want to be blundering around trying to find it in the cold. It was winter, and I'd never been in there before. I'd just been told the community centre was there when I walked past it with someone, and that there was a cafe in there.

"I don't know if me asking him to guide me put him off the idea of meeting me, but at about midnight the night before we'd arranged to meet up, he contacted me by email and said he'd realised he had too much work to do to meet me. I emailed him back asking what would be a more convenient time, but he never responded, so I wondered if what he said was just an excuse.

"I wondered if he could have been working himself up with worry about the idea of guiding me. I thought maybe he thought, 'Oh no! What else might he ask me to do? If he wants the loo, will he ask me to go in there with him? What would linking arms with and going into the loo with another man do to my credibility! And how incapable must Tony be when he can't even get around the corner by himself but needs me to go with him? Could such a person really do a radio show?'

"But I thought I could probably do shows that were better than his! He interviews people from the local community about things they've done; but his interviews sometimes sound as if they're being done in a toilet, since there's quite an echo on them. The radio station rents a local recording studio to do some of their shows, and I had a laugh thinking, 'Maybe they can't afford it any more, but the studio owners said to them, "Don't worry; you can rent out our toilet at a special discount price, and we'll put a bit of radio equipment in there for you," so some of them do their shows in there.' Can you imagine if a presenter contacted people to ask if he could interview them, and when they said yes, he said, 'I hope you don't mind, but I'd like you to come into the toilets in the building where the studio is with me to do the interview, since we can't afford to go in the actual studio.' "

Becky and Barbara laughed. But Rita said, "You're not being very nice! I hope the man doesn't know you're this rude about him! Poor thing!"

Tony replied, "I don't think he does. Anyway, he visited me in my flat in the end and he turned out to be nice after all. And a couple of the others were nice to me. I spoke to another man there not long after the first man said he couldn't meet me, and he listened to a demonstration show I'd done. He said he thought the music was good and he liked the idea of me having a show, but he said the sound quality ought to be improved first; he said the music sounded 'crunchy'. I don't know what he meant by that. Actually I think he might have said it sounded both too crunchy and too punchy. I wondered whether if I managed to change the sound of it but he still didn't like it, he might say, 'Well it's not crunchy or punchy any more, so that's good, but this time it's too Munchy!' "

Some of the others giggled again.

Tony said, "Anyway, they said I could have a show in the end. So I started playing music and telling funny stories in between the songs."

Rita said, "I think you're good! I like the music you play, and I enjoy the funny stories you tell. I hope you don't make any more jokes about the people who gave you a show though; it wouldn't be nice. They didn't Have to do that for you!"

Tony looked a bit sheepish and said, "Oh I know. Actually, I know I've just made jokes about them, but I do appreciate them for letting me do a show. And also, I Am grateful for all the support I've had from other people over the years, like you, Mum and Dad; I know I wouldn't have been able to achieve anything like what I have in life if it hadn't been for you helping me over the years, like buying me my computer equipment and working on setting it up for me and things, helping me move into my flat, driving me around to places over the years, and things like that."

Rita responded, "It's nice of you to say that. Actually, I'm sure we could all be thankful for what other people have done for us; everyone probably needs to rely on help from other people from time to time. And as well as that, we're better off because of what other people have achieved over the years that helps us do the things we do, like the people who invented computers, and the people who got loads of them into the shops, and the people who make sure lots of food gets into the shops that we can buy, and all kinds of people like that. We all depend on other people for our survival and quality of life. But I'm glad all the things we've done for you over the years have paid off, and you're now reasonably happy and successful, and you've got hobbies you enjoy."

Tony said, "That's nice. I do appreciate the *extra* help you've given me because I can't see.

"It's funny actually though: Me and Barbara have spoken so much about being blind today, Becky might think that's all we ever talk about! Well, hopefully she doesn't. But actually, when I've got everything I want around me so I can just get on with things, which is most of the time, since you helped me get everything I need set up, I don't think about being blind at all. I just be me. I bet that's the same for Barbara too."

Barbara said it was.

Becky said she'd expected as much really, since she and Barbara often happily talked about other things.

Then Tony said, "Anyway, about the funny stories you wanted to hear, Becky: One I told on my radio show was something I found on the Internet about a man who kept going into his local library and taking his shoes off, despite the fact that the librarian would often ask him not to because some of the people there would often complain about the smell of his feet. Some would even leave because they thought it was so bad.

"The man got banned from the library in the end for causing a nuisance by still taking his shoes off, but he still kept going in there and doing that, so they took him to court for trespassing. He was ordered to pay a fine, but he didn't like that, and said he'd take the case to a higher court to appeal the fine. He did, but they had no sympathy and doubled it! He spoke to the international press and said he was going to take the case to an even higher court! I don't know what happened in the end. Can you imagine him going to a solicitor and saying, 'I want you to fight a case for me! I've been fined by a court just because I've got smelly feet and I like to take my shoes off in the library!'"

The others laughed, and then Tony said, "Another story I told was about a 2000-year-old joke book that's been found, written by the Romans ... or one Roman at least. There were jokes about absent-minded professors, and fake prophets, and lots of other things. One was about a great big sporting event called the Millennium Games, about how an athlete was really upset that he didn't win his race, and one of the spectators tried to comfort him, saying, 'Never mind; you can always try again at the next Millennium Games.'"

They giggled, and Becky said, "Imagine an athlete competing in an international competition when he was over a thousand years old! Maybe his body would have been preserved in ice all that time, and they would have defrosted him not long before and resuscitated him."

Barbara said, "Actually, that Roman joke reminds me of something someone said at school. We had to do some of our washing ourselves, by hand, which was good really, because it meant we learned how to do it, and they taught us how to iron and sew and things, making sure we knew how to do them safely, so we could end up being more independent than blind people whose parents do all that kind of thing for them.

"We used to put our clothes in a spin dryer when we'd washed them by hand. There was a laundry room over the top of one of the classrooms, and one day one girl said she was going to do some washing, but someone said the spin dryer might make a bit of noise when a lesson was going on in the classroom below, so, not really thinking about what she was saying but trying to be considerate, she said, 'Oh, maybe I'll put my clothes in the spin dryer first and wash them afterwards then, so I can finish using the spin dryer before the class begins.' Then she realised what she'd just said."

The others chuckled. Then Tony said, "It's nice working at the radio station. People email me requests sometimes, and I play them on my next show if I've got the songs on my computer. I ask people to email me little funny stories about themselves or things they're interested in that I can tell on air too. Maybe I'll tell that one. I hope the person it happened to wouldn't mind.

"A fan of pirate radio emailed me a funny story he'd heard once. It said there was once a ship on the North Sea near where Radio Caroline was, and they were broadcasting this pirate radio station, and the authorities wanted to close it down, because they were sure it was causing interference on the emergency channel the coastguard used. But one day the pirate radio station stopped broadcasting for a while, and the interference was still there! It turned out that it was coming from two completely different stations, one of which was the BBC World Service! That must have caused a bit of a scandal! I don't know what happened in the end."

They giggled again.

Tony said, "It's not just funny stories I do. I make my own daft wacky jingles too. I've got software that works with the electronic speech on my computer where I can mix things like sound effects together with my voice. I've downloaded some sound effects from the Internet, like the sound of ducks quacking, the sound of an elephant, the sound of a train, and other things. I made a sound effect where there's the sound of a big splash, followed immediately by the sound of an elephant doing that trumpeting noise they make, so it sounds as if an elephant's just jumped in the water and doesn't like it. Then I put the sound of ducks quacking noisily afterwards, as if they don't like the elephant being in it either. And over the top of the quacks, I put my voice, saying the name of the radio station.

"And another jingle I've made has the sound effect of people talking in a restaurant; and then the sound of a train comes in, fading up and then down as if it's coming into the restaurant and going out the other side. And then the sound of chatting and cutlery on crockery continues, as if people are just carrying on eating and talking as if nothing happened. And I've mixed my voice over the top of that, so while the train's fading out, I say, 'The sound of ...', and then I say the name of the radio station, so it sounds as if I mean the sound of the radio station is the sound of a train going through a restaurant, while people eat their meals in a leisurely way as if they're just used to trains passing through it because it happens all the time in that restaurant.

"And I've made some daft promos for other shows on the station too, that I play on my show. Like there's one where I mixed my voice with a famous song by Diana Ross that has the words 'I'm missing you' in the chorus. I recorded my voice saying what time one of the other programmes was on and what was on it over its introduction, and then I edited quite a lot of the song out so the chorus would come straight in then, saying 'I'm missing you', and then I faded it down a bit to talk over the top of it again, so it sounds as if straight after it says that, I say, 'Oh well don't worry about that; if you miss it the first time, you can hear it when it's repeated', and I say when it's on again.

"There's another promo where I say what's going to be on over the introduction of a song, which I edited a lot out of so the chorus comes in next, and it says, 'Just ain't good enough'. Straight after it says it, I've made the music fade down and I say, 'Come on, how do you know?' as if the artist singing the song's really saying the programme just isn't good enough. Then I made the song fade up again, and it says, 'Just ain't good enough' again, and after it does, I've faded it down again and put my voice on it, saying, 'Oh go on, I bet you haven't even heard it yet; give it a listen!'

"The station management haven't complained about me making that promo, so I'm assuming they don't mind."

The others thought that was amusing.

Then Tony said seriously, "It's interesting though: I never realised how much preparation you have to do for a radio show. I used to hear DJ's on the radio, and what they do sounds effortless, and I used to think it must be an easy job. And I'm not saying it's hard or anything. But since I've been doing radio shows myself, I've realised there's a lot more involved in putting them together than I thought. So it's made me realise DJ's must work harder and put more thought into what they do than I ever thought they did.

"I mean, since I've been doing shows, I've discovered it takes a lot more time and planning than I expected:

"You've got to keep trying to think of new ways to introduce your show and say goodbye so you don't start to sound repetitive; you've got to do your best to make what you want to play and say fit exactly into the time you've got, and if it's going just under the time or just over, you've got to try and work out what to do about it; you've got to make sure you know how long the introductions of all the songs are and plan things you can say that fit into the time you've got before the vocals begin on any song you'd like to talk over the introduction of so you don't crash the vocals; you've got to find out before a show if the songs you're planning to play fade down slowly at the end so you can talk over the endings, or whether there are any with a fancy vocal bit at the end that it would sound horrible to talk over; you've got to find new things you can talk about every time you do a new show so it doesn't sound boring; if you record yourself telling a story or something before the show so you can edit out any mistakes you make before it goes out on air, for me, anyway, it takes me longer to do the editing than I would have ever expected; you've got to remember to announce the name of the station and say your name and whatever the station owner wants you to say during the show, at whatever times they want you to say it, and the number of times they want you to say it; and you have to do other things like that.

"Well, I suppose on big radio stations, DJ's have probably got a team of people helping them with all that. But it's at least what DJ's have to do on little stations like the one where I do my show.

"There are other jobs people do that I just used to assume must be easy; but finding out there's a lot more involved in putting a radio show together than I ever realised there was has made me realise there's probably a lot more involved in lots of other jobs than I ever thought there was too, and they might take a lot more skill or stamina than I ever realised."

Becky said, "I know what you mean. I used to think doing a radio show must be easy, until I did one with some other students as part of our media studies course on the local community radio station. I thought it was fun to do, but there was a lot more work involved in putting a show together than I'd realised – you know, like making sure things stayed within the time we had, and editing the interviews with local people we did before we put them on the air. Sometimes we had to take out bits of them we'd rather have left in, to keep the show within the time we had.

"And I think we all made a few embarrassing or funny mistakes from time to time, like once I started talking, thinking the microphone was on, not paying attention to it, because I just expected it to be on, but I realised halfway through what I was saying that it wasn't on, and instinctively I quickly switched it on, but when I'd finished talking, I realised it must have sounded funny to listen to, with a silence, and then people suddenly hearing the second half of a sentence, which probably began halfway through a word even. I didn't just start what I was saying again when I switched it on, because I'd started playing a record and the vocals were coming up, so I thought that if I started what I'd said from the beginning, I'd be talking all over them.

"After that, I made up my mind that I was always going to test the equipment every time before the show started to make sure it was working. Sometimes I did. But often I still didn't remember or couldn't be bothered, thinking it was probably alright. Thankfully it was, most of the time. Just as well, because we were being assessed by our tutors on how well we did!"

The others sniggered.

Tony grinned and said, "I've made mistakes too. I accidentally did something recently that's against the station rules. Thankfully I don't think anyone noticed! They've got this rule that you're not supposed to play songs with swear words in them. Well I didn't think any of the music I've got had any swear words in it, but ... actually I'm not sure I should be admitting this with Mum and Dad here ... but oh well, I've started now, so I may as well finish because they'll probably be able to guess what happened anyway now."

He went a bit red with embarrassment. Then he carried on, "Well I didn't think any of the songs I play had any swear words in them, as I said, but I don't listen to the lyrics carefully; I just like music as a nice melodic background to what I'm doing; but I found out that at least a couple of the songs I've played actually Do have swear words in them! The thing is, I didn't find that out till they were actually playing on the radio station for everyone to hear! ... Well, if anyone was listening, that is! I must have been listening to the first parts of them more carefully than I normally do when they were going out on air. But it was too late, since they'd just played by then. I hoped no one would complain, and that no one from the management was listening carefully and heard them!

But no one said anything, so I think they can't have noticed, thankfully!

"It was odd, because I'm pretty sure all the songs I'd played on the shows I did before that one didn't have any swear words in them, and then somehow I managed to go and play two that did in the same show! It wasn't as if the swear words were smattered all over the songs and really noticeable; there were only one or two in each song; but still!

"And then I went and did it again a few weeks later, playing a couple of songs that turned out to have swear words in them, only I just hadn't realised before because I'd never listened to them closely enough to pick them up. I just noticed when they were going out on air! They weren't all that noticeable."

Barbara giggled and joked, "You know, I could blackmail you with that story now! Whenever you're being horrible to me from now on, I'm going to threaten to tell the station management you played songs with swear words in them!"

Tony grinned broadly and said, "You dare! If you do that, I'll tell the management you were the one who gave me those records to play, and that you told me that if I didn't, you'd invade the station headquarters and throw rotten apples at the management just to embarrass me!"

Barbara laughed and said, "Oh as if they'd believe you! You might have to come up with a more convincing story than that!"

Everyone laughed.

Then Tony said, "Actually, I recently did another thing that must have sounded a bit daft to anyone who noticed. Hopefully no one did. I played a few songs that were in a foreign language, and I said before them that I didn't know how to pronounce their titles so I was just going to have to guess.

Well I did guess, but then I noticed, for the very first time, that at the very beginning of a couple of them, the first words they sang were something that sounded just like their titles were probably supposed to sound, and I realised I'd pronounced them wrong. At least I could pronounce them better at the end of the songs when I repeated the titles; but if anyone did notice, they must have thought, 'What a twit! Saying he doesn't know how to pronounce that song title when it's the very first thing the song says!' And maybe other people wondered why I pronounced it differently at the beginning than I did at the end, and thought, 'He just can't make up his mind how to pronounce it, can he!' "

Tony sniggered, and everyone else laughed.

Then he said, "Actually, I did something else that was a bit daft when I first started at the station. I told my local society for people with sight problems that I'd started doing a show there, and they said if I liked, I could write something about it and send it to them, and they'd put it in one of their newsletters that they send out to members. So I did. And they did put it in one. I was pleased when I discovered it was in there.

"But I wondered if the first sentence had been edited. They say in their newsletters that some things might be edited so everything will fit in the space they have. It said, 'I've been blind since birth, but that hasn't stopped me doing what I want to in life.' I thought, 'Surely that should say, "some of what I want to in life"! Of course I can't do Everything I want to in life! Almost every day there are things I want to do but I can't! I can't just saunter out to the shops like most people can; I have to learn the way to one in great detail before I can go to it, and when I get shopping delivered, I want to be able to identify everything I've been given immediately; I don't want to have to play "guess the item" every time I buy things that feel the same as each other or they're new and feel unfamiliar so I can't tell which new thing's which! I wonder if someone edited what I said to fit in the space. If they did, it's silly to have edited something that completely changes the meaning of a sentence! What can they have been thinking!'

"So I thought those things, and grumpily found the file on my computer with what I'd written in it to check what that said. And guess what! It said exactly what it said in the newsletter! It hadn't been altered at all! I myself had written that sentence! I must have been feeling particularly optimistic that day! Or maybe when I wrote it, I had the big things in mind, like my dreams, whereas when I read it back later, I was thinking about little day-to-day problems. So the people who put what I wrote in the newsletter didn't deserve all the grumbling I did in my mind after all!"

The others chuckled. Barbara said amid her laughter, "You twit!"

Then Tony said, "There was a bit of controversy one week when one thing I did in preparation for a show was to download a short speech from the Prime Minister from the Internet, and download some burp sounds, and I edited out some of the Prime Minister's words and replaced each one with a burp. And I played it on a show! And I did a similar thing with a member of the Royal Family, but replaced words with horse neighs and dog barks. I thought it was funny. They usually repeat my show a few days later, but that week, they put a different one on instead. I thought someone must have complained, or the station management must have disapproved of what I'd done, so I emailed the station manager and asked them who'd complained, or whether it was just them disapproving. I said,

'Oh well, if someone's complained, at least I know someone's listening!'

"The manager emailed me back and said no one had complained, but they'd just played the wrong show by mistake."

Becky and Barbara giggled, and Becky said, "Actually, I messed around with mixing sound effects with famous people's voices and altering them myself once, on the radio show I used to do with other media studies students, with my tutor listening!"

Barbara and Tony grinned.

But before they could find out any more about what Becky did, their mum said, "You want to Keep your show, don't you, Tony? You'd better not take too many risks like that!"

Tony replied, "Yeah, true. Mind you, I do do some nice things sometimes. On the last week of every month, I tell a heartwarming story on the show that I found on the Internet. I record myself reading them in braille, and then edit out any mistakes I make from stumbling over words or whatever before I record the show. Mind you, that didn't stop something else that sounded a bit daft happening recently: My show was on one of the last days of the month. The story sounded good. But the repeat of the show was a couple of days into the next month. I listened to it, and I realised that at the beginning of the show, I'd said, 'Since it's the last week of the month, I'll be telling a heartwarming story.' Anyone listening to the repeat, not knowing it was a repeat, must have thought, 'What a twit! He thinks it's the last week of the month this week when it's really the first!'

"And just recently I did something else that was a bit embarrassing: I edited a story I wanted to tell, but I didn't take as much care with it as usual; I just edited out some mistakes and then thought it would be alright, not listening to it again to check to see if anything else needed editing. The recording was quiet, so I amplified it with my editing software. I'll know to check things I edit properly in future! I only realised when it went out on air, but it turned out that it had amplified all the breaths I took a lot, and some sounded really loud, especially where I'd paused for a second or two to take a breath and took a long one! I would have edited them out if I'd checked it! I will in future. Oh well, you learn by your mistakes."

The others laughed.

They chatted on for a while. Then Barbara's parents decided it was time to go home, and they and Tony left.

Chapter Three

Becky and Barbara Make a New Friend, and They Discuss Faulty Eyewitness Testimony and Other Things

Becky started going swimming with Barbara sometimes, guiding her from her hall of residence to the pool and back, with Barbara linking arms with her and Becky steering her out of the way of objects so she didn't bump into them, and telling her whether she needed to step up or down when they were about to encounter a kerb. Then in the pool, she would tell her when it was safe to start swimming at the beginning of each length they did when there was no one near enough for Barbara to bang into.

They both enjoyed swimming, or at least felt pleased that they'd done some worthwhile exercise when they'd finished.

One day, they got chatting to another student, Pauline, while they were drying their hair after a swim, and Barbara told her about the things Becky did to help her with her work, and at the swimming pool and so on.

Well-meaning, Pauline said, "Oh, I hope you give her something nice in return, like buying her treats!"

Barbara looked guilty. Becky saw her expression and wanted to quickly say something to reassure her that there was no need to worry.

She grinned and said to Pauline, "Don't encourage her to do too much of that! We've just been swimming partly to get healthier and lose a few calories. If she goes and buys me a treat, I'll end up putting on all the calories I've just taken off!"

Pauline exclaimed, "You're a bit young to be worrying about calories, aren't you?"

Becky replied, "Maybe. But anyway, that's not the only thing. I wouldn't want Barbara to feel as if she's indebted to me; I help her because I want to, not because I'm hoping for something in return.

"Besides, I'm doing a psychology course, and we recently read a book that said rewarding someone for something can have the opposite effect from the one you expect, after a while anyway. It gave some examples. It said one is that if a health service is trying to get more people to donate blood, if they offer a small amount of money for it, thinking that'll incentivise more people to donate their blood, they might find the opposite happens: A lot of people might feel insulted, thinking, 'My blood's worth more than that!' and not donate, whereas if the recruitment drive had just publicised how much the blood was needed, people would think about the need instead, and make a decision to give blood depending on how much they cared. Of course, it might make a difference if they really needed the money, or if the amount on offer was larger."

Pauline said that was interesting.

Becky continued, "And there was a study of nursery school children where the ones who enjoyed drawing were given some attractive drawing equipment. They were split into two groups, and the kids in one group were given a nice-looking certificate for drawing a picture, which they'd been promised they'd get if they did well before they started; but the kids in the other group weren't offered anything.

"A few days later they were all given the drawing equipment again, but weren't promised anything if they drew something nice. The kids who'd been given the certificates before showed a lot less interest in drawing than the ones who hadn't been given them, even though they'd enjoyed drawing as much as the others had, as if the ones who'd been given a certificate before thought not being promised one was a bit disappointing, and it put them off drawing the second time.

"I mean, just because that study found that, it doesn't mean every study would; but you can easily see how that would work, can't you."

Pauline responded, "Wow, it sounds as if people need to be careful about what they do! Mind you, it must be possible to go too far the other way. I mean, I've heard people say things like, 'I did all that work for her, and she never even offered me a cup of tea!' "

Becky became thoughtful and said, "Yes, perhaps there's a happy medium somewhere.

"But it seems from what I've read that when people are given things every time they do someone a favour, after a while they come to expect it, so they're disappointed if it stops happening, and it puts them off doing the favour from then on. I wouldn't want to end up like that. Mind you, Barbara does give me cups of tea and biscuits and things sometimes when I go to her room."

Pauline tried to be reassuring and said, "If you don't want to end up like that, you probably won't. You must be helping Barbara for other reasons, and those reasons are still going to apply even if she does give you treats."

Becky replied, "Maybe. But I'm wondering if that kind of feeling could come on without me really wanting it to. I was surprised by what I read. And it's not just children who can have attitudes like the ones I've been talking about. You'd have thought grown-ups would know better, but maybe they don't. At least, not all of them. So if that kind of thing can happen to grown-ups, I'm wondering if it might be even more likely to happen to people of my age.

"A chapter in a book I read about that kind of thing said there was a school in America that was started by people with a vision to give kids a different style of education from the norm, where teachers put work into helping the kids develop their own individual talents and creativity, and there was a more easy-going atmosphere than there is in most schools, where the kids were allowed to wear what they wanted, and decide for themselves whether they wanted to go to classes. Teachers were paid quite a low salary, but they were all dedicated to putting in a lot of work to make the school successful.

"But the time came when they seemed to forget about how much they'd wanted to actually teach the kids things.

"Schools got the opportunity to become independent from government regulations, and the teachers and other school staff were pleased. But for a school to be allowed to do that, they needed to come up with some new and interesting plans to improve the performance of pupils who weren't doing so well. All the teachers got together and had a think about what to do.

"They'd noticed that there seemed to be two main categories of pupil, one group who were enthusiastic about the work and keen to come to classes and learn, and another where the pupils didn't like school and would often skip classes. The teachers came up with the idea that if they could improve attendance rates, the kids who weren't so dedicated to learning would start getting better grades, because they'd be there more often, so they'd learn more things. The school didn't have a bigger problem with kids skipping classes than other schools did, but still the teachers thought improving attendance rates was a good idea. They decided to try to both stop kids giving up courses they'd started, and to get them to turn up for lessons more often.

"They didn't come up with any good ideas about just how to do that, but they left it up to individual teachers to think up ideas for themselves, and made it the rule that they'd calculate how many kids were still attending courses some time after they started, by getting someone to go around to classes on one day in the last week of term, not warning the teachers in advance of which day it would be, and the teachers who had more than eighty per cent of children attending their classes on that day would get a huge salary bonus.

"A few years into the new system, school inspectors found that the number of children finishing the courses they'd started had gone up from around half to around three quarters, so it seemed the new system had been a great success.

"But when it was looked into more thoroughly, it was found that although far fewer kids were dropping out of their courses than they had before, they weren't attending more of the lessons; and worse than that, average grades, far from rising, had actually fallen! So it seemed kids weren't learning as much as they had before.

"Some researchers investigated the problem, interviewing staff about what had changed since the new system had been introduced. They discovered that teachers simply weren't teaching the way they had before; they were trying to entice pupils to stay on their courses and attend their lessons so they'd get their big salary bonuses. So they were doing what they hoped would make the kids want to come to classes more, instead of what they thought would help them learn. They were all trying to make their courses more interesting and fun, but not in a way that would make actual learning more enjoyable; they were having more field trips, and parties in class.

"They were still doing a lot of teaching, just less than they had before, because their bonuses were the main thing on their minds; so they did what they knew was pretty much guaranteed to make a lot of the children stay on the courses, instead of doing experiments to find out what helped children most, which might or might not have worked.

"But they were all teachers who'd had good intentions when they started working there."

Pauline thought that was interesting. She said, "Wow, so even teachers can behave like that!"

Becky replied, "Everyone probably can. But maybe part of the reason the teachers did that was because no one had given them any better ideas about how to get attendance rates up, and they thought they'd feel embarrassed and annoyed if other teachers got bonuses because they had more parties in their classes, while they didn't get bonuses because they tried to do as much teaching as they had before."

Pauline said, "It's interesting that things can work like that. Mind you, I don't suppose it means people's attitudes would change no matter what. If you knew there was a possibility that you'd start thinking more about a reward than about what would help someone, and you didn't want to, you'd probably catch yourself beginning to do it if you did, and then you might have a good think about what was really most important to you."

Becky replied, "Yeah, maybe. Perhaps it would partly depend on how dedicated you were to doing what you were doing, and how strong the emotion was that made you want the reward, as well as other motivations. I mean, maybe some of those teachers felt really enticed by the idea of getting a bonus, and the emotion was stronger than their principles; or maybe some of them thought they could really do with the bonus because they were struggling because of the cost of living. Or maybe they knew they'd feel really left out if other teachers got bonuses but they didn't, and they didn't want that to happen. Or maybe for some of them, it wasn't about the bonus; they just felt under pressure to raise attendance rates a lot so as not to let the side down. Or maybe they just didn't predict that the kids would get lower grades if they spent more time having fun instead of learning.

"I don't know why they created a competitive atmosphere by deciding on the bonus scheme, instead of making it the rule that they'd all try to find out information about what had worked in other schools, and think more about what might work themselves, and try any new ideas they found or came up with, and then pass the information on to the others if they succeeded, so they could try it too. Maybe one of them suggested the bonus idea, and everyone fancied the idea of getting more money so they just went along with it."

They'd finished drying their hair, and walked outside. Pauline was going in their direction, so they walked together and chatted.

Becky and Barbara Start Joking About How to Make Swimming More Fun

She asked them, "Do you feel better after doing exercise?"

Barbara replied, "Not particularly. I do quite like going swimming though."

Then she grinned and joked, "Of course, I might feel a lot better if the water was made of ... say, lemon squash! ... Or maybe I wouldn't, because I'd spend so much of the time drinking it I'd probably feel really full when it was time to get out, and be twice as fat as I was when I went in there!"

They chuckled, and Pauline said, "Surely you wouldn't really want to drink the water ... or whatever it was! Not when it would have chlorine in it, and dirt from other people, and who knows what else!"

Barbara smiled and said for fun, "That's true! Maybe what would be really nice is if everyone else could be banished from the pool, so I was the only one allowed in there!"

The others giggled, and Becky said, "It wouldn't be nice for everyone else!"

Barbara grinned and replied, "No, I suppose not. Alright then, maybe it would be good if everyone here could have their own individual swimming pool. Then people could have whatever they liked in them. Imagine if some people had honey instead of water! If you could resist the temptation to eat it all, imagine how fit you'd end up after spending hours trying to swim through that! ... Well, I doubt anyone could really eat a swimming pool full of honey! Imagine how fat you'd get if you tried! And sick! But maybe anyone who wanted to swim through it could start off by swimming through yoghurt, and gradually build up their muscles and their fitness till swimming through honey was easier."

Becky giggled and said, "Oh really! What if there were no showers? People would have to walk around all sticky, covered in honey or lemon squash or whatever else they had in their swimming pool. But if everyone had a private swimming pool here, there wouldn't be any room for lecture theatres or anything else!"

Barbara grinned and joked, "That's true. Maybe we wouldn't need lecture theatres though; maybe lecturers could just sit at home and talk into their computers, and what they said would be beamed into all the swimming pools so everyone could hear it while they were swimming. And if there was no room for any student accommodation because of all the swimming pools, then maybe at night, people could just stay in the pools, some sleeping on beds of honey that they'd been swimming around in all day, and some floating around on a sea of lemon squash, and that kind of thing."

The others giggled.

Becky remarked, "Somehow I think a lot of students would end up with severe sleep deprivation! And if all the lecturers were beaming their voices into the swimming pools at once, it would just sound like a muddled cacophony, and no one would be able to understand what any of them said!"

Barbara grinned and replied, "That's true! OK, that idea needs work!"

The Conversation Turns to How Barbara Manages to Cope With the Work and Finding Her Way Around When She's Blind

Then Pauline said seriously, "Actually, that's given me a thought. How do you take lecture notes – you know, not being able to see? And for that matter, how do you write your essays?"

Barbara explained, "I've got a little laptop computer that has software on it that makes it talk, so I can type something and then get it to speak it back to me; or if someone emails me course handouts and things, I can get it to read them to me. It reads in an electronic voice; but actually it puts some good expression into it. It's funny though, because if I ask it to read the same few words twice in quick succession, say if I didn't hear what it said properly the first time, it sounds irritated the second time, as if it's thinking, 'I've just told you that! Why are you asking me to tell you it again? You should listen more carefully!' "

The others chuckled.

Then Barbara continued, "I take my computer into lectures, with headphones so I don't disturb everyone around me when it's talking. Then I type notes on it. I can turn the speech off while I'm doing that if I want so it doesn't make it harder to hear what the lecturer's saying."

Pauline commented to Barbara, "I think you're really brave to have come here and done what you do!"

Barbara grinned and replied, "Thank you. But it's probably really just that I haven't got the imagination to think of all the things that could go wrong. Actually though, it's been easier for me than I thought it would be. I assumed I'd have to try to get in touch with someone who runs the student newspaper or the local paper in the area and advertise in it, asking for volunteers who could help me, like by reading the course material to me that I'm supposed to study. But it turned out that there was an organisation already set up to help students with disabilities; on the very first full day I was here, one of the staff introduced me to someone who helps recruit volunteers to read course-work for blind people.

"That's how I met Becky. They introduced me to her. At first I was surprised, and wondered if someone that young could really help me, or should. And I wondered if someone of her age should really even be at university! But I was impressed with what she told me, and it turned out that she's been good at helping me, and she seems to still cope with her studies alright so she's never said it's a burden on her or anything. I don't suppose many kids of her age could do all that; I'm sure I wouldn't have been able to cope with learning the kind of stuff we have to learn at university when I was her age, let alone help people at the same time! I think she must be pretty exceptional! But then, she tells me people have told her she could even talk as soon as she was born. I find that difficult to believe! But she does seem to have some surprising abilities for someone of her age!

"And other people have been helpful here too. It was good, because someone on the staff here got in touch with people from the local society for blind people, maybe before I even got here, and they organised for someone to come here and teach me the way to my lecture theatres, and to a little shop on the campus where I can buy food and drink, where the people who work there help me by guiding me round and getting me what I want.

"Learning the routes to places meant me going over and over them till all the details were in my memory, with the person teaching me them supervising me and giving me instructions at first, and then just telling me if I was going wrong when I got more used to them, until I could go to the places on my own because I'd remembered all the details. I got the person teaching me to write down the instructions for how to get there so I could refresh my memory if I hadn't been there for a while so I'd become less familiar with them, like I might in the holidays. But actually, they're easy routes to remember, so I think I'll always be alright.

"Lots of people have come up to me and asked me if I need help when I've been walking to places too, so I don't think I'll ever need to worry about it."

"That's good!" said Pauline.

The Little Group Starts Talking About Distorted Memories, and How and Why Eyewitnesses to Crimes Can Remember the Details Inaccurately

They started talking about the ability to remember things, and then Barbara said, "Some people seem to feel sure they remember things that didn't really happen. My granny thinks I murdered a little baby bunny rabbit once!"

"What?" exclaimed Becky. She and Pauline were a bit shocked.

Barbara explained, "Well, I'll tell you what happened: When I was little, my family used to keep rabbits. We sometimes had quite a few because they had babies. Not long ago, my granny was around for tea, and we were talking about each other's memories of what other people in the family did when we were younger. Some memories were funny, but then my granny said she remembered me sitting on a baby rabbit when I was little and breaking its back so it died. She said I told her I'd sat on it because I wanted to keep it warm.

"I was a bit shocked to think I could have done that, and asked her why she didn't tell me off. She said it was because I was only little so I wouldn't have known any better.

"But when I thought about it, I was convinced I'd never done such a thing and that she must be confusing a few things in her mind. I'm sure I'd have remembered something as dramatic as that, and I'm sure I had the sense even at that age to know that sitting on a delicate little animal would kill it! What I do remember was that once, a baby rabbit was born that was deformed in a serious way; I don't know what it looked like, but it felt as if it wasn't properly developed at all – not that I felt it that carefully. It didn't seem to have any legs. My granny was there at the time. She thought I might like to cuddle it, so she gave it to me and I just sat there holding it and stroking it for some time, and then she put it back in the hutch with its mum. A few hours later, just before she went home, she came and told me it had died. I thought it must have died because it was so badly deformed that there must have been something badly wrong with it.

"Another thing was that I used to enjoy playing with the baby rabbits. I sometimes wheeled them around our garden in a dolls' pram, and a few times I picked a bit of grass and a few leaves and put them on top of the rabbits, saying I was doing it because I wanted to keep them warm. I know my granny saw me doing that.

"I reckon she must have had the memories of the two things in her mind, and somehow over time, they got blurred into one memory, and she just started misremembering me sitting there with a deformed-looking baby rabbit saying I wanted to keep it warm or something, so she thought I must have squashed it, because she'd forgotten it was born like that. I don't know. But it's the only reason I can think of why she would have said such a thing."

The others sympathised a bit.

Then Barbara said, "I've got another story a bit like that. In the summer holidays after I left school, me and some of the people I'd been at school with went to this campsite for disabled people where they had a holiday week especially for blind people. There were volunteer helpers there, to help us with things like getting around when we went for a walk or on outings to places like museums, and getting from one bit of the campsite to another, like between the places where we slept and the place where we had meals, before we learned the way ourselves.

"There was this girl there who'd been in my class, who embarrassed me in front of one of the helpers one day. My school was a boarding school for blind and partially-sighted people, Pauline. There were kids there from all over the country, so we didn't get to go home that often, and they let us keep rabbits there, which was nice. I had a couple, and this girl had one too.

"She told a lot of stories about things that had happened at school, which was interesting; but I don't know how much of what she said was actually true! Someone teased her about making stuff up after she asked me if I remembered something and I couldn't. She protested that she didn't do that. But I don't know if she often got some details wrong without realising.

"She told this helper about how we'd had rabbits at school, and said I had this really nice cute docile male one that liked cuddles. He did. But then she told the helper that me and her had decided to mate my rabbit and hers, but that hers had turned out to be male when she'd thought it was female, and its personality changed and it got aggressive after that.

"She might have tried to mate him with one of the rabbits, but I'm pretty sure it wasn't mine, unless she'd got him out of his hutch when I wasn't there, without telling me! I couldn't remember deciding to mate my rabbit with hers at all! I might have been a bit stupid – well, maybe I still am; but I can't imagine being irresponsible enough to ever have decided it would be a good idea for hers to have babies, when I didn't even know what she'd do with them! So she was making me look irresponsible in front of this volunteer helper. ... Well, I suppose she was making herself look irresponsible too.

"But it was worse than that, because she said it was me who'd first told her her rabbit was a female, when it was actually another girl, who'd been reading a braille book about looking after rabbits and thought she'd learned how to sex them. At least I remembered who it really was, so I corrected her on that, and then she remembered it was this other girl.

"But I couldn't tell them it definitely hadn't been my rabbit she'd tried to mate hers with, because I couldn't remember what had really happened. I just remembered her saying her rabbit had gone aggressive. But I was pretty sure I hadn't had anything to do with her rabbit mating with another one!

"But it made me wonder if it really is possible for people to feel sure they can remember things when they're really getting a lot of the details about them wrong."

Becky said, "We've got a rabbit at home. My mum bought him a couple of years ago. When she first brought him home, she gave him to me to hold, and I think he might have been a bit scared because he didn't know where he was or what was going to happen, because I could feel his heart beating fast. I said, 'Hello bunny, wow, your heart's beating ...' and then he moved, and I was worried he was going to jump out of my arms and run away, so I stopped talking to concentrate on trying to stop him doing that. I'd been about to say 'fast', but I didn't. My mum said, 'I should hope it is! If it wasn't beating, he'd be dead, wouldn't he!' "

The others chuckled.

Then Becky said, "But as for what your granny said about you killing that poor little bunny rabbit, and what the girl at the campsite said, Barbara, yes, I agree with you, memories can get distorted over time. This reminds me of something we've been studying on my psychology course, and some things I've found on the Internet on my own, about how the memories of eyewitnesses can be unreliable. I think a lot of people probably assume that people who were right there at the scene of a crime must have a very good idea of what happened so their memories must be trustworthy. I used to think that. But the things I've been learning have been interesting:

"It turns out that even people who are right there at the scene of a crime can be mistaken, or miss things. And of course, the longer it is since a crime was committed, the more likely they are to get things wrong, because memories fade, and then people have to do their best to bring them back to mind. But sometimes people mistake other things for real memories, for a few reasons:

"One example is that say a person's in a pub just relaxing and chatting to a friend when someone asks them if they'd like to buy some jewellery for their wife or something. They might just say no and then get back to their conversation, not thinking anything of it. But a few weeks later, they might be sitting there again, when a policeman comes up to them and tells them there have been a lot of burglaries in the area and he believes the burglar has been trying to sell what he's stolen in pubs around the area. The policeman might ask the man if he's been approached by anyone selling something recently.

"The man might say yes, and hope to help the police solve the crime because it sounds nasty having a burglar around. So when the policeman asks for information, he might do his best to remember what happened.

"He might tell the policeman what he thinks he saw. But there might be quite a few reasons why he doesn't get things right: It was a few weeks ago and his memory's faded, especially because he quickly put the incident out of his mind at the time to get on with his conversation, and because it didn't seem to be of any significance; and he wasn't talking to the man for that long so he didn't have a really good look at him, especially because he was concentrating on looking at the jewellery the man was offering him, not on the man himself.

"So he might do his best to piece together his memories of what happened. According to what we learned, one thing people tend to do is to use what they would expect to happen and the way they believe the world tends to work in such a situation as a guide to piecing their memories together, whether they realise that's what they're doing or not. Here's an example of the kind of thing I mean: Say this man believes that some of the people most likely to commit crimes in the area are people with accents that are associated with the poorest neighbourhoods. He might remember he heard a person talking loudly in an accent that sounded like that nearby, and think, 'Oh yes, I bet he was the one who's been committing these crimes!' He might be so convinced it's almost certain to be true that he might tell the policeman that he thinks the person who asked him if he wanted to buy the jewellery had one of those accents.

"And imagine there was someone wearing white shorts nearby at the time. The image of the man wearing them might flash into the mind of the man talking to the policeman, and he might ask himself why that's happening, and think it must have some significance, and that it's probably because the man wearing them was the criminal, whereas it might really be just some random thing that stuck in his memory. So he might give the policeman a completely false description of the one committing the crimes."

The three students got to Barbara's accommodation; but because they were engrossed in the conversation, they decided not to go their separate ways just then, but hung around outside talking for a while.

Barbara said, "I've heard about lawyers trying to trick witnesses they're cross-examining into incriminating themselves or changing their stories in court to ones that contradict what they originally said. One thing they can do is to pretend they're having a really hard time believing what the witness they're questioning's saying, so if the witness isn't absolutely sure about it, they might admit to that. But that must be why lawyers do that kind of thing – because witnesses' memories can be unreliable sometimes."

Pauline commented wryly, "And because they're doing their best to win their cases for their clients!"

"Yeah, that too, I expect," said Barbara. "I've heard that lawyers can act as if they're scornful of a witness and as if they really don't believe them, when really, they're just putting on an act to do the best they can for their client, trying to intimidate the witness they're cross-examining a bit, in the hope that it'll mean the witness isn't confident enough to say what they believe happened as clearly as they would otherwise because they'll know that the more they say, the more they'll be challenged on it. And if that doesn't work, the witness might still get distracted into an argument with the lawyer so they don't get to say what they came to say.

"So I heard it's best if people try not to take anything a lawyer cross-examining them says personally, but they just think of it as the lawyer trying to do their job as best they can, to try to win their case for their client, as if they're playing a part in a drama and trying to do it well. If witnesses think of what the lawyer's doing as just playing a role, they might be able to keep calmer, and to patiently explain what they think really happened when they're questioned about the truth of it, as many times as they have to do it."

The friends Tell Each Other Funny Stories They've Read

Pauline said, "That sounds like good advice.

"You know, the subject of crime's bringing to mind some funny stories I read about people who committed crimes and thought up novel ideas to try to get away with them not long ago. There was one who got charged with assaulting a police officer in America, and he tried to get out of it by claiming he'd declared himself to be an independent country, so American laws didn't apply to him. He didn't get away with it!

"And there was a man who was stopped for speeding in America who threatened to sue the police under copyright laws if they wrote down his name. He said his name was copyrighted, and every time it appeared on one of their documents he'd launch a lawsuit against them for copyright violation, claiming half a million dollars from them, and if the money wasn't paid within ten days, they'd have to pay three times as much. He said if they didn't pay, judgments would be taken out against them to get the money by confiscating their properties and selling them.

"The police asked to see his driving licence, and he said he refused to give it to them unless they gave him a receipt. They called their supervisor in the end, and the motorist said he'd sue him for copyright violation too.

"But his tactics didn't help Him get away with his offence."

Barbara said, "I read about a drunk driver in Belgium who crawled out of his car and started eating grass in a field. Maybe he was fantasising about being an animal. Police found him munching grass and grunting like a pig. They took him to hospital, and there they found out he was drunk. He was taken to court for drink driving, and he told the judge he enjoyed eating grass, especially when he was drunk, because it tasted nice, like spinach.

"He was fined the equivalent of hundreds of pounds, and banned from driving for 45 days."

Becky said, "I heard there's a mental illness where people become convinced they're animals."

Barbara said, "I wouldn't want that! Another story I read was about a drunk driver who was stopped by the police in Holland, and he claimed that he was immune from being charged with anything because he was the Pope. He turned his music up and refused to get out of the car. The police knew he wasn't really the Pope but just pretending. In the end his son, who was in the passenger seat, persuaded him to get out of the car and do what they wanted. They confiscated his licence after he failed a breath test."

Pauline said, "I read about a team of designers who invented a chocolate-powered racing car! It was made of all kinds of foods: the steering wheel was made of carrots; the seats were made of soya beans, and the body of it was made of potatoes. But somehow they made it so it could really be driven, and go really fast, at about 145 miles an hour! The team who made it said they'd like it if in the future, all racing cars had engines that ran on chocolate, and were made of potatoes and carrots and other things that came from plants."

The new friends laughed. Then Pauline said, "Another story I read was about a man in Germany who called the police because he thought his house was being broken into, only for them to find it was his budgie flapping around loudly in its cage. And another man in Germany thought he was being shot at, but the police found out it was just seed pods bursting loudly on a big cactus plant in his garden."

Becky and Barbara giggled.

The Little Group Talks About Sly Tactics They've Heard Lawyers Can Use to Try to Discredit witnesses in Court, and Other Such Things

There was a little pause in the conversation, and then Becky asked Barbara, "What other tricks have you learned that lawyers play in court?"

Barbara replied, "Well, I've heard they can do a variety of things. One thing some do is to deliberately mispronounce the name of the witness they're talking to, more than once, to try and draw their thoughts away from what happened onto something irrelevant so they won't be concentrating so hard on remembering the details of the crime, or to divert them into talking about the correct pronunciation of their name instead of what happened, and maybe to try and get them flustered so they'll get into an argument with them about that instead. The best thing a witness can do is to just ignore it if a lawyer mispronounces their name, or very quickly say what it really is before immediately moving on to answering the question they've been asked. If the lawyer mispronounces their name too many times, the jury will probably think they sound like a twit anyway, since people have to say what their names are at the beginning of the court case. So they probably won't mispronounce it too much.

"Some lawyers will try to get witnesses to argue with them, in the hope that they'll get agitated so they can't think so clearly, and that they'll get distracted from telling the court what happened, and might start coming across as not a very nice person, which will make the jury less likely to want to listen to them. So it's best if people can do their best to keep calm, and just think of the lawyer's provocations as tactics.

"And some lawyers will deliberately claim the person they're questioning said things they didn't really say in testimony they gave before, and try to get them to agree to that version of events, to confuse them and make them wonder if they really did say what the lawyer's claiming they said, so if they say they did, the lawyer can point out that they're now saying something different to what it says they said in their police statement and what they said earlier in the court case, so they'll lose credibility with the jury. So if a witness is fairly sure they said something different from what a lawyer's asking if they said or giving the impression they said, it'll be best if they calmly explain what they really said, not worrying about contradicting the lawyer.

"Since court cases can happen months after the crime was committed, things can be vague in a witness's memory by then though, so it's best if they read through what they said when they first spoke to the police after the crime was committed, before they take the witness stand, and if possible the day before the court case too, to jog their memory.

"Another thing is that sometimes a lawyer will pick up on something a witness mentions while they're answering their questions that they didn't say to the police at the time of the crime, and they'll ask them why they left it out, to try to give the impression they might be making it up. A witness doesn't have to feel bad about not having mentioned it before; it's best if they just calmly explain that they forgot or didn't think it was important enough to mention at the time, or whatever the reason was. The calmer a witness can keep themselves, the more things they're likely to remember, since it's more difficult to think clearly when you're put under pressure and you start getting nervous or angry.

"And sometimes lawyers will try to create the impression that the witness wants to avoid making eye contact with the jury because they might have something to hide, so they'll move to a position where the witness will be looking away from the jury if they look at them. So it's best if a witness starts off looking at them, and then turns to look at the jury while they carry on talking."

Becky said, "That thing about not looking at the jury reminds me of a joke I read on the Internet about a lawyer playing a trick. It said:

"A criminal defence lawyer thought he'd use a dramatic tactic to convince the jury of his client's supposed innocence. The man was accused of murder, although the body had never been found. The lawyer turned and pointed to the courtroom's clock and announced, 'Ladies and gentlemen of the jury, I have some astounding news. I have found the supposed victim of this murder to be alive! In just ten seconds, she will walk through the door of this courtroom.'

"Everyone waited silently in suspense. But nothing happened.

"Then the lawyer grinned and said, 'The very fact that you were watching the door, expecting the alleged victim to walk into this courtroom, is clear proof that you have far more than even a reasonable doubt as to whether a murder was actually committed.'

"He was pleased with himself, and sat down, fully expecting the jury to decide they just had to find his client not guilty.

"The jury was sent out to discuss what verdict to choose, and came back in just ten minutes later and pronounced that they'd found the defendant guilty.

"When the court was dismissed after the judge sentenced the criminal, the dismayed lawyer chased after the jury foreman and protested, 'Guilty? How could you have found him guilty? You must have thought it was possible he hadn't committed the murder; you were all watching the door!'

"The jury foreman said, 'Well, most of us were watching the door. But one of us was watching the defendant, and he wasn't watching the door.' "

The three new friends giggled.

Pauline said, "Good one! I wonder what other tricks lawyers use!"

Barbara replied, "Well, I've heard another one is that they might get the witness to do something like drawing a diagram of the scene, and while they're concentrating on that, they'll ask them a question, in the hope they'll be too busy concentrating on drawing to give a good answer. So it's best if the witness stops the task they've been asked to do so they can give their full attention to the question, politely asking the lawyer to repeat it if they didn't quite catch it.

"And another thing I've heard they sometimes do is to try to make the jury think the witness isn't credible by pointing out any inconsistencies in what they say, even minor ones, when they know really that just because someone can't quite remember all the details of what happened entirely accurately because they happened quite some time ago, it doesn't mean the whole of their story's a lie. So it's best if the witness tries not to worry about what the lawyer's saying, and just calmly explains why they think their mistake happened.

"And some lawyers will interrupt a witness quite a bit while they're in the middle of answering a question, to try to stop them finishing telling the jury about something that happened, and maybe to try to get them flustered or make them look bad if they interrupt back or don't stop talking and it turns into an argument and they start losing their temper."

Becky remarked, "If lawyers do that many things to get witnesses to argue with them, it sounds as if they must really enjoy arguing!"

Barbara laughed and said, "Maybe they do! Maybe they don't want to stop when a court case has finished, so they go home and start arguments with their families just for fun, or for the adrenaline boost they get from it!"

Becky grinned and said, "Yeah, maybe some of them go home, and if their dinner's ready for them and it's something they really like, they'll think, 'Oh no! I can't argue about it now! What else can I think of to argue about? This won't do!' "

The others giggled.

Then Barbara said seriously, "Another thing I've heard is that sometimes lawyers will be nice to a witness they're cross-examining at first, giving the impression they're being sympathetic and understanding, in the hope that the witness will think the lawyer's not as intimidating as they might have expected, and that they must genuinely want to hear things from their point of view, so they'll drop their guard, and start agreeing to go along with things the lawyer says happened, even if they don't quite agree really, because they don't want a confrontation with someone who's being friendly; and then the lawyer will say things that'll make the witness look bad or dishonest if they do go along with them, because it'll sound as if things happened a bit differently from the way they said they did before. Or the lawyer will suddenly start questioning them more aggressively, and because the witness is off their guard, they might not be as prepared to stand up for themselves as they might have been when they first went in to the courtroom.

"And lawyers use other tricks too."

"That's not fair!" said Pauline.

Barbara replied, "No, it doesn't sound fair. But at least it's good if people know about these things, so they can recognise what might be happening if they ever have to go to court and a lawyer uses the tactics on *them*."

"That's true," said Becky.

She grinned and said, "Imagine how it would be if a lawyer was using tactics like that on a witness, and instead of answering the questions they were being asked, the witness kept announcing things like, 'I believe you're now using the common lawyers' tactic on me of trying to make me think you've befriended me so I won't feel like contradicting you so much when you say I said things I didn't quite say, hoping that'll make it sound as if I've sneakily changed my story since I spoke to the police.' "

The others smiled.

Then Pauline said, "Mind you, I don't think it's just in court where lawyers use tricks. I remember a television programme where it was saying that some people who want to take former employers and organisations to court for things like really stressful working conditions, or post-traumatic stress disorder caused by serious accidents at work or other things, can worry that the more they recover, the less money they'll be awarded, because if the case takes a long time to get to court and they've recovered by the time it does, so they stand up in court fully healthy, and they're living life to the full again with a good job, the jury or judge will think that since there's nothing wrong with them any more, they don't need to be awarded much money, because part of what they take into account when deciding how much money to give people is how the problem will likely affect them in future, and whether they're likely to be too ill to work so they need compensation for loss of earnings.

"I think the programme said something about people wondering if it's really in their interests to get help to recover before the court case is over. If they decide not to, or their lawyers advise them not to, they might be suffering their symptoms for quite a bit longer than they need to, since cases can take ages to get to court. I wonder if some people's lawyers let them know in some kind of way that it's in their best interests not to recover till the court case is over."

Becky exclaimed, "It'll be a shame if that does happen."

Then she joked, "So you think someone might go to see their lawyer, and happily tell them they're feeling much better since they got a therapist to help them develop strategies to overcome their psychological problems, and that their family are being really supportive and that's helped them a lot too, and the lawyer might fume and say angrily, 'This is no good at all! How can you expect to win a lot of money if you keep this up? You must sack your therapist immediately; they're doing you a great deal of harm! And don't go anywhere near your dreadful family and friends again till the court case is over!' "

They laughed, and Pauline said, "I don't know about that! But I expect the person would soon feel really stressed again if they had a lawyer like that!"

Barbara said, "I don't know if people ever deliberately decide not to get help before a court case. But I have heard that lawyers advising organisations that are being taken to court by people who want compensation for trauma and stress they say they suffered when they were working for them can try to get the court case delayed for as long as possible, because they know the alleged victims will often get fed up of it dragging on, so they'll prefer to agree to settle out of court and be paid less money than they might possibly be awarded in the end if they take the court case the whole way, since the alternative will be to have it hanging around their necks for maybe years, with the possibility that they'll lose in the end and maybe have to pay really expensive court costs themselves."

Becky exclaimed, "That's not good!"

As if the sky was agreeing with them, a little squall suddenly blew up and it started raining a bit. They all thought about sheltering indoors. But a minute later, the shower blew over so the rain stopped. So they just carried on their conversation.

Pauline said, "I heard something interesting on the radio the other day about how not so many doctors in America are being sued for making bad decisions that have led to people dying or being injured as they used to be, partly because quite a few of them are reacting in different ways from the ways they used to to patients and angry relatives who want answers from them about what happened. Apparently it used to be common for doctors to try to cover up their mistakes and keep denying they'd done anything wrong, because they thought it was best to do that so they wouldn't incriminate themselves and give away anything a patient or their family and their lawyer could use against them if they sued them.

"But they've started meeting with patients and their families and apologising instead, explaining the reasons why things went wrong, and maybe talking about things that can be done to try to prevent such things happening in future; and it's been found that after meetings like that, patients and their families don't feel nearly as angry and upset as they did before, and they can understand better why things went wrong, so they're less likely to sue them than they were before when they would often feel more and more angry the more they thought about things, because they were convinced they were being lied to, and no one would give them information about why things happened the way they did, and because as far as they knew, similar things might happen again and again to people, because if the doctors didn't seem to think they'd done anything wrong, they likely wouldn't change the way they did anything."

Becky said, "That's interesting. I think if something bad happened to me, especially if it was because of some kind of mistake that was made in an organisation that was set up to help the public like the health service, I wouldn't rush to sue, if that would mean I would get money that could otherwise be used to help people; as long as I was well enough, I think I'd try to arrange a meeting with someone in authority who could do something about it, and tell them about all the changes I thought ought to be made to prevent what had happened to me happening to anyone else. I'd try to get promises from them that they'd do something about it; or if I didn't know what ought to be done, I'd ask them what They thought ought to be changed, and still try to get assurances from them that they'd do something about it. And then I'd contact them again a few weeks later to check that they really were trying to do something. If they weren't, and didn't seem to be interested in changing things, I might eventually tell the media what had happened, or my local MP."

Pauline replied, "That sounds like a good idea. Mind you, I think some people sue because they've been prevented from working by the way they've been injured, so they might have had to go into debt, and they just want to get money back to pay their debts off and make sure they can stop having to worry about money. Also, I think it's often a doctor's insurance company that pays the person who sued, not the doctor themselves, or the health service."

Barbara said, "I think companies that deliberately do bad things deserve to be sued and to have to pay out a lot of money. I think they should be ordered to change their ways as well, and monitored to see if they are, or made to stop trading altogether if what happened was really serious."

The Conversation Turns Humorous Again

Becky agreed. Then she grinned and said, "Hey I wonder if it ever happens that a doctor makes a mistake and causes someone to get a medical injury, and instead of thinking to go to another doctor to get it fixed, they just think, 'Right! I'm going to go to a lawyer and get advice on getting this doctor sued!' "

Pauline giggled and said, "Yeah, imagine it! Imagine if someone had appendicitis and the doctor kept misdiagnosing it, and then their appendix burst and they were really ill, and they said, 'I'm sure I could go to that doctor or a different one and they'd cure me if they could, but the important thing is to go to a lawyer instead and get that doctor sued!' "

The others chuckled, but then Becky said, "Really though, I wonder if the people who are injured the worst are the least likely to sue, simply because they're not well enough. I suppose their relatives might sometimes sue on their behalf if they die."

The others became thoughtful for a little while. Then Barbara said, "I had a music teacher at school who told us that when she was little, she got a burst appendix, and she was seriously ill and had to stay in bed for six months!"

Becky responded, "Yikes! That must have been painful! And probably boring once the pain wore off quite a bit. Mind you, maybe she ended up being lucky to be alive to tell the tale!"

Barbara replied, "Yeah. She was the great great granddaughter of a famous composer. She had the same surname as him, and the braille label on her door just said her surname, for some reason, so it was as if it was saying it was the room of the composer, since I think he was just known by his surname. I know it's a bit rotten, but we used to make fun of her a bit, just for a laugh, pretending we thought she was the composer himself so she must be really old, and that she either must have had a sex change, or she was really a man. We mainly used to make fun of her when she wasn't there; but one day, someone in my class called her Sir. She was surprised, and said, 'Sir? Do you think I'm a man?'

"And one day someone else asked her what life was like at the beginning of the 20th century. That was when the composer was composing. She said, 'I'm not that old!'

"We sometimes had a laugh when she wasn't there, imagining other things we could say to her; but no one really said them. We came up with ideas for questions like, 'Were you around when the first ever chocolate bar was invented? Did you taste some of the first ever chocolates? What were they like? Were you there when cars were invented?'

"Then someone came up with the idea that if she really was the famous composer, she must have lived to a remarkable age to still be teaching us, and if she had, maybe she had the ability to live for thousands of years, and she was really old when she'd started composing music. So we thought up daft questions like, 'Did you visit Egypt when they were building the pyramids?' 'Did you witness the Great Fire of London?' 'What were the Neanderthals like?' 'Were the summers as hot as they are now in the 6th century?'

"She was a good sport, actually, so she probably wouldn't have minded if we'd teased her like that just for fun. We thought we'd better not though."

The others giggled.

Then Pauline said, "I read that archaeologists have actually discovered a bottle of Roman wine! They found it in someone's tomb. Apparently it had gone off a bit though in the couple of thousand years it's been around – it had gone a bit waxy and gritty, as if it had a bit of mud in it or something, I think."

Becky responded, "Wow! That's interesting! I wonder what it's like to taste!"

Pauline replied, "You wouldn't be allowed to taste it!"

Barbara grinned and joked, "Gosh no, she's underage!"

Pauline smiled and said, "Well there is that; but I mean I don't suppose *anyone* would be allowed to taste it, since I don't suppose the archaeologists who might have spent years excavating the place it was found in and then eventually dug it up would be very happy if no sooner had they done that than an alcoholic or someone who was after a good time snatched it from them, gleefully shouting, 'Whine!' and then they just gulped it right down in front of them! ... Mind you, the man drinking it might be disappointed too, since apparently all the alcohol in it had long since evaporated; and also he might realise halfway through drinking it that whine that tasted of ear wax really wasn't what he wanted after all!"

The others chuckled.

Then Becky grinned and said, "Hey Barbara, maybe you could have asked your old music teacher, 'Were you around in Roman times, and did you taste Roman whine? What was it like?' and, 'Were you around at the time of the dinosaurs, and did you ever hunt them for food?' "

Pauline grinned and said, "Yeah. And maybe you could have asked, 'Were you alive when the first ever criminal committed a crime? That must have been before courts were thought of. What did they used to do to criminals in those days?' "

Barbara chuckled and said, "Yeah, maybe."

The Little Group Starts Talking About Things That Can Influence People Unfairly in Court Again

Then the conversation turned serious again, as Becky asked Barbara, "What other tactics have you heard about lawyers using to win their cases in court?"

Barbara replied, "Well, I've heard that one thing some of them can do is to advise the person they're trying to convince a jury to acquit to present themselves nicely, because research has found that juries tend to be influenced by outward appearances, such as by assuming people who look smart must be too nice or well-educated to burgle houses, and suspecting a scruffy-looking man of doing it more because they think he looks the type. I mean, that might be a reasonable judgment to make on the whole, but lawyers can use people's tendency to make it to try to manipulate things in their favour.

"I even heard that lawyers will sometimes tell a man being charged with a violent crime to get some glasses and wear them to court, since it's apparently been found that juries will often assume that people wearing glasses are less likely to be violent, maybe because they assume they wouldn't want to take the risk of getting their glasses broken by getting into a fight, or that if they've got sight problems, they'd be less likely to get into a fight because they would know they might not see an opponent's moves as quickly so they might be at a disadvantage.

Or maybe they often just think someone wearing glasses looks more like the kind of person who'd sit studying a book than the kind who'd get violent – I don't know.

"I don't know how much difference it really makes. But apparently some lawyers think it's a tactic worth trying, although if the crime's something like fraud, rather than a violent crime, it seems it's been found that juries are actually *more* likely to think someone wearing glasses committed it, maybe because they can give off the impression of a nerdy person who's more likely to sit cooking up schemes than to get out and do active things, I don't know. It might not be that at all. And again, I don't know how big or small the effect is."

"In any case, that's bad!" said Becky. "It sounds as if lawyers like flicking through psychology books to see what the latest research is on the behaviour of juries."

Barbara said, "Yeah. And another tactic I've heard they've been known to use is telling their clients to talk faster than usual, since it's apparently been found that that gives an impression of intelligence, since I suppose you have to be quite intelligent to think of what to say fast, although I'm not sure about that; maybe some people who talk fast are often talking rubbish. But anyway, I heard that the most likely reason it can influence juries is that the faster you talk, the less time they'll have to take in any incriminating things you accidentally say; they'll be so busy concentrating on taking in what you're saying that they won't have any brain power left for thinking it through as you're talking. I heard that salesmen use that tactic with people they're selling things to for that reason."

Becky grinned and said, "If salesmen talked Too fast though, people might not be able to take in all their hype about their products either."

The others smiled, and Becky carried on, "Hey imagine if a salesman was trained to talk very fast when he was talking about the bad things about the products he was selling, like they do on those adverts where they spend most of it doing a mini entertaining drama, and rattle off all the details they'd probably rather we didn't think about too much really fast at the end, but he was trained to talk normally when he was talking about the good things. But imagine if he got things muddled up, and he started talking really fast when he was telling the people he was hoping would buy things from him about the good things, so they couldn't really take what he was saying in, but whenever they asked an awkward question and he had to say something unfavourable about the product, he'd always slow down; and he'd answer far more honestly than he should have done too.

"So say if he was selling a chair, he'd talk about how comfortable it was too fast for people to understand him properly, and they'd all be puzzled about what on earth he could be talking about, but then he'd slow right down to say, 'It will only last about five years though before the springs start coming through, so sitting on it will eventually start to feel as if you accidentally dropped your keys on it before you sat down and they've somehow found their way into its cushioning, and you're sitting on them without realising.' "

The others sniggered.

Then Becky said to Barbara, "Sorry, carry on talking about tricks lawyers use."

Barbara said, "Well, it's not just tactics lawyers use that can influence a jury unfairly. One thing that can apparently influence a jury to think a defendant's more likely to be guilty is if they're ugly, or if they come from the kind of neighbourhood you'd expect there to be a high crime rate in. It doesn't happen if the evidence is strong or in very serious crimes, but in cases where there's some doubt, and the crime's more minor, some studies have found that some jurors are more likely to think a defendant's guilty if they look like the kind of person who would commit a crime, if even through no fault of their own, they, say, look a bit sinister, because, say, a bully broke their nose when they were a kid and it mended crookedly, and it makes them look as if they might get into fights easily to people who don't know why it really happened.

"I read about a study that found that some people tend to judge people just based on the evidence and by thinking things through logically, whereas some people are a lot more likely to choose a verdict partly because of how they feel about the person on trial, such as if they feel sorry for them because they find out they were very poor growing up, or if they feel as if there might be something a bit sinister about them because they look ugly. The researchers said that everyone judges by a mixture of logic and their feelings, but that some people are more likely to do mainly one thing or the other for more of the time.

"Funnily enough, I heard that it's been found that if witnesses are really polite and respectful, they're actually *less* likely to be believed by some jury members, maybe because their politeness makes them sound a bit fake; or it might be because polite people might be more likely to let lawyers get away with using some of their tricks on them, like the one where they interrupt them with a new question to try to stop them finishing telling the jury what happened, instead of them standing up for themselves and insisting they be allowed to finish answering the question they were answering before they were interrupted, before they answer the latest one.

"But apparently, it's also been found that judges can be influenced too. You might think they're less likely to be influenced by things that are in reality probably irrelevant like politeness, or tactics meant to mislead them, because they must be well-educated; but it seems they can be. If what I heard is true, then if a criminal is found guilty, even if he's been insisting on his innocence throughout the entire trial, if before he's sentenced, he confesses his guilt and says he's sorry for what he did, especially if he's fidgeting awkwardly as if he's feeling uncomfortable about having committed the crime, he's more likely to get a lighter sentence than if he doesn't, since a judge might think that if he's sorry, he's less likely to commit the crime again because he must regret it, so he's safer to be let out into the community again soon than a person who doesn't seem remorseful.

"But really, some people are good at faking remorse. And other people might feel a bit sorry at the time, but as soon as they later remember how much fun it was to commit the crime or to enjoy the results of it, they might start thinking it'll be nice to do it again."

Becky said, "Yes! I've heard that men who abuse their wives can be really good at fake remorse, or they can just have temporary upset feelings, saying they're sorry and even crying, only to do the same thing again the next time they feel like it!"

Pauline exclaimed, "That's bad!"

Barbara said, "I've even heard that judges can make different decisions according to when they last had something to eat! If they're making decisions in parole hearings, I've heard that the prisoners whose cases they judge first thing in the morning and straight after their lunch are more likely to get treated leniently than the ones they see just before their lunch break, as if the judges aren't so much in the mood to think deeply about their cases when they're hungry, so they can just decide to be on the safe side and keep the prisoners they see in prison. Or maybe it's that they're fed up of being there after judging cases for hours, so they're in a bad mood, so they maybe get irritated with prisoners more easily or don't feel so generous, so they're more likely to just decide they don't deserve parole than they will be with the prisoners they see after they've had refreshments. That's what I heard anyway. How common the effect is, and what the real reasons are, I don't know."

"Yikes!" said Becky. "I think I'll look up information about that myself and see what I find! Mind you, it might be useful for prisoners to know; maybe if they did, they'd start taking packets of sweets and snacks into their parole hearings and offering the judge some in the hope that his decision would go in their favour!"

They sniggered. Barbara said, "I wonder if that would really work! It would backfire though if some judges accused them of trying to bribe them! Maybe a few would think, 'Bribes have to be bigger than that to influence me!' "

Becky commented, "I don't understand why judges don't bring their own sweets with them if they're always in a bad mood before their dinner. ... Mind you, I suppose it could seem like really bad manners if they were scoffing sweets all through the parole hearings, especially if they didn't offer any around!"

They chuckled.

But then Pauline said seriously, "It's depressing to learn about how flaws in human nature, like not thinking as logically as it's best to, or feeling more generous just because you've had a nice dinner, can influence people though!"

The Conversation Becomes Light-Hearted, as Becky Imagines How it Would Be if Nothing Ever Died

Becky said, "Yeah, it's not nice. But those things are definitely worth knowing about."

Just then, a fly landed on Becky, and she aggressively brushed it off, accidentally squashing it. She said, "Oh yuck, I just gave a fly the death sentence when I brushed it off me. It's a good thing there aren't masses of flies around the place, or we might have to subject them to a mass execution. Poor flies.

"Still, it would be worse if no flies ever died. Imagine if nothing at all ever died. Imagine if there were people still alive from hundreds of thousands of years ago, or from when humans first existed on earth; imagine if every human who ever lived was still alive, and every animal. It might be interesting to ask lots of ancient people what things were like when they were young. But imagine how overcrowded the world would be!

"You'd go outside the front door and wonder where to put your feet, because the place might be so full of little animals like rabbits and cats and squirrels and things, you'd wonder how you could walk without stepping on them!

"You might gather up all the ones in front of you to try and clear a space to walk in, and find it really difficult to hold all these heavy struggling animals that didn't want to be all packed together in your arms, only for the gap you left when you picked them up to be quickly filled by other animals; or you'd only be able to walk one or two steps before you'd get to a load more animals all packed together you wouldn't know how to pass by without stepping on. You'd have to turn round, put all the animals you'd just picked up down again, some on top of each other because since you were standing where some of them had been, there wouldn't be room for them all to stand side by side any more, and then you'd have to turn back around again and gather up the animals in front of you, walk the few steps in the gap they'd left, turn round and put them down, and carry on like that till you'd got where you wanted to go. And what if you wanted to walk miles? People would never get anything done!

"And just imagine if people kept growing for all their lives, so people who were hundreds of thousands of years old would be as tall as trees! They'd have to shout all the time to make themselves heard because some of us would be so far below their heads! Or they'd have to bend down all the time. What would it be like being surrounded by a group of people who were all hundreds of thousands of years old and all as tall as trees?"

Pauline said, "There would probably be a time when the world stopped getting more crowded, because if that many creatures were packed that tightly together, they wouldn't have room to manoeuvre themselves into a position where they could mate! So at least no new ones would be born."

The others chuckled.

Barbara said, "When you think about a world like that, you realise that maybe it's a good thing people die, although it's sad when nice people die young. Wouldn't it be horrible to witness someone being killed! ... Well, unless you could stop the killer in the act, like by throwing him head-first out of a window into a big pile of manure or something and then quickly phoning the police."

Becky laughed and said, "The police would probably find him quite easy to identify after that, wouldn't they! If he managed to get out of the manure and started running away, the police might chase him and radio to other police to ask them to help them, and say, 'You won't need a detailed description of this man; you'll be able to identify him best by the smell, and the fact that he'll be covered in manure!' "

They giggled.

Becky Talks More About Eyewitness Evidence Sometimes Being Unreliable

Then Barbara asked Becky, "Hey, do you know any more about what you were saying before about eyewitnesses sometimes being unreliable, and the reasons why, like them forgetting some of the details of what happened and getting them wrong when they try to remember them?"

Becky replied, "Yes. I was talking about quite minor crimes before. But it turns out that people's memories are often no better for violent crimes they witness. That's partly because they often won't be expecting them, so it won't be as if they're concentrating on taking in every detail they can, so as to tell the police later. They'll likely be too much in shock to pay close attention to all the details of what's happening, and if a weapon's being used, they'll likely have their eyes on that, not on the person committing the crime. So they might be vague about what he looked like later on; or they might be sure they know, but give the police a false description by accident, because in the same way I mentioned before, they might be trying to assist their recollection to come back by using their ideas about the way the world works to help them.

"So, say if there was a man who had a big scar across his face and it made him look a bit sinister to the witness because the witness thought it made him look as if he was the kind of person who'd get himself into serious fights, and he'd been standing right near the criminal when the crime was committed, the witness might remember a man with an ugly big scar on his face, and feel convinced that must have been what the criminal looked like, because he can't remember the criminal's face, but he's just trying to piece together the bits of memory floating around his brain into something that makes sense, and it seems to make the most sense to him that the man with the scar on his face committed the crime. So he might tell the police it was him, and the more he relives the crime in his mind, imagining it was perpetrated by the man with the scar, the more he might be convinced it really was him, because he's pretty sure he's reliving the events accurately. He might even tell a court he's really sure it was him, because he assumes his memory's accurate.

"And if a few witnesses think the same way, they might all tell the police it was that man. If there's another witness who gives a correct description of the criminal, it might look to some people as if he can't be telling the truth, because, say, three other people say it was someone else. But people shouldn't assume that the majority must be correct, just because they are the majority. The fact that they are makes it more likely that they're correct, but it won't be a certainty.

"Even if the witness in the minority might have a hidden agenda in identifying a certain person as the criminal, say if he's a known racist and the person he's identifying as the criminal comes from another race, so in theory he might be more likely to misremember or lie about how the criminal's a member of another race, when all the other witnesses are saying it was someone in the same ethnic group as everyone being interviewed, it's unsafe to assume that what he's saying Definitely isn't credible just because of that, and to argue that after all, he's in the minority, so he's more likely to be the one who's wrong. It does mean that what he says should be treated with suspicion; but then, maybe everyone's testimony should be treated with a bit of skepticism till more evidence is gathered, because of the reasons why everyone's memories might be a bit distorted.

"Another thing is that there have been informants who have outright lied on the witness stand because they've been hoping to gain something, because they've been promised that if they testify against a suspect, they'll get released from prison or get a lighter sentence for their own crime, so they make things up or exaggerate what they know so it sounds more impressive to the police."

Pauline said, "That's bad! Why do the police use people like that as witnesses when they must know they might do things like that?"

Becky replied, "I don't know; maybe they sometimes just haven't got any other witnesses, or only ones who are a bit vague about what really happened."

Pauline Says Something Worrying, Before Humour Breaks Out Again

Pauline said, "I've got a cousin who knows a man who got put in prison for violent crimes, and I don't know if there was some dishonesty going on, but he seemed to have completely changed his personality in prison, and he didn't do anything violent for years, so they eventually decided he was a lower risk than he used to be and transferred him to a prison for more minor offenders, and they started letting him out on day release to go and work somewhere; but as soon as they did, he went and committed another serious crime! Goodness knows why, when he must have known he was risking never being let out on day release again!"

"That's bad!" said Barbara.

Becky agreed. But then she had an idea, grinned and joked, "Maybe they should let prisoners they let out on day release out in cages at first, that have to be pushed around by prison officers, or people employed specially for the purpose, so the prisoners can talk to people in the community, to get used to it, but they can't commit crimes against them."

Pauline grinned and said, "Oh Becky! Imagine what human rights groups would say! And imagine the headlines in the papers! 'Prisoners to be wheeled around the community in cages!' "

They giggled.

Then Becky said, "Well maybe the authorities could tell the people from human rights groups that being wheeled around in a cage wasn't really that bad, and that if they thought it was, they could get in a cage and be wheeled around all day themselves just to see if it was as bad as they thought. I wouldn't be surprised if no one from a human rights group would want to do that, so they wouldn't be able to prove it was bad, so no one would have to take their complaints seriously."

The others grinned, but Pauline said, "Apart from the fact that a lot of prisoners themselves might be complaining!"

Becky replied, "They wouldn't dare, since the prison officers could always tell them that if they were unhappy with the idea, they didn't have to go out on day release. Only people who agreed not to make noisy or public complaints would be allowed to go.

"And imagine if the prisoners were sent to work in various places, but they still weren't allowed out of their cages, so they had to put their fingers through the bars of them to do the work. So, say, if they got put to work in an office typing on a computer, they'd have to stick their fingers out the bars to put them on the keyboard."

The others chuckled. Barbara said, "Yes, and they'd have to put their fingers through different bars to reach different keys, which could slow them down a fair bit! And maybe when it was time for them to eat, the prison officer wheeling them around would have to open a little door in the cage to put food in."

Becky grinned and said, "Imagine if prison officers gave the prisoners bird seed like you'd give a bird in a cage, or rabbit food or something.

"Hey imagine if a new theory became popular about how prisoners could be made safer for everyone else if they could be transformed into animals, and a way was found to do it, so from then on, they'd be given a special kind of new food that would actually transform them! And they'd have to eat it, because it was a choice between eating it or starving. And imagine if it took quite a while for them to be fully transformed into animals, and they wouldn't be released until they had been; and when they were, they'd be sold to zoos and safari parks and places as if they were just ordinary animals, and tourists would go and see them, thinking they really were just ordinary animals, since they'd be sold in secret."

Barbara chuckled and said, "Yeah, and imagine if some were accidentally sold before they'd been fully transformed, while they could still talk! Maybe really fat prisoners would transform into elephants. Then tourists would be driving slowly round a safari park, enjoying the view, looking at the elephants, and then get a shock when they heard one suddenly shout, 'Oy! What do you think you're staring at!' "

The others laughed.

Pauline said, "There are thousands and thousands of prisoners though; zoos and safari parks wouldn't want them all. What would they do with all the spare ones?"

Barbara replied, "Maybe they'd transport them to Africa and release them into the wild in the jungle, and animal rights groups would think they were being kind and humane, thinking they were real animals."

They all grinned, and Becky said, "Hey imagine if they had that policy for about fifty years, and lots of animals that could still talk were transported to Africa by mistake, because they kept quiet till after they'd been released so their ability to talk wouldn't be discovered, since that would mean they'd have to stay in prison for longer. And imagine if they kept on being able to talk, because they stopped having to eat their transformation diet. Imagine if governments abandoned the policy of transforming prisoners into animals after about half a century, and people forgot it had ever been a thing, and the new animals bred with each other in the jungle, and then a couple of hundred years later, some scientists discovered them, and were surprised to hear them talk, and announced to the press that they'd discovered this new species of talking animal, and that amazingly, their language even sounded like English!

"Or imagine if some people were making a nature documentary for a television channel, not knowing some animals could talk, and the presenter was watching some giraffes, getting as close to them as he dared, giving a commentary on their behaviour like those people do, when one of the giraffes leant down and said, 'Oy! Get that camera out of here! We don't want to be on the telly!' "

They chuckled. But Barbara said, "They might like being on television though. But how would they know televisions existed? Well, the oldest ones might; and I suppose the others might have come across them in their travels. Hey imagine if they thought it would be nice to watch television! Imagine if a lion walked into a village, and everyone who saw him screamed and ran away, till he bawled, 'Oy! Come back! All I want to do is buy a television for my family! I was thinking I could work for one of you to make some money, say, catching rats and things, and then I can use the money to buy a television.' "

Becky said, "Yeah, and imagine if he got some money and went into shops where they sold televisions, and people kept shouting, 'Oh no, a lion's come into the shop!' People would scream and try to hide, and the lion might say, 'Oh I wish people would stop doing that whenever I want to talk to them; I'm really fed up of it! How am I supposed to buy a television if everyone's run away!' "

Pauline said, "I wonder if they'll even have televisions in a couple of hundred years' time."

Barbara replied, "Maybe in Africa, they'll have solar-powered televisions! They probably couldn't do that here, but maybe they could in countries where there's lots of sunshine."

Becky said, "Maybe in a couple of hundred years' time, they'll have the technology to put huge pipes in the sky that suck loads of sunshine halfway around the globe to places like here, so places that have got way more sunshine than they need can share some of it with us."

Barbara responded, "Yeah! Maybe they'll make one huge

pipe to bring it to this country, and then it'll split off into a huge network of little pipes that'll go to lots of different areas of it, and empty the sun out over lots of people."

They tittered. Pauline said, "But if there were too many, the pipes would block out the sun that should have been shining down here. Then again, maybe they'd be quite thin, or made of something transparent, so they wouldn't. But imagine if it's raining and the sun comes zooming out of the pipes, and it's really hot. It might warm the rain up, so standing underneath it will be like standing under a hot shower."

"Wow, that would be good!" said Barbara.

Becky replied, "I'm not sure about that; the police might make some arrests for indecency if people took their soap and sponges outside and took all their clothes off because they thought it would be nice to have a real shower in the rain underneath the sun pipes!"

They laughed.

Then Barbara said, "Actually, that reminds me, I'd better go and rinse my swimming costume out soon."

"Yeah, maybe I'd better go and do that too," said Becky.

They agreed it had been nice meeting up, and went their separate ways.

They soon met up again though.

The Three Meet Up on Another Day, and The Conversation Turns Again to Problems With Eyewitness Evidence

Becky and Barbara were walking back to Barbara's accommodation together after doing a bit of work in the library a few days later when Pauline spotted them and came over to say hello. They decided to walk back together.

Pauline said, "Did we finish our conversation about eyewitnesses last time? Do you know anything else about what can make eyewitness testimony unreliable, Becky?"

Becky replied, "Yes I do. But I can't quite remember what I've already told you and what I haven't."

Pauline and Barbara told her what they remembered.

Then Becky said, "Well, another reason the memories of eyewitnesses might not be as accurate as you might expect is that if a violent crime's happening right near them, they might be really stressed; and if a person's brain's full of strong emotion, it's going to be more difficult for it to concentrate on doing things like remembering the details of things.

"Another reason people's memories can get distorted is that after they've witnessed something nasty, they'll likely want to tell other people about it, and some people who do that might fill in the gaps in their memories where they're a bit vague about the details of what happened with information they imagine, because they want to be able to tell a good story, or they'd feel stupid saying they can't remember some of the details.

"People might ask them questions, like, 'Did the criminal look angry?' And because they were looking at any weapon there was or what the criminal was actually doing most of the time, they might not be able to remember the expression on his face at all, but they might think that if they say they can't, they'll look silly, or the people listening might start doubting they were even there, thinking they might be lying about the whole thing. So they might lie and say yes, just to avoid an awkward situation like that. People might ask them more and more questions they're not sure about the answers to, so they might make up more and more things to avoid looking silly or like someone who wasn't really there, or because they want to be entertaining by telling as dramatic a story as possible.

"But then because they keep repeating the things they're making up to fill in the gaps in their memory, over time, as their memory of the whole thing gets a bit blurry, they might forget which are the bits they made up, and start really believing some of them must have happened, so they might tell the police they did.

"Or they might hear media reports where other witnesses were interviewed about what happened, and the other witnesses might be saying certain things happened that the person hearing them can't recall; but if the person's memories of some of the details are a bit vague, they might assume the other witnesses remember what happened better than they do, so they might decide they must be right, and tell the police the details the others gave as if they remember them themselves.

"Mistakes like that have led to serious miscarriages of justice in the past, since people have identified the wrong person as the criminal. Other witnesses might have even backed them up. Now DNA fingerprinting technology's been developed, there are cases where it's been found that people in prison who were identified as the criminals by eyewitnesses probably didn't commit the crimes really, because other people's DNA was all over the crime scenes but theirs wasn't there.

"But false convictions can happen for a number of other reasons, not just inaccurate eyewitness statements. They can have nothing to do with the witnesses."

Pauline said, "Wow, how do you think you'd feel if you were falsely convicted of a serious crime and put in prison?"

Becky grinned and replied, "I think I'd be annoyed, especially because I'm way too young to be sent to prison, so that would mean that in their effort to enforce the law, they'd be doing something illegal!

"Imagine if they were often doing illegal things to try to enforce the law, or just things that actually made things worse, genuinely believing they were for the best. It reminds me a bit of that saying about the remedy for some things being worse than the disease. A bit like if the government decided to get rid of a lot of the little flies that cause a nuisance by releasing big flies into the environment to eat them, and then after they did, they wondered what to do to get rid of all the big flies, that were causing much More of a nuisance!"

They tittered, and Barbara grinned and said, "Maybe they'd release loads of spiders into the environment to eat all the flies, and then wonder how to get rid of all the spiders."

Pauline joined in, "Yeah. And then they'd release ... what eats spiders?"

Becky said, "I'm not sure anything does. Maybe instead, they'd broadcast public service announcements, encouraging people to catch them and make spider pies with them; and maybe businesses would turn spider-catching into a big commercial operation and catch millions, and can them, and try and sell spider casserole and spider stew, and things like that. Maybe they'd advertise them by boasting, 'There are thousands of spiders in each tin of spider stew! More than enough protein for all the family! Heaps of goodness!' "

Barbara giggled and remarked, "People would have to be daring to eat products like that!"

Becky said, "And maybe the government would invent ideas for what people could do with all the cobwebs, and try to encourage people to actually do them, doing their best to convince everyone they were good things to do, like claiming, 'If you plait lots of cobwebs together, you can make handy string, that you can use in all sorts of ways all over your house. And if you plait and tie loads more cobwebs together with them, you could even make cobweb rope! It'll be very strong, so you could even do things with it like tie one end to the back of your car and tie the other end to a broken-down car, and tow it along with the cobweb rope.' "

Pauline giggled and said, "I wonder if a member of the government themselves would be willing to try that, live on television! Hey imagine if there was a government public service broadcast specially for children that said, 'Start making cobweb rope. Then you can tie your brother up in it if he's annoying you, and do all kinds of handy things like that!' "

Becky exclaimed, "I can imagine that government being soundly voted out at the next election!"

They laughed.

Then Barbara said, "Actually, I read a true story about a man in America who bought or inherited a farm, but at first he was discouraged and a bit unhappy, because it turned out that the soil was so poor that nothing would grow there except manky scraggy bushes, and no animals could graze there; and worse, the place was full of rattlesnakes! But then he had an idea to turn what seemed to be a disadvantage into an advantage: He started catching the rattlesnakes somehow and canning their meat.

"He must have managed to advertise it really well somehow, because his rattlesnake farm became a big tourist attraction, with about 20 thousand visitors a year coming to watch the process of canning rattlesnake meat. He sold it all over the world, and he sent the rattlesnake venom to scientific laboratories where they were developing an antidote to snake venom."

Pauline grinned and asked, "What could they do with that? Did he send it to them because it can somehow be turned into an antidote to itself, or was it just like a trollish thing to do, you know, like the way someone who's feeling a bit mischievous might post a load of pope jokes on the blog of someone trying to promote Catholicism?"

Barbara sniggered and said, "I doubt he would have done a thing like that. I don't suppose he'd have had such a good reputation if he had! No, I don't know how the laboratories used venom to make an antidote to venom, but I've heard they can do it somehow. Or else maybe they experimented with injecting it into cells to see if the anti-venom they were trying to make out of something else could neutralise it; I don't know."

Pauline said, "Actually, I'm a bit curious: You know you said you read the story? Does that mean you read it in braille?"

Barbara replied, "No. Actually, what really happened was that I came across it on the Internet while I was browsing it, using the electronic voice on my computer which was reading me the things on there. I tend to just say I read things when I mean that, since it's the equivalent of reading, and saying exactly what I did would be a bit of a mouthful. It's like the way I say I 'watched' the television, when I really only listened to it. I just say what everyone else says, because it's really more like a figure of speech than meant to be a precise description of what you're doing; after all, if people wanted to use a precise description, they'd say, 'I was watching and listening to the telly', instead of saying something that makes it sound as if all they were doing was looking at it, without listening to it at all."

The others grinned.

Then Becky joked, "You were talking about something being a mouthful just now. Just out of curiosity, would you like a mouthful of rattlesnake meat?"

Barbara giggled and said, "Ugh! No, I don't think I would! Mind you, some people must have been brave enough to eat that stuff, or they just kept it as a souvenir, because apparently this farmer I was telling you about sold lots of it. The story said he became quite rich, and in the end, the village where he lived was renamed Rattlesnake in honour of him! He also sold rattlesnake skins at fancy prices to make women's handbags and shoes."

Pauline laughed and said, "I don't think I'd fancy a handbag made of rattlesnake skin! And I think I'd feel a bit squeamish wearing shoes made of it!"

Barbara replied, "Yeah, I think I would, although you'd know it was harmless; all the venom would have been taken out of the snakes before their skin was made into things, and the skin wouldn't be able to bite you or anything ... wow, just imagine your handbag suddenly seeming to come to life and trying to bite you, or your shoes suddenly starting to nip your toes!"

They giggled and squealed and made faces.

Becky grinned and said, "It might be even scarier if you were eating some rattlesnake meat, and that suddenly came to life on your fork and tried to jump off and bite you on the nose! Mind you, if it succeeded, it might not be much more painful than eating curry, and a lot of people seem to enjoy doing that!"

Pauline replied, "Yeah, but I think quite a lot of people who eat that are young men trying to impress their friends for a dare or to look macho ... or at least that's the opinion of someone I heard. Some people go for the hottest curries going, don't they!

"Hey imagine if for some reason, this country was overrun with rattlesnakes and other pests, and the government wanted to get rid of them, and they came up with the idea of holding events they called Days of Dares, where they would dare people to eat weirder and weirder things, or more and more dangerous animals – or at least meat that had once been dangerous animals. So they might advertise them by saying things like, 'Come and see how much courage you have at the Day of Dares on Saturday! Are you bold enough to eat a dollop of Rattlesnake stew? Could you be courageous enough to eat spider casserole? If you dare do that, would you be willing to chew on Rat Roast? Come and test your bravery at Saturday's Day of Dares!' "

Becky grinned and said, "And imagine if they made it so people had to be even more daring, by mixing the animal meat with sweet things, so the adverts would say things like, 'Come and taste mouse ice cream! Then if you dare try that, try fox crumble, and mosquito and orange mash, and caterpillar chocolates!' "

They giggled, and Barbara said, "Oh yuck! Hey you know you were talking about eyewitnesses to crimes sometimes not remembering the details well? Well if the government did that, I can imagine that another reason they might not remember things happening near them too well is if they were feeling sick because they'd just been to a Day of Dares, and all their attention was focused on trying to crawl under a bush in the hope they'd fall asleep till they felt better.

"Hey imagine if official course textbooks about why eyewitnesses sometimes can't remember things accurately said things like, 'Another reason eyewitnesses sometimes fail to remember things well is if they've just been to one of the new government-sponsored Days of Dares, and eaten so much weird novelty food they've made themselves too ill to be paying attention to what's going on around them.' "

They sniggered.

Becky Tells the Others a Couple of Stories About How It's Possible to Fail to Notice Dramatic Things Happening Very Nearby

Then Barbara asked, "Hey Becky, do you know any more about why eyewitnesses sometimes have problems remembering the details of crimes that happen near them?"

Becky replied, "Yes I do. Another problem is that a person might use what they think is their common sense to try and work out what happened if they didn't see it all that well, and they might get it wrong, say if they saw policemen chasing someone, but they all went by in a flash so there wasn't time to notice much at all, but since they saw it, they seem to be expected to know what the suspect looked like. If they're asked whether he had a weapon, for instance, they might try to imagine him with one to see if it seems right, and the more they imagine it, the more they might convince themselves they did see one; and they might think that the police must have been chasing him for a good reason so it's most likely he did have one, since they might think people who are chased like that usually do have them, so they might say yes, thinking they're more than likely right, and that in any case it's better to say that than to look silly by admitting they didn't notice, when the suspect ran past just in front of them.

"But actually, people can't really be expected to notice much if the event happened quickly, especially if they were concentrating on something else at the time. The longer a crime goes on in front of them, the more likely they are to get a good impression of the details of the suspect's appearance and other things.

"And it's even possible to completely miss something dramatic that's happening right near you if you're concentrating hard on something else. There was a police officer in the 1990s who claimed he'd done that, but he wasn't believed, and he got convicted of lying and obstructing justice and put in prison for a few years, when he probably wasn't lying at all. The conviction was overturned after a while and he was released. That was after a psychologist investigated and did experiments to see if it really is possible to be completely unaware of something serious happening right by you if you're concentrating hard on something else.

"What had happened was that a policeman had been shot, and the man who'd shot him was escaping in a car with his friends. Lots of police were ordered to chase them. So there was a big police chase, but then the friends in the getaway car drove up a cul-de-sac, maybe by accident. They stopped the car, and all jumped out and ran off in different directions. A police car close behind them stopped and the police jumped out. The first one to jump out was a plain-clothed one. Somehow in the dark, the other police mistook him for one of the suspects and grabbed him and beat him up badly.

"Another policeman involved in the chase was after one of the suspects, and while he was running after him, he went past the police beating the other policeman up. Later, he claimed he hadn't even realised it was happening. But he wasn't believed. All the other policemen who were working in parts of the neighbourhood at the time claimed to have been nowhere near the scene, and they were believed. But the one who said he ran by and yet didn't notice it wasn't believed and was taken to court. The jury didn't believe it could be possible that someone could run past someone being beaten up and not realise it was happening. They just thought the man must be trying to protect his fellow policemen who'd beaten the other one up by not saying anything to incriminate them. So they convicted him.

"But there was a psychologist who'd been doing experiments to try to prove a theory he had that it was quite possible for people to be looking at one thing so intently that something else coming on the scene could go by completely unnoticed, even though it should have been easy to spot. The experiments he was doing seemed to be proving it was possible, with people in his lab being told to concentrate on watching one thing on a screen, to see if they'd notice something else that happened on it while it was going on, and a lot of them didn't; but he wanted to find out if a similar thing would happen in a real-life situation.

"The nearest he could come up with was asking people to chase a jogger, counting the number of times he put his hand up to his hat while he was running. The reason he asked them to do the counting was to make sure they concentrated on him the whole time, just as the policeman who'd been put in prison would have been concentrating on keeping one of the police shooting suspects he was chasing in his sights the whole time he was trying to chase him, to try to make sure he didn't give him the slip or pull a gun, or throw a weapon over a hedge or something.

"Quite a lot of people took part in the experiment, sometimes at night, and sometimes in the afternoon. The experiments went on for two years, I think. While the people were running after the jogger, concentrating on observing him, three students would stage a fight on the grass verge right by them. The people running hadn't been told that would happen. When each person chasing the jogger had finished, they were asked whether they'd seen the fight. When it was dark, about two thirds of them said they hadn't; and in broad daylight, about 40 % of them still said they hadn't.

"I suppose there might have been a flaw in the research. Maybe some people claimed they hadn't seen the fight because they were afraid that if they said they had, the next question would be, 'Why didn't you stop to try to help?' Then they would have felt uncomfortable.

"But if they genuinely hadn't seen it, it wouldn't have just been because they were concentrating hard on something else, but that when you're running, you go past what's near you so fast that you haven't got much time to observe it.

"After the experiments, the authorities decided to give the policeman the benefit of the doubt, and he was released from prison.

"I've heard of other situations where people have just not noticed things going on near them. I read about a paramedic who drove an ambulance as fast as he could to a house where two little twins had just fallen into a swimming pool and started drowning. When he got there, he jumped out with the other paramedics and ran over to the children. They started working hard to revive them. After a while, he stopped and asked where the mother was. It was only then that he realised she was less than ten feet away from him, screaming. He literally hadn't noticed her until then, despite her being so close and noisy! So it seems that it really is possible to be concentrating so hard on doing one thing that you miss even dramatic things happening near you."

Barbara said, "The poor mum! And the poor twins!

"I think that stuff's astonishing though, about being able to concentrate so hard on one thing that you're completely unaware of another thing going on right near you, even though it might be really noisy and dramatic!"

Pauline said, "You know, I'm finding all this stuff about eyewitness testimony often being unreliable a bit worrying! I mean, how can people in courts know what to believe?"

Barbara responded, "Well, it's a good job some people believe some things, or just think of the number of criminals there'd be roaming around!"

"That's true!" said Pauline.

The Three Start Joking Again

Becky grinned and said, "Hey imagine if the technology was invented that made it possible for criminals to be shrunk till they were about an inch high. Then maybe you really could leave them to roam around instead of putting them in prison, since they wouldn't be able to do much damage. I mean, just imagine if a couple of shrunken burglars somehow broke into your house; they might only be able to steal, say, a couple of bread crumbs, or a couple of copper coins that they'd have to haul off with a great effort."

The others laughed. Barbara said, "Yeah! And just imagine if they were all sentenced to live in criminal colonies, in tiny little criminal houses, and they were given punishments, like one could be made to roll a peanut up a hill; he'd be so small it would be like rolling a boulder up a hill for a proper-sized human. And just imagine if every time he'd managed to roll the peanut up the hill, someone in authority would push it back down again and order him to push it back up, again and again and again for years."

Becky said, "What a horrible punishment! But then, the clever criminals would probably eat more and more bits off the peanut every time they rolled it up the hill, so they might enjoy themselves, and the peanut would get lighter and lighter. Mind you, I suppose whether they could do that would partly depend on how closely they were being watched."

Barbara remarked, "Ugh! The hill might be all muddy though! I don't suppose they'd enjoy eating muddy peanut! And if they nibbled bits off it, it would get misshapen instead of smooth and roundish, so it might actually become harder to roll up the hill!"

Pauline said, "My brother once put a crisp on a quiet railway line in the countryside when he was little, to see what would happen when a train went over it. He expected it to bust the crisp to bits, but he said he was surprised because instead, it went all flat and soggy."

Becky asked, "He didn't eat it afterwards, did he? That sounds like something my uncle Steven would do!"

The others giggled. Barbara said, "Hey imagine if train-flattened crisp became a delicacy in restaurants in a country that didn't have good safety regulations, and rich people were willing to pay hundreds of pounds to be served one to eat."

Becky said, "Or imagine if crisps could be made of dried frog skin and things like that, and rich people were willing to pay hundreds of pounds in restaurants to be served up one of those!"

They laughed.

Then Becky said, "Hey imagine if an auctioneer deceived rich people into believing he was selling genuine coats and other clothes that had been worn by famous shrunken criminals in criminal colonies, and they sold for hundreds or thousands of pounds each, but really, they were just clothes made for little dolls' house figures, and he'd bought them cheaply. If he got caught, he'd be shrunk and sent to a criminal colony himself, maybe to roll muddy peanuts up a hill for years; and he might end up wearing some of the clothes he'd been trying to sell!"

Barbara sniggered and said, "Yeah, and if they were little dolls' house dolls' dresses, he might be given those to wear, and told it was either that or wearing nothing. I expect all the other shrunken criminals in the colony would laugh at him for that. I wonder how he'd feel, having to wear dolls' house dresses while he rolled muddy peanuts up a hill for years."

Becky was so engrossed in the conversation, she forgot to warn Barbara to duck her head to avoid some overhanging branches that were in front of them, and Barbara banged into them and they brushed her head and face as she walked through them. Thankfully they were covered in young leaves, so they didn't feel as hard as they would have done earlier in the year.

They stopped, and Becky apologised to Barbara and asked her if she was alright. She said she was.

A few leaves had come off in Barbara's hair. Becky joked, "You've got leaves in your hair, Barbara. Hey look Pauline,

Barbara's sprouting leaves out of the top of her head as well as hair; maybe she's ingested some kind of toxic chemical that's turning her into a tree."

Pauline grinned and joked, "Watch it! If she takes you to court for banging her into a tree, and you want me to tell them it didn't really happen but she just got leaves in her hair because she must be turning into a tree, and I really do tell them that, my eyewitness testimony might be considered the most unreliable ever!"

They chuckled.

Becky Tells the Others About Methods Police Use of Trying to Increase the Reliability of Eyewitnesses' Evidence

But then Pauline turned serious and said, "Actually though, I really do find this stuff about eyewitness testimony often being unreliable a bit discouraging."

Becky replied, "Well, I expect lots of it is still reliable, or they wouldn't be able to catch so many criminals. But anyway, it isn't all doom and gloom. I've been learning about techniques the police have started using to try to make sure what witnesses say has a higher chance of being reliable.

"It turns out that if the police say things to jog witnesses' memories of what really happened, and encourage them to think things through carefully from beginning to end as if they're reliving what happened, instead of just asking them questions that mean they have to answer by trying to pull specific memories about it out of their minds straightaway that might be from somewhere in the middle of the crime, their memories can be more accurate, because they might find it easier to recall things if they can gradually go through the whole thing and slot them into place, with one remembered detail jogging their memory for the next, than they will if they have to just try and dredge what might be a hazy memory of one of the details from the middle of it up on the spur of the moment.

"It's been discovered that one important part of the police interview is at the beginning; it might not seem to be anything to do with helping a witness retrieve their memories, so it might seem a waste of time, but it isn't. Apparently it's been found that witnesses give more accurate information when they're feeling relaxed. So it can help if before the witness starts trying to remember what happened, when they first meet, the policeman greets them by name and tells them theirs, so they sound more informal than they would otherwise so it might put the witness more at their ease, and if they just chat to them for a little while at first, in the hope that they'll start feeling as if they're on more friendly terms with them than they might have done otherwise, and so they'll hopefully come to think of them as an individual and more of an equal instead of an authority figure who might seem a bit intimidating so it might make them a bit anxious."

Pauline quipped, "That was a long sentence. I'm hoping my memory will be able to get the stuff you're telling me to stick in itself. ... I wonder if people's bodies burn off calories when they think or try to remember things extra hard. If they do, then witness interviews might be good for witnesses!"

Becky smiled and said, "Maybe. Anyway, what I was about to say was that people can think more clearly when they're not nervous, so it's a good thing if the policeman doing the interview seems friendly, because it might reassure the witness; and also, if they get to think of the policeman as more of a friendly person, they might be less likely to think of them as a representative of an organisation where people know a lot more about crime than they do who might know more than they do about what's happened; so they'll be more likely to feel confident enough to correct the policeman if they think he's got a detail wrong.

"I mean, say if the policeman says something like, 'So the crime happened at around 10 in the morning?' but the witness being interviewed feels sure it happened at around 11 o'clock. If the witness feels a bit anxious and thinks the policeman's bound to know better than they do, because they'll have other information they're going by and might even have official records saying it happened at about 10 o'clock, they might say yes, even though they don't really believe what they're saying, because they might doubt what they remember, and won't want to look silly by saying something different to what might be in the official records.

"But the more at ease they feel with the policeman interviewing them, the more likely they will be to have the confidence to say they don't think things happened in quite the way the policeman seems to think they did. At least, that's the theory. And if the policeman comes across as friendly and a nice person, and interested in them, and a fan of some of the same hobbies as they have too, such as having the same kinds of pets or liking the same sports, it might also make the person being interviewed feel as if the policeman's just an ordinary person, so if they felt badly about the police before, some of the bad feeling might melt away, so they might feel like putting more effort into helping them, which might make them work harder on concentrating on remembering things than they might if they feel as if the whole thing's just an official process, or as if they'd rather not be there really.

"Actually, I've heard that salesmen do something like that, only for motives that aren't so good; they're taught that the more they get people to like them, the more likely they will be to buy something from them.

"Anyway, when the policeman starts the interview, they need to make sure the witness doesn't feel rushed at all, so they won't feel self-conscious and leave out information because they're worried that the policeman doesn't think it's relevant and thinks they're wasting time. And they'll ask the witness to remember as much detail as possible, and to talk about it even if they only half remember it, to try to make sure they don't leave out things they assume the police will already know or might think aren't important, or else things they'd have to make a special effort to try to remember so they don't feel like it, only for it to turn out that they're leaving out useful information.

"And they ask them to imagine they're back in the place where the crime happened, not just to try to remember what the criminal did there, but to try to remember all kinds of things that were going on at the time, like what smells were around, what else they could see, what they could hear, and so on, because thinking of all the things that were happening at the time can jog a person's memory, so more of the important things that happened come to mind.

"The policeman will also ask them to try and think through what happened backwards as well as forwards, in case that helps them think of things they didn't remember before.

"And if the policeman thinks there are still things left unclear after the witness has been talking, they'll ask them questions about them; but they need to be careful not to ask leading questions, which are questions that give clues as to what answer the person who's asking the question thinks is the right one and is expecting to hear, for instance, 'The suspect is unusually tall, isn't he?' If a witness can't really remember how tall he was, they might just say yes, to avoid the embarrassment of having to admit they can't remember, when they think they should really know.

"Or even a question like, 'Was the suspect carrying a weapon', could be a leading question if it leads a witness to think the policeman's expecting them to say yes. They might say yes, even if they can't really remember, to try and avoid the embarrassment of being unsure, or because they remember being scared of the criminal, and think if they were that scared, it must have meant they had a weapon.

"Apparently it's even been found that if a person's asked, 'How tall was the suspect', they'll estimate them as being taller than if they're just asked, 'What do you think was the height of the suspect?' as if just putting the word 'tall' into a person's mind will make them imagine someone as being tall. I don't know what percentage of people would be affected by that though. But anyway, the police are advised to try and do their best not to say words that suggest any one kind of answer.

"So that's basically the kind of thing that happens, and it's been found that witnesses can often remember and give quite a bit more information in interviews like that than they can in just a normal interview where they're just asked to say what happened."

The Friends Talk About How Questions Can Influence People to Give Certain Answers If They're Worded in a Certain Way, and Then Have a Laugh Again

Barbara said, "That's interesting! Mind you, I can't imagine leading questions influencing everyone. I mean, imagine a teenager trying it on their parents, saying things like, 'Mum, you did say I could eat all the leftover cakes from the party, didn't you?' 'Mum, you did say you wouldn't ask me to do any housework for the next two months, didn't you?' 'Dad, you did say I could borrow fifty pounds, didn't you?' 'Dad, you did say you'd do all my homework for me, didn't you?' 'Mum, you did say I could play my music really loud, didn't you?' 'Dad, you did say I could stay out really late tonight, didn't you?'

"Somehow I don't think leading questions like that would lead their parents to say yes to any of those things! So I don't know how careful you really have to be with them. Maybe not as careful as the police think."

They all giggled.

But then Becky said, "It's possible there's something in that. But it might make a difference that the parents would be in charge of the teenagers asking the questions; leading questions might only influence people who think the people asking them must know better than they do, or if they assume it'll be best to give the answers it sounds as if an authority figure who's asking the questions wants to hear."

Barbara said, "That's a point! ... Actually, that thing about questioning, and having to be careful not to 'put words in people's mouths' reminds me of something. I was with a little group of people once where someone read us out an article from a newspaper where a man was interviewed about a crime he'd witnessed, and one of the group commented that he sounded more educated than you'd expect him to have been, given the neighbourhood he came from. He reckoned the reporter writing up the story had just put words in his mouth, writing something based on a few interview questions he'd answered and checking it was OK with him, and then just passing it off as something the man had actually said.

"I found it hard to believe any journalist would do such a thing, and I still doubt that someone working for a national newspaper would do that, but I'm not entirely sure. Have you ever been told about it happening on your media studies course, Becky? I'm wondering whether if it does happen, sometimes journalists might write something on behalf of someone they want to write a story about, and some of the details might not be quite accurate, but the person accepts what they've written because of this thing about some people not wanting to voice opinions that contradict what a person they think of as an authority figure seems to think, because they don't want to risk getting into some kind of disagreement with them, or they want to be liked.

"The reason I'm wondering about this is because when my brother Tony first started doing shows on the Internet radio station he told you about, the management thought they could promote it by sending a press release out to the media, telling them they had a new blind DJ, hoping that would spark interest in the station. I don't think it worked.

"What happened was that a man who worked there who'd worked on quite a big commercial radio station before wrote an article and emailed it to Tony, saying, 'I've put words in your mouth. Let me know if you're happy with what I've written.'

Tony altered some of it because it wasn't the kind of thing he'd have said, and then he emailed it back. He didn't find out what happened to it in the end, like who it got sent to."

Becky said, "Well, I'm pretty sure that kind of thing doesn't happen all that much. But I have heard there's an old journalistic trick of getting a story from interviewees who are quiet or who don't want to say much by writing something you think they might say, and then asking them if it'll be alright if you say they said that."

They thought about that for a few seconds, and then Pauline said, "That reminds me of something I heard on a news programme on television once when Yoko Ono was being interviewed – you know, the widow of John Lennon, the ex-Beetles star who got murdered in about 1980. She got interviewed on the news on the telly after someone brought out a biography of him she didn't like. The news headline at the start of the programme said, 'Yoko Ono calls John Lennon's biographer his second assassin!' Well that sounded like strong wording!

"But it turned out that she didn't say that at all! I heard the interview, and what happened was that the reporter interviewing her said, 'Would you call the biographer who wrote this book John Lennon's second assassin?' and she just said yes. Well it's difficult to know whether she really did think that, but I doubt it. I mean, reading a book that says bad things, no matter what they're like, surely can't be as bad as finding out your husband's been murdered! So maybe the reason she said yes was just that on the spur of the moment, it seemed a lot easier than saying something like, 'No; that would be quite an exaggeration! I think the book's horrible, but I actually find your question a bit offensive. Do you really think I'm going to think writing a book like this is as bad as murdering someone? What do you think this country would be like if the justice system worked like that? I mean, imagine if people could be put in prison for life, just for writing books some people don't like!'

"You know, she would feel as if it was a bit of a bummer, wouldn't she, if she'd gone on the telly to criticise this book, and ended up sounding as if she was defending it and its author, by speaking up for his right to say what he said!"

The others giggled.

Then Barbara said, "That reminds me of something. I used to go to a church where after the service, the pastor's wife would always come up to me, and I think she was just trying to be nice, but she would always ask me the same one question – she'd ask me what I'd been doing during the week, and I never did anything all that exciting, so it was hard to remember, and I tend to find it hard to dredge up memories about that kind of thing on the spot anyway unless I've done something especially eventful. I wished she'd ask me more interesting questions or tell me interesting things instead.

"One day when she asked me the question, I told her I found it hard to think backwards and remember what I'd done, and she said, 'I suppose all the days just blur into one, do they?' I mumbled something that probably sounded like a yes or maybe, but I was actually thinking, 'I don't really know what that means.' I didn't ask her what she meant, because I thought it didn't really matter, and not asking seemed easier than getting into a conversation about what the question really meant, or explaining myself some more. Maybe she was thinking my days might be so similar that I might not be able to distinguish any difference between them, which wasn't quite true. But I just mumbled some kind of half-hearted agreement because it seemed the easiest thing to do at the time.

"But I wonder if witnesses being interviewed by the police might do that kind of thing if, say, a policeman asks them a question they think they should really know the answer to but they don't, and they feel awkward not knowing. Anyway, it sounds good that the police have got this sophisticated interviewing technique nowadays."

Becky asked, "What kind of questions would you like that pastor's wife to have asked you instead of the one she kept asking?"

Barbara thought about it, and then replied, "I don't know."

Becky grinned and said, "Well they couldn't have been anything too weird, could they; I mean, what would people listening have thought? What about if she'd come up to you one day and asked out of the blue, 'Do you know tortoises live to an astonishingly great age?' "

Barbara replied, "That might have been interesting!"

Becky said for fun, "Hey, imagine if someone went up to a total stranger, and the very first thing they said to them was, 'How do you think you'd feel if you had five noses on your face?"

Barbara laughed and said, "Maybe they'd say, 'It depends whose they were!' "

Pauline commented, "I don't think I'd want five noses on my face whoever they belonged to!"

Becky said, "Imagine going up to a total stranger and asking, "If you had five noses, would you prefer to have been born with them all, or would you prefer it if you just woke up one morning and discovered they'd grown there in the night?"

The others laughed. Barbara said, "If you went up to a stranger at a party and said that, they'd probably think you were drunk!"

Becky replied, "But what if you went up to someone you'd never met in a railway station waiting room or somewhere like that and asked them? How about if you asked, 'What do you think you'd do if you were a really talented musician playing in a band that was recording a new album, and the band's manager said, "On our new album, I don't want you to play the normal instruments you play; I'd like you to just play the fog horn!" ' "

The others giggled, and Pauline said, "The person you were asking might have a hard time deciding who was nuttier, you for coming up to them and asking the question, or any record company manager who'd make such a weird decision!"

They all grinned, and Becky said, "And just imagine if the next question you asked was, 'Or how about if the record company manager said, "On our next album, I don't want any of you to play any instruments, but I'd like some of you to make werewolf noises instead, as if your voices are the instruments. I want you to do the werewolf noises in harmony with everyone's singing so it sounds nice." '

"Or Barbara, what if that woman at the church you went to had come up to you one day and said, 'If you were making a cream cake for some visitors who were coming to see you one day and you realised halfway through that you didn't have any cream to put in it, do you think it's possible you might think, "Oh well, I've got some cream for grazes and bruises in my first-aid kit; I'll put that in the cake instead; maybe they won't notice the difference." '?"

Barbara laughed and said, "I'd probably think she was a bit strange if she said that! ... Well, either that or I'd wonder if she thought that's the kind of thing a blind person might do. I think there's probably a balance between asking more original questions than she was, and asking really way-out ones like that!"

They all chuckled.

Becky Finishes What She's Been Saying About False Convictions For Crimes

There was a little pause in the conversation, and then Barbara asked Becky, "Did you finish everything you wanted to say about eyewitnesses?"

Becky replied, "Nearly. The only other thing I thought of saying is that besides things like the kind of police interviewing I was talking about, there are other things that can make it less likely that the wrong people will end up being convicted of crimes. There's an organisation calling for reforms, such as making sure that when witnesses are asked to pick a person from a line of people in an identity parade to see if they pick out the person the police suspect of having committed the crime, they're told that the suspect may or may not be in the line, so they don't feel pressured to pick one person if they're unsure of whether the person who committed the crime is in the line.

"And they say witnesses should be asked how confident they are that the person they pick is the perpetrator of the crime, and their answer should be written down and told to the court, so if they're not all that confident it's the right person, the jury will hopefully find out."

Pauline said, "That sounds like a good idea, although I suppose criminals might take advantage of it by changing their appearance a bit before they go on an identity parade. Then again, a lot of them might do that already."

Then she suddenly grinned and joked, "Hey, do you think people who work in courts or go there to do jury service are called courtiers?"

"Somehow I doubt it!" replied Becky, and they all laughed.

Becky Tells the Others About Something Controversial She Once Did On Her Little Radio Show

Then she said, "Actually, thinking about royalty reminds me of something I did once: In my first year here, I did a radio show once a week for about a term on the little local community radio station with some other students on my course, and one week, I invented this game. I found this free audio editing program on the Internet that you can use to put all kinds of weird special effects on things you've recorded, or on music and things you've downloaded from the Internet, and you can mix sound effects with them too. I downloaded the audio editing program, and then I downloaded some recordings of some famous people's voices, like Prince Charles's and Winston Churchill's. I downloaded some sound effects as well.

"One sound effect I downloaded was the sound of a traffic jam, with loads of car horns beeping at different pitches. I thought it would have been funny if the drivers had all managed to beep their horns at certain times and in a rhythm, so they made a good tune, so it sounded as if it could have been an introduction to a pop song. I didn't try to edit the sound effect to make it do that, but I faded it in at the end of a song one day and said, 'Oh, this band must have just gone on tour.

Listen to all the congestion that must be being caused by lots of their fans going to see them!

"I put some funny effects on the famous people's voices. I made Prince Charles's voice go backwards and really low-pitched, and then I played it on the radio and told listeners to email me if they could guess who was speaking.

"And I made Winston Churchill's voice go all high-pitched and trembly, as if he was a talking frightened mouse shaking in his shoes!"

Barbara exclaimed, "Oh! What did your tutor think?"

Becky replied, "He didn't like it! I don't see why though! At first he blamed us all for it, but then I told him it had been my idea, and that I was the one who'd edited it that way. So he told me off for it. I didn't think it was fair of him to have disapproved of it, so I went into this rant about how I thought the speech deserved to be messed around with.

"I said something like, 'I don't understand what the problem is! It wasn't as if I was making fun of part of a speech where Churchill was talking about casualty figures or Britain losing a battle; I know that would have been in gross bad taste! But I was just making fun of a bit where he was saying stupid things!'

"I told him how stupid I thought they were, going through the part of the speech I messed up line by line.

"The first bit I messed up was a bit where Churchill announced, 'Upon this battle depends the survival of Christian civilisation.'

"That sounds like a really daft thing to have said! He was talking about the Battle of Britain. I know that was a great big battle that lasted for quite a while. If we'd lost it, the Nazis might have invaded this country and been a lot harder to push out of the countries they'd already taken over. But that would still leave countries like America, Canada, Australia, New Zealand and other ones that were probably called Christian at the time. The Nazis might have had a hard job taking over all those too! America wasn't even in the war when he said it!

"And it sounds as if he'd somehow forgotten that even if we won the Battle of Britain, there were bound to be lots of other battles the Nazis might win! It wasn't going to end the war! He must have known that really.

"And then he said something even dafter! He said, 'If we can stand up to Hitler, all of Europe will be free, and the life of the world will move forward into broad sunlit uplands.' I mean, I don't even know what that's supposed to mean!"

The others tittered.

Becky continued, "Well I don't like it when people talk in flowery figures of speech like that; I like them to talk in plain English and say just what they mean, although if Churchill had done that, he might have sounded even worse!

"I said to my tutor, 'It sounds as if he was saying he thought that if Britain won the war, everything on earth would suddenly be fantastic and life would be really easy. Well what a stupid thing to say! I bet he didn't even believe it himself! I mean, he must have known that after the war, there would be loads of grieving families, loads of bombed-out families who needed new homes, lots of bomb damage to clear up, and lots of other problems! He probably just said it to try to give people a feel-good feeling about following him, that he was hoping would be such a feel-good feeling they'd support him even if he ordered British soldiers into battles where loads of them would probably die! If that wasn't quite his motive, I bet it was something similar! If he did believe what he was saying though, he was stupid and not fit to be prime minister, because anyone who spouts nonsensical drivel like that probably makes nonsensical decisions too!' "

Barbara commented, "I think you might be being a bit judgmental there!"

Becky replied, "Maybe, I suppose; but I wouldn't be at all surprised if I'm right!

"Anyway, then I carried on explaining to my tutor why Churchill deserved to have that speech messed around with! I said, 'The next bit of his speech says that if we lost the war, the whole world would be plunged into a new dark age. Just how he thought he knew he could be so sure of that, I don't know! I mean, for all he knew, Germany might have been in too much chaos to make much trouble for anyone even if they did win the war, or countries far away might not have been affected much at all, so they'd keep going on the way they had before; he had no way of really knowing. He was probably just hoping people would believe him anyway so they'd carry on supporting the decisions he was making. ... Not that I think the Nazis should have been allowed to win, of course!' "

"That's a relief!" said Pauline.

Becky continued, "Obviously I'm glad we won. I just don't see what's wrong with criticising politicians if you think they're talking rubbish or making bad decisions. I finished what I said to my tutor by saying, 'In the last bit of the speech I played around with, Churchill said something just as silly as that hot air about sunny uplands! He said, "Let us so bear ourselves that even if this country and its commonwealth last for a thousand years, men will still say that this was their finest hour."

" 'That was just more illogical gibberish! I mean, for one thing, it sounds as if he meant he thought there were men around at the time he was making that speech who'll still be around in a thousand years! Just how long did he believe people live for?

" 'And if he didn't mean that, he must have meant that despite all the technological and medical advances and other achievements that might be made by British people between now and then, people then ought to be looking all the way back in the history books, which will be about the equivalent of us looking back to 1066, and saying, "The thing this country can be most proud of ever was fighting the Second World War!" It's just more nonsensical mindless blithering, probably just designed to stir up people's patriotic emotions so they'd be more eager to do what he wanted them to!

" 'I mean, anyone who thought about it for more than a few seconds would realise it was just silly! Maybe people were too busy worrying about what was going to happen to them to think about anything he said much at the time. They might have just been comforted by the impression the speech gave that they had a strong leader. But still, stupid things like that deserve to be made fun of!'

"Then I said, 'I think people should be careful to pay attention to any politician's speech they – for some reason – really want to hear, to see if it really, truly does make sense, or if it's just gibberish really, probably designed just to make people enthusiastic to support them!' "

The Friends Talk About Things in the Media Offending People, and Then Come Up With an Idea They Find Amusing

Barbara asked incredulously, "And you actually said all that to your tutor?"

"Yep!" replied Becky.

Pauline made a face and said, "I bet that didn't go down well! Did you have to get so heated about it? It's only some old speech that's nothing more than a thing of historical interest nowadays! Churchill probably gave it to motivate people. He must have known how tough the Battle of Britain was about to be. It was better that he gave some kind of feel-good but pretty much meaningless motivational speech than if he'd been hyper-realistic. I mean, just imagine if he'd sounded really pessimistic and said, 'We're going to need you men in the RAF to put a lot of effort into fighting, although the odds are very much against us so there's a very high chance we'll lose and you'll all be killed!'

"If he'd got everyone down like that, a lot of people in the air force might not have seen the point of putting so much effort into fighting, and then more of them might have been killed, since when people are depressed or discouraged instead of being fired up with enthusiasm, their reaction times are more sluggish, so they wouldn't have been so quick to dodge the enemy. Even seconds could have made a big difference to whether they got out of the way of enemy guns in time!"

"I suppose so," said Becky, "although once they started fighting and discovered for themselves how tough it was out there and they saw people they knew being shot down, a lot of them might have become depressed and discouraged anyway! But OK, what Churchill said could have been a whole lot worse than it was!"

"So why did you think what he said was worth making such a fuss about?" asked Pauline.

Becky replied, "I just didn't like the way my tutor seemed to think the speech was too special to play with, so I wanted to prove it wasn't. You're right though – what I said didn't go down well! He scolded, 'Rebecca!' – A lot of people seem to call me Rebecca instead of Becky when they're cross with me, for some reason. Anyway, he said, 'Rebecca! It doesn't matter what our personal opinions are of people and what they say; the fact is that on a community radio station, you have to respect the wishes of the community, and be careful to try not to offend anyone!'

"I suppose he had a good point really; but I was annoyed at the time, because I thought the way I made Winston Churchill sound by playing around with his voice was good! And I was disappointed he didn't like it, because All the students doing the show with me thought it was a laugh!"

Pauline said, "Yeah, well I think tutors think differently from students a lot of the time."

Becky replied, "Yeah, but tutors must have been students themselves once."

Pauline responded, "Yeah, but maybe as people get older, they start worrying more about offending people, or tutors just concentrate on how something's going to affect your grades, rather than caring about whether it's fun or not. You'd better be careful, because you wouldn't want to do something that might get you marked down so you end up with a lower grade!"

Becky protested, "If he marked me down just because I disagreed with him, or just because I thought something was fun when he didn't, he's not much of a tutor! Doing that's probably not allowed!"

Pauline replied, "No, but I mean I'm guessing that on your media studies course, you might have to demonstrate that you're good at doing things without offending people, since if you go into journalism, you might have to do a lot of writing for some paper or magazine or other, and if you offended too many people, it would stop selling so well, so they might fire you. So the tutors might be assessing you partly on how good you are at not offending people."

Becky responded, "I don't think I'm that bad! It's not as if I go around offending people all the time."

Pauline replied soothingly, "No, I'm sure you don't."

Barbara said thoughtfully, "I wonder if the papers really do care about not offending people; I mean, I've heard that at least a few of them have sometimes had headlines or opinion pieces that could really stir up bad feeling about certain groups of people, which must offend people in those groups. And being offensive probably gets them more sales among certain groups, even if it gets them less among others, because some people probably enjoy reading that kind of stuff. Maybe they have to tread some kind of fine line between making the most money they can, and offending people so badly their sales drop; or maybe they make some kind of clever complicated calculation about how it'll be worth giving up selling their papers to certain kinds of people, because then they can say offensive things about them and that'll be so popular with lots of other people, it'll increase their sales among *them*, and end up making them far more money than they'll have lost by offending the other ones so much that they stopped buying their papers."

The others chuckled. Pauline said, "Somehow I can't imagine people who work for some of the papers busy making complicated calculations like that! Then again, maybe it really is more of a science than we think!"

She grinned and said, "Hey imagine if it really was classed as a science, and it was taught at school along with biology and chemistry – the science of calculating how much offence you can get away with causing, and of tactically offending people to gain some kind of advantage."

The others giggled. Then Barbara screwed up her face and said thoughtfully, "Wow, I wonder what it would do to your personality if that really was a subject at school, and you spent two years practising offending people in every lesson on it, and estimating how much offence you could get away with in different situations, and then you had an exam in offending people! I wonder what you'd have to do for that."

The others laughed. Becky said, "I bet that class would be popular with all the school bullies! Maybe it would be called bully class for short!

"Actually, tactical offence sounds like something you'd do in a war! Maybe all the pupils who were interested in war would take that class by mistake! Mind you, they still might like it, especially if they taught things like, 'How you can hint to a foreign ambassador that he's a cretinous pig and a repulsive creep in such a subtle way that he probably won't think you're saying anything all that bad, so you can do it without offending him so much he complains to his country's leaders and it risks causing a war'."

Barbara and Pauline sniggered.

Pauline Tells the Others an Interesting Story She Heard About a Clever Way Some Lives Were Saved

Then Pauline said, "Actually, talking about war, I read something interesting on a website the other day. Someone told the story of how during the Second World War in America, the military wanted to put armour on their planes to defend them against enemy efforts to shoot them down, since they'd already lost quite a few; but they thought putting armour all over them might cause problems, because it would make the planes quite a bit heavier, which would lead to a couple of difficulties: First, the planes would need to stop to refuel more often, because it would take more fuel to move them, and while they were refuelling, they'd be more vulnerable to attack, and they'd be out of action for a little while each time they stopped; and also, since they'd need refuelling more often, they wouldn't be able to fly so far in one go, so they couldn't get to so many places, because they'd only be able to get to places if there was somewhere they could land safely on the journey. Mid-air refuelling was still in early development.

"And for another thing, the planes being quite a bit heavier would mean it would be more difficult to change their direction quickly in the sky, because heavier objects can't be manoeuvred into different positions as fast as lighter ones can be, for whatever reason, and that would slow the planes down enough that pilots wouldn't be able to escape from the enemy so quickly, so they might get shot at more, and also they wouldn't be as good at chasing after an enemy who was dodging them.

"So the military wondered what the best compromise would be between putting no armour on the planes, and putting so much on that they'd slow down enough to have more problems. They decided to just put it on the parts of the planes where it would be needed most; but they weren't sure how much of them to cover.

"They asked a mathematician if he could help. They gave him information about the state of the planes that were returning to America from Europe after going on bombing raids, to see if he could work out where the most armour should go. A lot of them had bullet holes in the nose and the tail and the wings and their central parts. A lot more had bullet holes there than in their engines. So it could have seemed as if the best thing to do was to put more armour there than on the engines, since it seemed those bits were getting hit most. That's what the military did think they should do, but they wondered how much armour to put there so as to protect the planes more but keep them flying almost as efficiently as before.

"But the mathematician wanted to have more of a think about what was going on. It might have seemed natural that there would be more bullet holes in the main part of a plane than the engines, since after all, there was much more of it to hit, so someone just aiming at the plane in general would have more chance of hitting it there. But he thought a piece of the puzzle could be missing. A lot of planes were being shot down and not returning at all, so he wondered where the bullet holes were going in those.

"It occurred to him that if a plane was shot in the engines and they broke, the plane would likely fall out of the sky and never be seen in one piece again, so the military would never be able to tell where the bullet holes were on it, or even that there were any. And a bullet hole to the engine was much more likely to bring a plane down by stopping it working than a bullet hole somewhere less important. He thought that the fact that they were seeing planes come home with lots of bullet holes in the main parts of them must mean that it was often possible for planes to be shot there but for the pilots to still be able to struggle home to base, and even for the planes to still be useable for future raids, so it wasn't as important for there to be armour there.

"So he recommended something the military hadn't been expecting – that the most armour should go on the parts of the planes where the ones they'd examined had no bullet holes – the engines. They followed his advice."

Becky and Barbara thought that was interesting.

Pauline continued, "After the story, on the website I read it on, there were a couple of people talking about things that can be learned from it, and one said that ordinary people can make mistakes in their thinking a bit like the American military did with the planes, in little ways, only judging by the results of things that have happened successfully, assuming they represent the whole picture, instead of wondering about the failures and the reasons for them too, without realising that's what they're doing.

"For example, if someone's lived to 110 and you ask them the secret of their longevity, they might say they don't know but they've eaten slabs of chocolate and bacon every day for decades – hopefully not together! And they might say they've had a couple of glasses of whisky a day and smoked lots of cigarettes for as long as they can remember. And you might think, 'Wow, if they've done all that and still got to such an old age, it must be alright to do that after all.' But it might just be that they've got an exceptionally strong constitution because they've got very healthy genes, and that most people who live like that die quite young. So giving up a healthy lifestyle because of what they say and adopting theirs instead because you think it would be nice might be a mistake. It would be better to wonder whether there might be people you aren't taking into consideration, like all the people who live like that and die young.

"Or a company might be offering this new treatment for baldness, and they might have an advert where a man with a head covered in hair says it worked really well for him, and other men might be impressed and want to try the treatment, without wondering whether his success is typical, or whether the treatment doesn't work for most people, and might even harm anyone who was especially sensitive to the chemicals in it.

"Or the product might be quite good, but a lot of men might make the mistake of going for it rather than looking into whether there are better alternatives out there, either because they don't think to do that, or because they don't feel like devoting the time and energy to doing it, when they might actually end up better off if they did.

"Or imagine if a few psychologists did a survey where they interviewed quite a few couples who'd been married for decades about how much they argued, and a lot of them said they'd always argued a lot, but that they loved each other so much they'd still wanted to stay together. Then the psychologists published their survey findings and declared that the amount couples argue doesn't make a difference to how long they stay together. If they'd also interviewed divorced couples and people who were in relationships that didn't get near the stage of marriage before they broke up, Their survey results might have been very different, or even pretty much the opposite!

"Or someone might visit a school when they're thinking of sending their child there, and they might ask a teacher how successful pupils at the school are, and the teacher will want to give the best impression they can so as not to let down the school, so they might tell the parent that a couple of the students made it to Oxford University. The parent might be impressed and think it must be a good school in that case; but actually, it might be that those two pupils had very encouraging parents who expected a lot from them and paid for them to be tutored privately in the evenings after school, and the pupils were so motivated they gave up making friends to do their work, because it's a school where most pupils think working just isn't cool, and they tease ones who think it is.

"So a parent would be better off not getting too impressed quickly, but asking the teachers what the average exam grades of pupils are, and also asking questions like, 'When the kids play up in a class, how do most teachers regain control of it? And roughly how often does that have to happen?' "

Barbara exclaimed, "That's interesting!"

Becky commented, "I wonder how many schools there are that are as bad as that! I'm glad mine wasn't!"

The Three Have Fun Talking About Pig Latin, and Daft Make-Believe Compliments They Think Up

Barbara grinned and said, "Hey imagine if a parent was visiting a school to see if they liked it enough to send their child there, and they asked a pupil what languages they learned there, and they said they learned French, German and Pig Latin. If the parent hadn't heard of Pig Latin, they might be impressed, thinking the school must teach Latin, and that the child was just using the word 'pig' because they didn't like it."

Pauline asked, "What is Pig Latin?"

Barbara replied, "It's nothing to do with Latin really, although it might sound a bit like it when people speak it fluently. It's just like a simple code where you swap letters of words around a bit, to confuse people, or to play games to see if they can work out what on earth you're talking about, and that kind of thing.

"I was browsing a few websites about it the other day. They said the way it works is that if a word begins with one or more consonants, you put them on the end of the word instead of at the beginning, and then say 'ay' on the end. Or if the word begins with a vowel, you don't do anything to the beginning, but you say 'way' or 'yay' at the end of the word.

"So the way you'd say Becky would be Eckybay; and the way you'd say Pauline would be Aulinepay."

Becky and Pauline smiled.

Then Barbara said, "One of my relatives is going to have a baby boy soon, but they don't know what to call him. They think it might be nice to have an unusual or exotic name; but some of the things they've come up with! The other day they told me they'd decided Bear would be a nice name! The poor little kid! I think the father's some kind of lover of wildlife. Why he loves animals that eat people, goodness knows! Perhaps he's never been close enough to one of them to change his mind! But of all the animals he could have chosen from! I said, 'No, don't call him that! Just imagine how he might get teased at school! Some kids might call him an animal! And he might get asked, "Are you Bear?" And when he says yes, they might all snigger and joke that he just said he hasn't got any clothes on!'

"They came round to my way of thinking and decided to choose something else, thank goodness! But they're still looking at weird names. I suggested for fun that they could call him a foreign name, or even just a foreign word; even if it turned out to be dustbin in one language or something, it would be OK as long as no one here knew the word meant dustbin! It would at least be better than being called something that would make an embarrassing English name like Bear!

"But I had a thought that made me smile a couple of days ago: If they really want to call the poor thing something weird, and there's just no stopping them, maybe they could give him a Pig Latin name. You know, instead of Gary, they could call him Arygay; or instead of Robert, they could call him Obertray; or instead of Daniel, they could call him Anielday; or instead of Brian, they could call him Ianbray; or instead of Steven, they could call him Evenstay.

"I'd better not suggest that to them; they might like the idea and do that for real! Mind you, it could be worse if they decided the word the boy's name was based on didn't even have to be a real name! If they decided they really didn't like their poor new baby, say if he screamed all the time for the first few days, they might feel like calling him Ashtray, which is Pig Latin for trash. Or they might think it would be a laugh to call him Outstay, which is Pig Latin for stout. ... Well, I'm pretty sure they wouldn't really do that; but maybe some people would.

"I think you might deserve to be punished for calling your baby a name like that though. A punishment that fits the offence – one that might embarrass you. Like maybe you could be put on a chain gang and made to pick litter, and every time you picked something up, you'd have to say its name loudly in Pig Latin; so if you picked up an old beer can, you'd have to shout, 'Eerbay Ancay!' And if you prized a bit of chewing gum off the pavement, you'd have to yell, 'Ewingchay umgay!'

"People might think you were nuts! That would teach you! Then you'd know how your kid felt when people laughed at the embarrassing name you'd given them!"

The others chuckled.

Then Pauline said, "The other day I came across some funny surreal compliments on the Internet – you know, things that don't make sense because they're completely different ideas put together as if they do, like, 'Your coffee is as luxurious as a table leg discovered vibrating in the depths of the mossy ocean.' "

Barbara grinned and said, "We could try to think up our own. Hey Becky, I bet You'd be good at this if you tried! Have a go at thinking some up."

Becky replied, "Um, give me a minute."

Barbara said, "Maybe something like, 'Your face is the very picture of a coffee bean-headed cow dazzling us with its beauty in the bouncing night sky.' "

Becky said, "What about, 'Your belly is as delicate as the nightingale that sings atop the rubbery crocus clouds in the salty cornflake trees.' "

The others grinned. Pauline said, "Your hair is as glorious as the dust that settles on the teeth of a thousand wise carrots' grandmas."

Becky said, "You have the ears of a finely-sequined toothbrush that fights the flies that intrude into the stealthy ironing boards in the park."

Barbara said, "The fresh air that flits into your lungs will be forever blessed with the delicate fragrance of armchairs dancing in the spinning dishwasher."

Becky said, "The tulip petals of your nose sparkle as the great Brazil nut shines forth its music for the world to see from the tall steeple of your pillow."

Barbara said, "You enrich my life with the fifteen windows in your back and the eggshells that crumble deliciously above your shoulders every time you talk."

Becky said, "You keep me amused all day long with the seashell full of alphabets you put in the kitchen cupboard when you tripped over the big raincloud in front of the tennis ball in the mumbling sky."

Pauline said, "The grass on your face is as luxuriant as the peanut butter that flows cheerfully from my dandelion-stiffened radiator when I turn the television on in the evenings."

They'd reached Barbara's accommodation again. They arranged to all go for a swim together the following week, and then said goodbye happily.

Chapter Four

Becky Gets Into an Argument After Barbara's School Reunion, Which Spoils Much of an Old Friends' Evening Get-Together

One day, there was a reunion of ex-pupils who'd gone to Barbara's old school. It was at the school, which was nearby, and afterwards, Barbara invited a few of her old friends back to the university for a chat.

Her brother Tony, who'd been to the same school as her a few years before her, had gone to the reunion too; but afterwards he went to the pub with his own friends, and then got a taxi home.

Barbara thought of inviting her friends to sit in her room, but realised it would be a bit of a squash with everyone there, especially since a couple of them had guide dogs, and some were with one of their relatives who'd come with them for the day to help them out wherever help was needed, since they were blind. So they decided to go to one of the university bars.

Barbara asked Becky if she'd like to come along to meet them, and she said she would. Barbara said it would be convenient, since then Becky could guide her to the bar and around it, since her mum, who'd been to the reunion with her, went home soon after they got back to the university. Barbara wasn't familiar enough with the bars to know her way around them by memory. Besides, with all the people who might be standing around in them, she didn't want to risk banging into people. So she needed someone to guide her.

The group sat down in a bar that was much more quiet than the other bars, so they could hear each other talk easily.

The Group Has Fun Talking About Old School Memories

They had a nice chat for a while. At first it was humorous. Not long after it started, one of Barbara's old friends, Esther, said, "I enjoyed talking about old school memories at the reunion. There are more I can think of: I remember when everyone in the dormitory I slept in one year, where there were about six of us, once had a midnight feast, and one or two people thought it would be fun if we went for a walk around the school grounds. So we did, all linking arms. But the headmistress caught us! She must have decided we were doing something dangerous and wanted to scare us to teach us a lesson ... well, either that or she thought we were being naughty and she couldn't tolerate that ... or else she just thought it would be fun. She came up to us silently and grabbed the arm of a girl on the end, Samira, who must have thought she was a prowler and screamed.

"Then she told us off, and went back indoors and locked us out, which must have been to carry on teaching us a lesson. But it was funny, because we decided to try and get in another way.

"Remember the winter garden? For anyone who doesn't know, it was a great big room, which I suppose must have been meant to be an indoor garden, although I've got a feeling there weren't many plants in it at all, if any. ... Well, none I could see anyway, which no one's going to be surprised by, since I can't see. It was a place undercover where they used to teach us pottery in the cold. Actually I used to like the smell of some of the clay we used. I think it smelled a lot nicer than some of our school dinners, although I wouldn't have wanted to eat it!

"Anyway, there were steps in there leading up to a door that led into one of the other girls' dormitories, and someone had the idea of us all going up them and seeing if they'd let us in. So we went up to the top. But when we gently knocked on the door, they either didn't hear us, or thought we might be scoundrels or ghosts, or maybe both, because they wouldn't let us in. They just kept quiet, so we didn't know if they could hear us.

"We were standing there when we heard the headmistress come in and prowl around down below. She must have been looking for us to tell us she hoped we'd learned our lesson and that she'd decided to be merciful and let us in, even though we deserved to be made to stay out there in the cold. Well, maybe she wouldn't have said all of that.

"But we decided to all be quiet so she wouldn't catch us; and after she prowled around, she went away again.

"We decided to come down and try and get back in the door she'd locked us out of. So we did, and it turned out to be unlocked again. The headmistress was on the other side, and asked us where we'd been. We told her we'd been in the winter garden, and she wouldn't believe us, because she'd looked in there and hadn't found us. We told her we'd been at the top of the steps. Then the mystery was solved for her, and she let us go back to bed."

Everyone in the group giggled, and one of Barbara's friends, Vicky, said with a grin, "Maybe it was a good thing the people in that dormitory didn't let you in; imagine if they had! The headmistress wouldn't have known, and she might have been prowling around outside all night long looking for you! She might have even got all the other staff up out of their beds to help her search! And wouldn't you have been in trouble when you just turned up the next morning as if nothing had happened!"

They all laughed at the idea.

Then another ex-pupil, Joy, said, "I remember a local drama group came and did a play for us once. It was fun. There was a bit of swearing in it, and we thought it was funny, but when it was nearly time for us to go to bed, I went and had a bath, and I heard the headmistress telling the actors off outside the window, ranting about how it just wasn't right to expose her pupils to swearing like that! I felt sorry for them. There was only a little Bit of swearing after all! It was just done by a couple of bad-tempered cricketers in the play who accused other ones of daring to be better than them!"

They all giggled again.

Then Barbara said, "I remember I used to sidle slowly between the desks in the classroom to get to my own, to reduce the risk of me banging into the corner of a desk or into a chair that had been left out or that someone was sitting on, and one day the science teacher told me in front of everyone that I looked like an overgrown fairy. I remember thinking it was just as well she hadn't said that to one of the boys instead, or he might have been embarrassed!"

One of the group, Cheryl, said, "Do you remember the tests we had to do in the first year we went to the school, just to make sure we knew how to use the microwave and the toaster and the spin dryer without blowing the school or ourselves up? Well, maybe they didn't think of them in that drastic a way. Anyway, I passed all my tests first time, but maybe I wasn't quite as competent at using them as they thought, or maybe I just had a lapse in competence one day when I was supposed to be older and wiser in my last year there, when we were allowed to share a kitchen for older pupils, and there were shared rooms where there were just two of us instead of being in the dormitories.

"I remember a day when I decided to make this bread pudding in the microwave, and I don't know why, but I was silly enough to put it in this plastic container. I should have checked to find out if it was microwaveable first. And I probably shouldn't have put it on for as long as I did. I found that one out afterwards, when I opened the door and discovered that some of the plastic had melted and broken in bits. I took the bread pudding out and tried to carry it to my room, but some of it fell out of the bottom of the melted bowl on the way, till there was a trail of currants and bits of bread all the way from the kitchen to my room, and all around the room! I still thought some of it was worth eating though, and thankfully I'm still alive to tell the tale! I was still finding currants on the floor the next day. I didn't eat those though."

The others chuckled. Barbara asked with a grin, "Was it you who put a whole egg in its shell in the microwave one day, wanting to boil it, and it exploded and splattered all over the microwave?"

Cheryl replied, "No. But I do remember when we first went there and we had lessons with the horrible cookery teacher Miss Nitpick or whatever she was called, and we were doing school tests a few months after we first went there when we were 11, and we had to boil an egg each. Well, I thought I'd turned the cooker on properly, but somehow I can't have done, unless someone maliciously or accidentally turned it down, for some reason, I suppose. Of course, being blind, I couldn't see what temperature it was on. When I thought my egg must be cooked, it turned out to be just warm, and just about raw. I knew I'd fail if Miss Nitpick found out, so I decided to get rid of the evidence quickly, and wolfed it down, shell and all! ... Well alright, I didn't eat the shell, just the egg, ... or should I say drank it! Thankfully I didn't suffer any ill effects!"

Then Vicky made a confession, saying, "This didn't happen at *our* school, but at my primary school, which was also a boarding school for blind and partially-sighted people. When I was about seven, I went through a short phase of wetting the bed. I don't know why I did it. It only happened a few times, and always at home, never at school.

"One evening my parents were driving me back to school after a weekend at home when they brought the subject up. They asked me if I was wetting the bed because something was stressing me out, like one of the staff at school. I didn't think it was anything to do with stress, but I thought that just supposing it was, it would be because my parents shouted at me so much. I thought I'd better not say that though in case they just had a go at me for it. So I mentioned one of the care staff at school. She supervised us in the dining room sometimes and put us to bed and stuff.

"She was cold and stern and unsympathetic and a bit bad-tempered, but she didn't stress me out. I'll call her miss Scolding. I heard she got sacked in the end for smacking boys with a hairbrush, although one of them told me it was more like show-tapping, since it might have stung a bit but there wasn't real force behind it.

"Anyway, I think I grumbled a bit to my parents about miss Scolding. What I did not see coming was that they were going to complain to her about what I'd said!

"That night, when I was in bed, she came up to me and told me my parents had complained that I'd told them she was stressing me out, and she ordered me to tell them that what I'd said was wrong.

"I agreed to; but I didn't really have any intention of doing it, since that would have been a pretty awkward conversation!"

Some of the Group Get Angry About Something That Happened to One of Them and Her Guide Dog in a Pub

There was some chuckling in the group. But then the conversation turned serious, and not long after that, a disagreement broke out between Becky and a few of the others.

It started when Cheryl's older sister, Brenda, who was also blind, said, "I was upset last night. I went out to the pub with some friends. I was following them to a seat with my guide dog when he stopped to sniff some people at a table. I jerked on his lead a bit and ordered him to leave them, the way we're taught to do in guide dog training to get their attention. A woman at the table told me it was OK to let him sniff around them, and I tried to smile politely, but said it wasn't OK because he's a working dog who's supposed to be paying attention to guiding me where I want to go. She said it was OK really and reached out her hand to stroke him, even though I was trying to move him away. I thought I heard her pat him, and put my hand out to see if hers was there, and she quickly took it away as soon as I touched it, as if she knew she shouldn't be doing it.

"I jerked on my guide dog's lead a bit harder than before, the way we're taught to to get their attention, and ordered him sternly to go forward. Then he guided me to where the others were and I sat down with him beside me on the floor. The couple at the table we'd just gone past were sarcastically calling me charming and saying I didn't seem very nice. I ignored them and talked to my friends. I sat with my foot in contact with my guide dog, so I'd be able to tell if he moved.

"Not long afterwards, the people at the other table got up to leave. Just before they walked out, the man who'd been sitting there with the woman walked past, and I felt as if something was making sharp contact with my dog, who suddenly jumped up. The man said angrily, 'Now yank him again!' before walking out. I wondered what he'd done, but my friends weren't looking so they didn't see. Thankfully my dog wasn't hurt at all. I said something loudly about how the man had tried to hurt the dog, but no one would take what I said seriously, since I didn't see what happened and the dog was alright. They just said the man probably didn't do anything on purpose and that he was probably just a bit drunk, and that he probably just moved the chair next to me a bit, or something like that. But what he'd said had sounded threatening. It's not nice to have to put up with that kind of thing, when all I want is a nice quiet evening!"

Joy said, "That's terrible! I hope that man gets what's coming to him!"

Joy's older sister Bridie, who'd come to guide her, said, "What an ignorant man! I'd like to have seen him banned from the pub!"

Cheryl said, "There are some scumbags out there, aren't there! It's a shame you couldn't report him to someone!"

Esther's older sister Sheila, who'd come to guide her, said, "What a cruel man, hurting your dog! Don't worry; he'll get what he deserves one day; what goes around comes around."

Joe, Vicky's sighted older brother, said, "It would have served him right if your dog had bitten him!"

Becky Disagrees With the People Getting Angry

Becky started feeling upset by the comments, because she thought they sounded way too harsh, and she said, "Hang on! We don't even know that man did anything that bad! Brenda, I can understand you being upset by what happened, because not really knowing what was going on must have made you feel a bit worried, and it must have been a bit scary to suddenly realise the man was there sounding a bit threatening, and for your dog to suddenly jump up as if something had just hurt him. But maybe what happened wasn't as bad as you thought; after all, you couldn't see what happened, and maybe you're misinterpreting the couple's motives a bit, and your misinterpretation's partly what's making you angry.

"I mean, it sounds to me as if when the woman said it was OK when your dog started sniffing them in the first place, you took it to mean that she was saying he could sniff them as much as he liked as far as they were concerned, so you said he wasn't allowed to. But what if she was really just trying to reassure you, because she thought that when you pulled him away, it was because you thought he was bothering them? And then what if when you said it wasn't OK, the woman felt sorry for him because she thought it was a pity that he wasn't even being allowed to stop to be petted in the relaxed environment of the pub, so she stroked him as a consolation; and then the reason she pulled her hand away when you touched it wasn't because she knew she was doing something wrong, but because she didn't want her hand to be in the way while you were doing whatever you were trying to do when you were reaching out to him?

"And then what if when you jerked the dog's lead hard and told him sternly to leave them, they thought you were being cruel to the dog? They probably wouldn't have known what you were taught in training about the way to stop guide dogs from being distracted, and how people aren't supposed to touch them when they're working. I've heard that people are told when they're in training to have a guide dog that they should use a stern tone of voice to get the dog's attention, but those people probably wouldn't have known that, and what if they felt sorry for the dog because they thought your voice sounded unfairly harsh, and that's why they complained to each other about you after you sat down?

"And then what if when the man came over afterwards, he didn't actually do anything to harm the dog, but the sharp sensation you felt was just the dog moving suddenly as he jumped up; and the reason he jumped up wasn't because he was being hurt, but because he was startled, or even pleased, that the man suddenly stopped in front of him? What if the man was holding out something for the dog to eat, and the dog just moved suddenly because he was reaching out to grab it?

"And what if when the man said, 'Now yank him again', he was thinking, 'Let's see if you dare be cruel to the dog with me right beside you!'? What if he was feeling sorry for the dog, and angry because he thought you'd been harsh with it, and he wasn't trying to hurt it at all?

"Or what if your dog suddenly jumped up because the man had his fists clenched in your direction, thinking, 'If you do another cruel thing to the dog I'll do it back to you', and your dog jumped up suddenly because he was planning to protect you, because it looked as if the man was threatening you, and the dog didn't know why, and thought he might be about to hit you for no reason? Maybe the man overreacted like that because he'd had a bit too much to drink. But it's possible he was still just concerned about the dog."

The Group Starts Talking About Badly-Behaved Animals, and Equally Badly-Behaved Humans

A young man called Christopher who had a guide dog with him was there. He was a few years older than Barbara, but had become friends with her at school after she met him while hanging around with his younger sister, who was blind like him and had been in Barbara's class. His sister hadn't come to the reunion, because she'd hated the school and didn't want reminders of it.

Christopher said, "I can understand you wanting to stand up for the couple who were annoyed with Brenda, Becky, and maybe you're right. But one reason people get worked up about this kind of thing is because it's common for guide dogs to get distracted by people, and blind people can really do without it when they're just trying to get somewhere. It would have been awkward for Brenda to have stopped to let the couple at the table pet her dog, because by the time they'd finished, her friends could have been out of earshot so she didn't know where they were.

"The public needs to be educated to leave guide dogs alone when they haven't got permission to touch them, because it really can get frustrating having someone trying to pet and talk to your guide dog when you just want them to carry on working for you so you can get where you need to be. I know that from experience. And even when the dog's not working, it can be a bit unnerving if someone starts doing something to it without asking you first if it's OK and you don't know what they're doing or what they're intending to do next. It makes you feel as if you're less in control than you need to be.

"I remember sitting in a pub one evening, and a man came up to me and asked me if he could give my dog some crisps. At least he asked ... at first! I said no, because for one thing, crisps probably aren't healthy for dogs – I mean, as much as they're nice, they're not even healthy for humans! But for another thing, we're trained not to let people feed our dogs, because the more people do that – at least so the theory goes – the more the dogs will be tempted to be distracted by people with food, hoping to get some from them, and we could be put in danger if they're supposed to be in the middle of guiding us when someone walks past with some food, and they forget all about guiding us for a few seconds and suddenly head towards the person, because they're hoping to be given some; what if we're walking past a lamp post just then? We might be banged right into it! We have to be strict with guide dogs to make sure they concentrate on their work when they're guiding us, for our own safety.

"Well, part of the reason we're told we're not supposed to let other people feed them is to do with trying to make sure they stick to a healthy diet as well, in the hope that they remain healthy enough to carry on working for us.

"But when I told the man who came up to me in the pub that people other than their owners aren't allowed to feed guide dogs, he must have got annoyed and just thought I was being unfair, because ten minutes later, I heard this rustling and crunching noise from where my dog was, and when I felt the floor to try to find out what he could be crunching, I found fifteen open packets of crisps there! I hadn't heard the man put them down, but I'm guessing he must have put them in front of my dog to spite me, because he thought I was being unfair to the dog. And maybe he was a bit drunk!"

Vicky said, "Wow, who would put fifteen packets of crisps on the floor for a dog to eat! Just imagine if he ate the lot! He'd probably be pretty sick after that!"

Bridie said, "I had a neighbour who had a cat that loved eating crisps once, and other kinds of party food too! It would jump up onto your lap to try and snatch food from you if you had some!"

Joy said, "One of my friends had a guide dog who loved party food! We had to be careful what we left within his reach. Mind you, that wasn't as bad as a dog that belongs to one of my relatives: It's a rescued dog; it used to be a stray dog on the streets.

It's very well-behaved most of the time, but it'll steal things if they're left within its reach. Mind you, it's not as bad as it was at first; they came into the kitchen one day not long after they'd got it, and found it had eaten all the bread in the bread bin ... and half the bread bin too! It was a wooden one, so the dog must have found it quite easy to gnaw through."

The others grinned.

Cheryl said, "I know someone whose guide dog was so naughty, one Christmas day they were invited round to a friend's house, and they must have left their guide dog unsupervised for a while, and the next thing they knew, it had jumped up and tucked into the turkey!"

There were a few sniggers from people in the room, while Becky said, "Yikes!"

Then Brenda said, "It can be worrying if a guide dog scavenges though, since you don't know what the things they've eaten might do to them. Some things that humans love are actually toxic for dogs, and can even kill them if they eat a lot, like chocolate, especially dark chocolate. That's another reason why people shouldn't feed guide dogs without their owners' permission, and dogs shouldn't really eat anything other than their dog food and dog treats. If someone feeds a guide dog a chocolate bar, it can make them vomit, and their blind owner might not know they've been sick, and might walk in it, or put something down in it before they realise it's there. So it's not nice!

"So if someone comes up and asks a guide dog owner if they can give the guide dog a treat and the owner says no, they're not just being grumpy and unfair; there are good reasons they might say no.

"Mind you, having said that, guide dogs aren't normally throwing up all over the place, so that probably means they're not normally eating things they shouldn't be. I know quite a few guide dog owners who've been ordered to leave restaurants because the managers weren't happy with them having their guide dogs there; but most guide dogs won't cause a health and safety hazard at all! Most will just go under the table and stay there; they won't sniff nearby customers' food or try to grab it, or jump up at anyone, or anything like that. They're trained to be well-behaved. They might sniff around under their owner's table after the meal and polish off any crumbs that have been dropped, but that's normally all. So no restaurant manager needs to worry that they'll be a nuisance or a safety hazard. ... Or at least the vast majority of them won't be. One reason we're taught to jerk their harnesses and say, 'Leave it!' to them sternly as soon as they seem to be getting distracted is to stop any misbehaviour they might be starting to indulge in, for all we know."

Barbara said, "I've known guide dog owners to get angry with restaurant staff who tell them they have to leave, and they say things that end up causing an argument, like that by law they've got no right to refuse to serve them. I can understand them being annoyed, but I wonder if trying to reassure the restaurant staff might work better, like if they say the kind of thing you just said, about how most guide dogs are well-behaved and won't be a nuisance to other customers."

Christopher said, "I don't know. Actually I do know someone who says she usually doesn't argue nowadays but just leaves, but then writes to the owners and explains what happened and how it was unfair afterwards, and she's often got free vouchers for more meals there."

Barbara responded, "That's good!"

Then she grinned and said, "Hey imagine if it was the law that instead of just not being allowed to refuse to let guide dogs into restaurants, restaurants had to entertain guide dogs too while their owners were eating!

"I came across an Internet forum where a woman said she had a blind work colleague, and they went on a training course for a few days, and someone opened a door to let some cool air in one afternoon, since it was hot. The blind woman just thought someone must have opened a window when she felt the breeze. But her guide dog was looking out the door, and it saw a rabbit hop by, and jumped up and ran out after it. Most of the people on the course jumped up and ran after the dog. It ran through a pond! The people running after it didn't fancy going in there, but one of them caught the dog by running round the pond and catching up with it. It must have been all soaking and muddy when they brought it back in! They probably wiped it down as best they could with a towel or something. The blind woman didn't let go of its lead for the rest of the afternoon in case it escaped again!

"It seems some of these beasts do a great job, but you've got to keep control of them if you don't want to risk them being naughty. ... Sorry, I don't suppose you guide dog owners will appreciate me calling them beasts!

"But anyway, I was just thinking: Wouldn't it be funny if there was a law that said restaurants had to entertain guide dogs while their owners were eating, and some restaurant managers who didn't think things through carefully tried buying rabbits that could run really fast, and set one loose in the restaurant every time a guide dog came in for them to chase, so once their owner had sat down, their guide dog would run all over the place. The rabbit would be dodging under chairs and running through all kinds of gaps that the guide dog couldn't fit through, so the dog would be haring around in different directions, probably knocking handbags flying, knocking empty chairs over, treading on people's feet as it ran under tables, and all kinds of things! Restaurants would long for the days when all the law said was that they had to let guide dogs In! ... Well, either that or they'd think up a different kind of entertainment for them!

"Or just imagine if every time a guide dog came in, one of the restaurant staff would bring some doggy toys out and play with the guide dog with them, and if other customers wanted a go, they'd let them."

Everyone in the group chuckled, and Vicky said for fun, "The guide dog owner would be lucky to ever get their dog back again if other customers were really enjoying playing with it! ... Actually, maybe no guide dog owner would ever dare go to a restaurant again, because they wouldn't know what might happen to their dog!"

One of Barbara's Friends Talks About the Hazards of Distracting Guide Dogs While They're Supposed to be Working

Christopher grinned and said, "Talk about distracting a guide dog!"

Then he became serious and said, "I didn't quite finish what I wanted to say to Becky about how we need to feel as if we're in control of our guide dogs. It's fair enough to play with a guide dog when they're not working, Becky, as long as the owner knows what's going on and approves, of course. Lots of owners play with their guide dogs when they're not working.

"But it can get irritating when people distract our dogs when they're supposed to be working, because they're supposed to be concentrating on keeping us safe and helping us get to places. Anything that tempts them to get distracted might be a safety hazard, or at least an inconvenience. That's one reason why we're told to give them stern commands when they start paying attention to other things when they're supposed to be guiding us.

"People occasionally get offended if they start talking to my dog or petting her and I tell them to stop while she's in the middle of guiding me somewhere. It's not very nice to say things I know people might be offended by; but I know it needs to be done for our safety really. I do try to do it nicely, like explaining that I've got a train to catch or that I'm in a hurry for some other reason, and people tend to be understanding about that. But it would be safer if no one ever distracted my dog while she was working, at least in some circumstances.

"Say if I was at the top of some steps with her, and I was hesitating because I was feeling for the banister and feeling with my feet to find out exactly where the steps started, but someone at the bottom called out enticingly to the dog to come down, trying to be helpful, or being a bit impatient, say if they were directing us to somewhere and they wanted to hurry us along because they were in a bit of a hurry themselves, and didn't understand that we were hesitating for a good reason, but assumed the dog was just dawdling or a bit anxious about going down steps, or that I was just fidgeting and flapping around for no good reason and that the dog was the one in control. If they did that, the dog might start down the steps when I wasn't expecting it, and either I might lose my balance and fall down and hurt myself, or the dog might suffer because

I'd still be holding her harness so she would be being pulled back up steps she was trying to go down. I heard about something like that happening to someone once, who fell down the steps because of it.

"I think the public needs to realise that guide dogs need to wait for our commands before they do things, for our safety. We have to be ready to do something before we'll want to give them the go-ahead. Otherwise, they could do unexpected things that could even put us at risk, like guiding us up or down steps we didn't realise were there. They're supposed to stop at steps till we tell them it's OK to go."

Barbara smiled and said, "I think it would be good if we could have robotic guide dogs, that looked exactly like real ones, but just wouldn't get distracted. Imagine if someone bent down to stroke one and it said in this butch electronic voice, 'Do not distract me! I am busy working for my owner!' They'd get a bit of a fright, wouldn't they!"

The others giggled, and Brenda said, "I heard about someone's guide dog that was trained to give people dirty looks when they distracted it by stroking it or talking to it while it was working."

They all grinned.

But then the conversation got serious again as Christopher said, "That sounds like a good idea! Another thing, Becky, is that apart from safety, it's just inconvenient sometimes to have other people stroking our dogs when they're guiding us, because as I hinted at before, while most dog owners out with their dogs might just be taking them on leisurely walks for exercise so they might not mind them being stroked, guide dogs are working dogs that we'll sometimes be using when we're hurrying to catch a bus or a train we might be a bit late for, or when we might need to walk somewhere else in a hurry, so we're going to get stressed if we keep being delayed because well-meaning dog lovers want to stop us so they can spend time petting our dogs.

"And if our guide dog's following someone and that's the only way we know what direction to go in, but then someone else wants to pet the dog so they stop us, the person we're trying to follow might not realise we've stopped, so they might carry on walking, and be out of earshot and out of sight of the dog by the time the other person's finished stroking the dog, so it might be really awkward for us to find our way.

"I don't mind people stroking my guide dog when she's not working for me, say if we're just in the park and I'm letting her relax for a while, or if I'm just standing waiting at a bus stop. Actually I've ended up having some really interesting conversations with people that started because they came over and admired my dog and wanted to pet her, so it can be nice. And sometimes when I haven't been sure of the way to somewhere, it's been nice when people have come over and asked me if I needed help, and I haven't minded them giving my dog a bit of a stroke then. It's just that when we're walking along purposefully, or about to cross a road and I'm listening out for traffic, sometimes I just need to get where I want to go, so it's awkward if she gets distracted."

Becky Becomes Controversial, and Others Feel Insulted

Becky responded, "That's interesting. But I'm wondering if you told me all that because you thought I was objecting to

Brenda not wanting her dog to be distracted. I wasn't. I was just thinking that maybe she wouldn't be so angry about what happened in the pub last night if she tried to think about how things might have seemed from the point of view of the people at the other table, who probably didn't know the rules about not distracting guide dogs, or about how their owners are trained to give them commands that sound a bit harsh and jerk on their harnesses if they start paying attention to things they're not supposed to instead of concentrating on obeying their owners.

"And I don't like the fact that so many people here condemned the man, when Brenda even said herself that she doesn't really know what happened. I think people should stop to think before they start judging people. I've heard this kind of thing before: Someone complains about someone else, and without even stopping to wonder what the other person's side of the story might be, lots of people can immediately take the side of the person complaining, and they can all start condemning whoever it was that did whatever made the person who's complaining annoyed, sounding way more extreme than is fair. I don't know why some people are like that. I think I can understand how Hitler found it so easy to get supporters now."

Barbara protested defensively, "Becky, you're not hinting that you think my friends might have been tempted to follow Hitler, are you? You've just complained about people saying things you think are too extreme, and now here you are being even more extreme yourself!"

Barbara would probably have been well-advised to have just let the Hitler comment go instead of drawing attention to it. Becky, who probably needed to learn the wisdom of picking her battles and the saying 'least said, soonest mended', replied,

"It isn't an extreme thing to say! I'm not saying your friends might have supported Hitler. It's just that some of them were so quick to condemn that man harshly that it shows how easy it must be to get carried along by feelings of anger against people when they're stirred up. Brenda wasn't even trying to stir them up. So imagine how easy it must be for people who do try to stir them up to succeed!

"I'm just saying it seems Hitler wouldn't have to have done much to work people up into having extreme views. All he would have had to do was tell some stories that made people angry, say about how Jews had been caught hurling abuse at some kids; and never mind that politicians have got a reputation for lying, people would probably have started angrily talking about how those Jews ought to be punished, just like the people who condemned that man in the pub, even though they don't really know what happened.

"And then if Hitler had told lots of stories about lots of different Jews hurling abuse at kids, he might have done a very good job of whipping up hatred against Jews in general, and a lot of people might have even started thinking it would be good to force all Jews to leave the country, at least if he put the idea into their heads.

"And what if some politician came along today and started whipping up hatred against some other group by saying the same kinds of things? Maybe they'd quickly get a lot of supporters, just like Hitler did, because a lot of people would get angry and be quick to believe what they said, not wondering whether it was all true or what the other side of the story was.

"But if Hitler had said that stuff about quite a few incidents where Jews had shouted abuse at kids, and people had actually stopped to wonder about what really happened, it might not have been so easy for him to get their support. I mean, what if they'd all thought to themselves, 'Did these things really happen, I wonder? If they did, did they happen in the way he's saying they did? Maybe crowds of Jews really did hurl abuse at some kids, but what if they did it because the kids attacked them or hurled a load of insults at them first? What if the "kids" were really big muscular teenage boys?'

"If Hitler didn't tell the crowd those details, they might have all assumed the abuse the Jews shouted was unprovoked, and that the kids were little, and they might have just got angry about it; but they might not have got angry and decided to support Hitler if they'd thought, 'Why might those Jews have done such a thing? If nothing happened to provoke them, what else might have made them do it? What about their backgrounds might make them more likely to behave like that? Is it something that can be fixed? If so, how can things be changed for the better? Do we need better policing in this country to root out individuals who behave in a threatening way? Roughly what percentage of the Jewish community behaves like that? If it's only a small percentage, is it fair to hate them all? And is it just Jews who behave like that, or do lots of other people behave like that too? I need to find out things like this before making up my mind what I think about Jews being in our country.'

"If they'd all thought things like that, it might not have been so easy for politicians to whip up feelings of hatred in them. And since it seems you don't even have to say anything that bad happened before people start wishing bad things on a person, judging by what people here have said about what happened with the guide dog yesterday, it sounds as if it could be easy to raise a rabble even nowadays!"

Barbara looked embarrassed and said, “Becky, you might be right, but I don’t think anyone here would ever want to be a follower of anyone as extreme as Hitler. Can’t you keep him out of this?”

Becky replied, “How do you know your friends couldn’t be persuaded to follow someone like Hitler? You might think you know them, but you might only know what they’re like when they’re not worked up with emotion. If someone came along and got them angry by telling them that certain groups of people deserve to be treated badly because they do bad things to other people, they might end up baying for their blood, without even stopping to think about whether everyone in those communities behaves that way and deserves to be treated badly.”

Most people were surprised to hear Becky talking that way. Barbara sighed wearily and said pleadingly, “Becky, it might be interesting to have a conversation about this kind of subject at another time, but can we talk about something else, please? I was hoping we were going to have a nice time this evening.”

She smiled and said to her friends in an attempt to be soothing, “Don’t mind Becky; she’s a psychology student. I bet they’ve all learned to analyse what other people’s friends say like that.”

Becky protested with a note of irritation, “I was doing that before I even came to university! But what’s wrong with that?”

Sheila sneered sarcastically, “I bet you make great company at a party! Do you criticise people all day, or just when you’re feeling grumpy because it’s getting near your bedtime?”

Barbara joked, “She isn’t normally that bad. Only when there are alcohol fumes in the air.”

If the conversation had been light-hearted, Becky might have made a joke about that. But instead she felt slighted by what Barbara said, since it sounded to her as if she was siding with the other people in the room against her and making fun of her. That wasn't Barbara's intention. But Becky interpreted what she said as being a bit demeaning. She got angry and said to Sheila and Barbara, "I don't see why you have to be like this! If you think there's anything wrong with my point of view, tell me what it is! It's not a good argument just to say scornful things about the person who thinks it instead, as if you want people to think that just because you can do that, you can make people think it's not worth taking seriously!"

Barbara said in a coaxing tone, "Becky, that's not what I'm trying to do at all! I'm just trying to keep the peace. You're getting way more worked up over what people have said than necessary. I don't want to argue at all. Come on, Becky, let's talk about something nicer. Any old thing ... I know, how about the weather even?"

The Conversation Becomes Humorous for a Little While

Christopher grinned and said, "Hey that's a good idea, let's do that! Do you know, there are genuine official weather forecasts for hell. Look it up on the Internet and you'll see; they say things like, 'Today it will be very cold in hell.' ... It's because there's a place in Norway called Hell. There's a place in America called Hell too. The weather forecasts are for those places."

The people in the room giggled. Cheryl said, "Maybe they talk about what the weather's going to be like in hell on the telly when they do the holiday weather. Imagine going on a holiday to hell! I heard someone on the telly say that in Iceland, people just can't understand how hell could possibly be a bad place, since they would just love to be in a place that was much warmer! Imagine if a travel agent somehow managed to do a deal with the Almighty and offer package tours to the biblical hell! Imagine a really posh person saying, 'My family are wintering in hell this year to avoid the cold weather.' "

They all laughed.

Christopher said, "There's a place called Useless Loop too, in Australia. Once I was fed up because the weather forecast said it was going to be sunny, but it was cloudy, and I put the search term 'useless weather forecast' into Google, looking for other complaints about useless weather forecasting so I'd feel better that at least lousy forecasts were being noticed, and a weather forecast came up for this place I'd never heard of at the time called Useless Loop. I wondered if it was a joke weather forecast at first, but it turned out the place really exists! Imagine telling people you live in Useless Loop!"

They giggled.

Becky had calmed down and begun to enjoy herself, and she said, "Imagine a weather forecast on the radio where they forecast the weather for quite a few places, and first they said what the weather forecast for Hell was going to be like, and then they said what the weather for Useless Loop was going to be like; people who'd never heard of those places would start wondering if they were dreaming, wouldn't they!"

Esther said, "Imagine if on days when the weather was especially cold and windy and nasty, weather forecasters would say, 'We're going to have hellish weather today!' That would confuse people, wouldn't it, because some people might think it meant the weather was going to be boiling hot!

"Or imagine if they would use words that would summon up thoughts of hate groups, because they thought the weather was going to be horrendous, and even dangerous for people out in it, so they'd say, 'We're going to have Nazi weather today!' "

They grinned. But then Barbara, even while she was chuckling, said, "Oh no, let's not get back to talking about the Nazis again!"

A Discussion Starts About Whether Debating Can Actually Lead to People's Views Becoming More Extreme Than They Were Before

Christopher had other ideas and said, "Oh don't worry. It can be quite good fun to have an argument sometimes. Actually, I wanted to say a few more things to Becky. You know, Becky, I don't think people could be as easily persuaded to follow someone who tried to whip up hatred as you think. I mean, I think people often say things in the heat of the moment that are a bit extreme, but then they get to have a more moderate view of things when they've cooled down and their strength of feeling's worn off a bit. And after all, if it was that easy to get groups of people to hate other groups, surely there would be a lot more conflict between groups of people nowadays than there is."

Becky said thoughtfully, "Maybe most people in Western Europe are too contented nowadays to get interested in joining hate campaigns against people. Maybe living standards are so high for a lot of people now that it would be a lot harder for politicians to recruit volunteers to go to war, because going would involve people immediately making way too high a sacrifice for them to want to, with everything they'd have to give up. That might be one major reason why there haven't been any big wars in our part of Europe recently.

"A century ago, a lot of men worked in such bad conditions that going to war might have seemed like a chance worth taking to escape them, especially since recruitment campaigns might have whipped up patriotic fervour and made war sound like an adventure, and they might not have thought far enough ahead to think about the possible bad consequences. Nowadays the effects of a war would probably be all over the Internet, which might be another reason why it might be harder to recruit people to risk their lives to do the bidding of politicians than it would have been in the past, at least when it comes to wars in foreign countries that there's no need for us to get involved in, rather than attacks on our own people.

"Also, things might work the way you say they do a lot of the time, Christopher, but if people keep listening to or reading things that keep their emotions heated, they might get more and more convinced to keep believing them over time, and feel more and more strongly about them."

Christopher replied, "I'm sure that can happen. But if people who've been listening to and reading that stuff spend time around other people who aren't being influenced by it, some of those people are almost bound to say things that contradict their views and make them think, so they'll start realising the hate preachers or whoever the people are who are stirring up their feelings are wrong, or exaggerating things."

Becky countered, "That might happen some of the time; but it can work the other way around too, maybe quite often, since when two people are debating something, anyone watching at the start might think, 'Oh good, they'll end up understanding each other's opinions better, and maybe one will persuade the other to take on a more sensible point of view', but it can have the opposite effect, since people don't normally like things they strongly believe in being challenged, so at least if the debate's going on online so there's time for people to think before they have to respond each time, they'll often think up or look for more and more reasons to justify their beliefs, to help them defend them against what the other person's saying, so they can just end up convincing themselves all the more that they're right, and even develop more extreme views than they started with, partly because of what they read at some of the places they go to search out information that supports them."

"Cheerful, aren't you!" quipped one of Barbara's friends, Malcolm, sarcastically. "Let's talk about something more enjoyable, like, err, I dunno, the time I stubbed my toe the other day! That'll at least be Marginally more fun than this!"

Some of the people in the group giggled.

Becky said, beginning with a note of reluctance, "Alright, let's talk about something else. But just one more thing first: I learned that sometimes, instead of debating with people, asking them questions that'll make them feel the need to think seriously about how sensible their beliefs really are if they want to give good answers will work better, ... at least if they're intelligent questions.

"Mind you, some people might think their questions are intelligent and that they're doing that when they're not really. And sometimes when people answer the questions, it can turn out that the person who asked them didn't really even want to know the answers, but was just trying to score points by making the other person look silly or ignorant, because they were so convinced they wouldn't be able to give good answers; so the person who answered the questions can just get annoyed. I've seen it happen on Internet forums.

"But the kind of questions I'm thinking people could ask others are ones about how much evidence for their beliefs there really is and how logical they are, like, 'Can you be sure it happened in the way that person says it happened?', or, 'Just suppose for a minute that it didn't happen for that reason; what alternative possible explanations are there for why it might have happened?' "

A Bit of Joking Breaks Out

Barbara smiled and said, "Hey, just imagine if a schoolteacher said to a pupil, 'You are lazy! You should have done more work than this by now!' and the pupil said, 'What evidence is there that the reason I haven't done much work is because I'm lazy? What possible alternative explanations can you think of as to why I haven't done much?'

"And imagine if the teacher said, 'Well I suppose it could be because you might have stupidly stayed up half the night playing video games so you're too tired to be at school', and the pupil replied, 'OK, so that's one possibility. Now what other ones can you think of?' And just imagine if every single time the teacher tried to come up with an insult, the pupil said the same kind of thing!"

The others giggled. Esther said, "Yeah, or when the teacher told the pupil they might be too tired, imagine if the pupil said, 'You're right! I'm too tired to be at school! Can I go home now?' "

Bridie said with a grin, "I wish I'd thought to say that to some of my teachers!"

They all laughed.

The Argument Gets Going in Earnest, as Becky Complains About Things She's Heard People Say, and Another Group Member Scornfully Challenges Her

The conversation could have become enjoyable at that point. Unfortunately, the argument suddenly became a lot more heated than it had been before, when Joe, who had a reputation for being argumentative, sneered challengingly to Becky, "I bet you actually did that, Becky. But you've been talking about showing people's arguments up as not very good by asking them what evidence they've got for their opinions, as if you think that when they tell you, you'll be able to show them what's wrong with them, or at least make them think more deeply about them so they discover it themselves; but why don't you take your own advice? After all, what evidence do you yourself have for thinking some of the things you've been telling us you think, such as that just because some of us criticised a man in a pub who sounded obnoxious earlier this evening, we're the kind of people who could easily be persuaded to become Nazis, and that we could easily be stirred up to go and harm people as part of a rabble? Don't think it's just other people whose arguments are bad!"

Some of the group grinned. But not for long.

Becky replied, "That's not quite what I said! But I wouldn't be surprised if you could personally be easily persuaded to be an extremist, because you were getting things out of proportion so quickly before, condemning the man when you didn't even have much evidence that he'd done anything wrong! Your behaviour reminds me of things people have said when I've been out with Barbara before, so you sound just like them.

"I like all the people in the disability rights group Barbara's a part of here at the university – they're all nice people with good ideas; but one day we went to meet a local group to chat and discuss what problems people have, and I went to guide Barbara around, and a few of Them were right bad-tempered grumps! They were just complaining, instead of trying to come up with ideas to solve problems! And they were getting things way out of proportion, just like some of you did! I don't suppose it's just those kinds of groups where this kind of thing happens – it probably happens in lots of different kinds of places with different people who are talking about different things. But I'll tell you about those people, since they're the ones who are coming to mind at the moment:

"One of them – not one of the horrible ones – a blind woman called Maureen, said she was annoyed because a couple of days earlier, she'd been sitting with some members of her family and some of their friends, when someone else came in and sat next to her without saying anything; she heard them sit down, but she didn't know who it was, and when she asked, one of her family on the other side of her said, 'Guess!' They were obviously thinking it would be entertaining.

"But Maureen thought that would just be humiliating, like being shown up as having disadvantages compared to everyone else in the room, and as if her blindness was being turned into a sport, since everyone else would have been able to tell who the person was as soon as they walked in the room, since everyone knew each other. She was the only blind one there. So she thought that if she got the wrong answer and people thought it was amusing, she'd be being laughed at for something she couldn't help, and she didn't think that would be funny. It would have been even worse if they'd asked her to guess again, and she'd got it wrong again, and they'd laughed again.

"So she told us she wished people wouldn't say that to her, and asked the group what they thought she should do when people said things like that, since it had happened before. She asked if they thought it was justifiable to feel like headbutting people who said that to her, since it annoyed her so much.

"Well, that reaction sounded a bit drastic, but I could understand her being annoyed. But then a few people said they thought it was perfectly justifiable to headbutt them for real, sounding as if they really meant it. They said people like that deserved a good punch. In fact, a couple of them even said worse things. One of them said he didn't think she should headbutt them, so at first he sounded nice, but then he said, 'It would be a pity if headbutting them hurt your head. I think you should break a glass and hit them in the throat with it instead!'

"They sounded horrible! I wondered what they'd recommend if Maureen had said one of the family had sworn at her – would they say they deserved death? I think Maureen herself got fed up of what they were saying in the end, because she said, 'Thanks for your opinions, but tell you what: Let's just leave it there and change the subject.'

"There was another blind person there who said people have done the same thing as Maureen's family member did to her to him, and he just tries to laugh it off, and he recommended that Maureen try doing that. But one of the others said that wasn't really a good idea, since then the family would think it was alright to do that and carry on.

"That was fair enough. I recommended that she try to make some kind of joke at the time, like maybe answering, 'I think it would be interesting if it was a famous dead celebrity, like Elvis Presley. Just imagine if we were the first people he revealed that he was really still alive to! Mind you, he'd probably be so old now that he might die for real right in front of us! So imagine if we went around telling people we'd seen Elvis just recently, and some of them said, "Oh, you're another one of those nutters who thinks he's still alive, are you?" And we said, "No, he's definitely dead now." ' "

The people in the room tittered.

But then Becky said, "Anyway, I said to her, 'Later, in private so they don't feel shown up, you could maybe speak to the person who told you to guess who the person who'd come in and sat next to you was, and tell them you don't like it when they do that, saying something like,

" ' "I know you don't mean any harm by doing this and you only do it because you think it's a bit of fun, but I really don't like it when you try to make me play guessing games, like when someone comes and sits beside me and I don't know who it is, and you tell me to guess when I ask. It makes me feel a bit embarrassed and uncomfortable, because I know there's a good chance I'll be wrong, and get laughed at for it, and that brings home to me that I'm at a serious disadvantage compared to everyone else, who'll instantly know who the person is, so it'll mean I start thinking about how much of a disadvantage I'm at, when all I want to do is enjoy a good chat. So that'll put me in less of a good mood. And it makes me feel shown up in front of everyone, because it brings it home to everyone else how much of a disadvantage I'm at as well, and if I guess wrong and I hear them giggling, it'll feel as if they're making fun of the fact that I can't do something they can.'

"I said she could say to them, 'I know you might not understand, but maybe you'll understand better if you try to imagine how you'd feel if something similar happened to you, like if you put on a lot of weight one year, and you were out with the family, and they were talking about having pudding, and someone announced loudly, "Who's the one who shouldn't be allowed to have ice cream this year? Yes, you, after all the weight you've put on!" They might only be joking, and it might be obvious to everyone in the room anyway that you'd put on weight, but you still might feel as if you were being shown up and embarrassed in front of everyone, and that the event was being spoiled by you having to worry about your weight, when all you wanted to do was have a good time.'

"Then I said to Maureen, 'I know it's not nice to have to confront people you know about things like that; but if you do, it might stop them doing it again, with any luck.' "

Joe, not a very sensitive soul at the best of times, and even less so when he'd had a few alcoholic drinks, as he'd had that evening, had been gradually getting more irritated with Becky for criticising people for expressing strong sentiments. He said, "That's long-winded, isn't it! If you could actually persuade anyone to stick around till you'd finished saying all that lot to them, they'd probably be asleep or not paying attention by the time you'd finished! People just don't like listening to lectures like that! They tune out!"

Becky got annoyed and said, "It wasn't long-winded! It needs to be long enough to make your point of view understandable to people! If Maureen and other people have decided to do what I suggested, then trying to explain things like that to people – even if it takes a minute or two – might actually change things, so it's better than just going behind their backs and talking with other people about how they feel like punching them in the face and things like that!"

Joe responded, "There's nothing wrong with saying things like that! It's just words! What are you, the thought police? Talking about having fantasies like that helps get anger out of the system. Sometimes people have had to put up with a lot of similar annoying experiences themselves and they just need to let off steam. There's no harm in just talking! All those things are mere comments! Only a child or a prude who'd lived a sheltered life and thinks they have the right to control other people's morals would object to people talking like that in the privacy of their own little groups! What is there for a sensible person to get all upset over?"

Becky wouldn't have minded debating Joe's point of view calmly with him if he'd expressed it in a less inflammatory way. But his insults and the scorn in his tone of voice made her annoyed. She got heated and yelled, "There's nothing wrong with getting upset about it at all! When people make comments about how much they'd enjoy committing violence against someone or how much they think someone deserves it, it shows you what kind of beliefs they have. People don't make comments that contradict the way they normally think; their comments show you what attitudes they have! And if they have the attitude where they think it's alright to be violent to someone just for saying something they don't like, how do you know they wouldn't really commit violence themselves, or egg someone else on to who really wanted to?"

Joe smiled and mocked, "You've been going on about people getting things out of proportion. I think you're getting things way out of proportion yourself now. Do you have to shout so loud? We're all going to need ear defenders if you carry on like this!"

There were titters from some of the others in the room.

Becky blushed, and replied just a little less loudly, "I wouldn't be annoyed if you hadn't just said something stupid!"

Christopher said, "Calm down, Becky! You don't need to shout in here; we can all hear you."

Becky tried to relax a bit.

But Joe continued the argument, saying, "It's time you learned to stop getting things out of proportion and calling them stupid when they're not!"

Becky protested, "But some of what you said *was* stupid! I'm fed up of people saying stupid things!"

Joe jeered, "You sound as if you think people are saying stupid things all the time; but maybe you can't count that well, since you haven't mentioned all that many things you've heard that you think are stupid. You've just kept mainly going on and on about the same one or two things."

Unbeknownst to Becky, Her Best Friends are Meeting Together Somewhere Else, Making Up Stories to Amuse Her On Her Birthday

Becky was getting a bit upset. She didn't like the argument, and she was disheartened to think that when the group had first met her early that evening, they'd been impressed that she'd made it to university at such a young age, and had praised her, only for their opinions of her to have sunk dramatically in a short time.

She might have felt less hot-and-bothered if she'd known that at the exact same time as she was having the argument, her best friends were together, discussing how they could give her an entertaining birthday party, since her birthday was coming up soon. They were thinking of giving her a party where they told her funny stories they'd made up, just as they had the year before.

They were busy thinking up stories they thought were amusing and asking the others what they thought of them. One of them, Luke, came up with one and told it to the others, saying:

"I think it would be fun to tell stories about pretend ancestors we make up. I will anyway. I've got an idea for a story about a pretend ancestor of mine who I could say rose from the grave and told me what happened to him after he died. It goes:

"I had an Ancestor called Pestilence Hornet. That was his real name! He was hated by most of the country, because he was a monster! Well, he wasn't a real monster at first – it was just that his behaviour earned him the nickname Monster, because it was the kind of behaviour you might expect from one. But he died and rose from the grave, twice, once just to tell me all about what happened to him after he died; and then he really did look like a monster!

"I'll tell you about the adventures he had after he died:

"When the time came for him to toddle out of the world and meet his maker, he tried to find his way to his maker's residence, hoping he could have an eternal party there; but he thought he must have taken a wrong turning, because he got swept up in a powerful wind, and couldn't do anything about it. He yelled obscene abusive threats at the wind, and tried to kick and punch it as hard as he could, but nothing worked. ... Or maybe it did, because it quickly dropped him.

"He ended up somewhere he'd rather not have gone though. It was a very hot stuffy hall full of frightening creatures, and one who looked especially frightening, who had a voice like thunder. PESTILENCE HORNET wouldn't have minded the loudness of his voice, since after all, he'd heard louder noises in the sleazy nightclubs he'd enjoyed going to on earth. But the way Thunder-Voice ordered people around really annoyed him, since he had a horrible feeling it might be his turn to be ordered around next.

"Sure enough, Thunder-Voice approached him. He introduced himself as Mr Devil.

"No sooner had he introduced himself than he ordered PESTILENCE HORNET to go with him to a big pile of rocks at the bottom of a fiery slope, and then commanded him to carry a heavy load up it.

"PESTILENCE HORNET was sure his feet would get scorched walking up the hill, especially since Mr Devil ordered him to take his shoes off, and although the thick layer of cheese on his feet was usually a formidable barrier against flames, nettles, nails and all manner of other things, he wasn't sure it hadn't all been blown off by that strong wind! Then it occurred to him that since he was dead, he might not be able to feel the flames anyway. With that cheering thought, he felt sure it would be easy peasy to carry the rocks up the hill, and picked some up and started walking briskly upwards, whistling merrily as he went.

"He'd only gone a few steps though when he realised the rocks were so heavy they were difficult to carry! His mood quickly changed, and a mere two steps later, he was exhausted! But the devil wouldn't let him rest. He poked PESTILENCE HORNET in the behind with a poker and told him to hurry up.

"PESTILENCE HORNET got more and more annoyed. But worse, when he got to the top and put the rocks down with relief, they just slid back to the bottom of the hill, and the devil ordered him to take them up it again.

"Angry, PESTILENCE HORNET asked him what the point would be, since they would only fall down again. The devil laughed, and told him with a sinister grin that he'd have to keep carrying the rocks up the hill no matter how many times they slid down. Then he laughed even more and said, 'I'll let you into a secret. Those rocks will *never* stay on top of that hill; they always slide down; and it's your job to keep carrying them up forever and ever. Just because I want you to.'

"Mr Devil threw his head back and laughed with a noise that made the rocks shake so much they fell out of the pile and rolled all over the hall. Flames came out of his mouth and swished down his chin and the sides of his face; but oddly they didn't burn him. He ordered PESTILENCE HORNET to run around picking up all the rocks, and then when he had a nice big pile again, to carry it up the hill again.

"PESTILENCE HORNET didn't know how he was going to be able to stand being in hell. He hated the idea of carrying rocks up the hill forever only to have them keep falling down again. But he thought he'd better get on and carry some more quickly, since he didn't want to get poked in the behind with Mr Devil's poker again! He was surprised at how much that had hurt, considering he'd thought he was dead.

"So he wearily picked up an armful of rocks and trudged back up the hill.

"He was irritated though by the fact that the devil walked close behind him all the time, chuckling to himself. PESTILENCE HORNET got more and more annoyed, till when he got to the top of the hill, put his rocks down and they just fell down the hill again, his temper flared, and he shouted, 'What are you doing stalking me, Mr Devil? You filthy creepy scumbag!'

"The devil was angry, and told him he'd be punished for saying that, by having rocks tied to his ankles as well as having to hold armfuls as he trudged up the hill.

"PESTILENCE HORNET had been a radio presenter! He wasn't used to being treated like a slave! He had certainly had slaves, and he'd enjoyed ordering them around. But he just didn't think it was fair to be ordered around himself, especially when he was being made to do such hard work!

"But worse, he was getting creeped out by the devil standing so close behind him all the time, poker raised, as if he was just longing to poke his backside again!

"As he trudged up the hill again, he said in irritation to the devil, 'Devil, why do you keep following me like this? Of all the millions and millions of people who must be here, it's *me* you want to be around. Why aren't you stalking any of *them*? Why don't you want to leave me alone?'

" 'Just keep walking!' ordered the devil.

"Then PESTILENCE HORNET felt sure he must know the answer to his question! Just as crowds of people had mobbed him on earth, at least in his dreams, he thought a similar thing must be going on now, surely. The devil must be in love with him! He must just be trying to hide it by being horrible to him.

"When the devil gave him a teasing poke on the backside with his poker, PESTILENCE HORNET became absolutely convinced of it. He turned round, accidentally dropping half the rocks on his feet in his haste, and then, with a mixture of pain and anger, he bawled,

"'I know what's going on, Mr devil! You're infatuated with me, aren't you! You can't bear to leave me alone! Well you'll just have to cry and pine for my love like a big sissy every day and every night, because I'm not that into you, you numbskull! Now leave me alone!'

"People turned their heads and started listening with curiosity. They were amazed that someone dared to talk to the devil like that. So was the devil!

"The devil became angrier as some people laughed. No laughter had ever been heard in hell before, apart from the devil's! In a mixture of confusion and anger, he yelled, 'Shut up, everyone, or I'll make sure you all end up in hell!'

"There was even louder laughter, as of course they were already there!

"God came down to see what the commotion was. From heaven, all the laughter sounded like a weird rattling noise. He walked up to PESTILENCE HORNET and the devil and asked in an interrogating tone what was going on.

"PESTILENCE HORNET thought, 'Oh no, not another one! The devil's after my body, and now God wants it too!' Before he had time to really think about it, he yelled,

"'So *you're* infatuated with me as well, are you, god? Well I'm sorry, but I'm not that into *you* either, especially since you sent me down here to this dump! You'll just have to cry and pine for me in vain every night and day like the devil will! The closest I'll ever get to caressing and kissing you the way you'd like me to is in your dreams!'

"God thundered, 'Why do you think I sent you down here? We wouldn't want this kind of behaviour in heaven!'

"Then PESTILENCE HORNET began to regret what he'd just said. He thought that if only he'd said something nice to God, he might have decided it would be OK to let him into heaven after all, and taken him away from that terrible dump! He was so annoyed and upset with himself that he kicked himself!

"He'd forgotten he now had rocks tied around his ankles. Boy did that kick hurt! He collapsed, and roared out in pain!

"The devil gave a loud laugh and said, 'Aha, so you *like* pain! You must do if you're inflicting it on yourself! You've come to the right place then. Well done. You won't mind *me* inflicting more on you then.'

"PESTILENCE HORNET had had enough of the devil's taunts. He couldn't get up after injuring his legs and with the rocks still tied to them, so he crawled over to the devil and tried to savagely claw at his ankles. He'd always had claws instead of fingernails.

"But quick as a flash, the devil jumped out of his way, grabbed a huge pair of scissors, bent down and cut his claws off.

"Then he trampled on PESTILENCE HORNET's hands. He had such clumsy great feet that that really hurt!

"Tears were coming from PESTILENCE HORNET's eyes now. He crawled over to God and begged, 'Please God, let me come to heaven. I'm sorry about what I just said and the terrible way I behaved on earth. I'll change, I promise! I'll never be nasty again!'

"God replied, 'I don't believe you'd change. If I let you into heaven, you'll probably just take it as another sign that I'm supposedly infatuated with you. Or you'll think I'm soft so you can get away with what you like. You'll just get abusive. I can't let you into heaven knowing you'll probably just do that.'

"PESTILENCE HORNET said pitifully, 'I promise I won't! I've been stupid! I'll change! Just give me a chance!'

"God replied, 'It isn't usually our policy to let people into heaven once they've been sent to hell. And I don't really believe you've changed your mind about believing I'm infatuated with you and want to stalk you. So I don't want you near me. In any case, if I'm going to make an exception for you and let you into heaven, you'll have to do something exceptionally heroic down here first to prove you're a reformed character. What heroic thing can you do?'

"PESTILENCE HORNET couldn't think of anything. He wondered what heroic things it was possible to do in hell.

"God interrupted his thoughts by saying, 'Well I haven't got all day. If you don't think of something quickly, I'll go and leave you here.'

"PESTILENCE HORNET got worried and blurted out, 'I can't think of anything I could do in hell, but I could be a bouncer on the door of heaven! If anyone causes trouble in heaven, I could rush in, drag them out and hurl them down to hell for you.'

"God replied, 'People *don't* cause trouble in heaven!'

"In desperation, PESTILENCE HORNET said, 'OK, I can't think of anything I could do in heaven or hell, but if you send me back to earth, I promise to do as many heroic things as I can think of there.'

"God thought about that. PESTILENCE HORNET had terrorised half the world when he was there, but God knew he had the potential to be a reformed character, at least for a few days, and the earth desperately needed people who'd be heroic.

"So eventually he agreed. As the devil howled in fury, PESTILENCE HORNET was transported back to earth.

"He felt himself returning to his body. Then he felt cold. Where was he? Worse, he was in a very enclosed space!

"Then he realised he was in a coffin!

"He felt the coffin being lifted up and carried. Then he heard a priest saying words a priest would say at a funeral. He realised it must be *his* funeral!

"He was concerned that if he didn't do something quickly, he'd be put in the ground and die again, buried alive! Wouldn't the devil laugh when he returned to hell so soon, he thought! After all, God would surely send him back there for breaking his promise to be heroic on earth.

"So he yelled, 'Help! Help!' He bashed on the lid of the coffin.

"He heard shrieks coming from outside. He realised people must think he'd turned into a spooky zombie or something, who wanted to come out and haunt them.

"But he shouted some more and banged louder.

"A creek was heard as the priest bravely lifted the coffin lid. PESTILENCE HORNET thought, 'My coffin creeks? Cheap-skates! Just how old is this coffin? It must be second-hand! When I find out who gave me this one instead of a nice new one, I'll ...'

"Then it dawned on him that fantastically, he was being rescued!

"A wave of euphoria burst over him, and he leapt out of the coffin with a triumphant yell.

"Hundreds of people cried out in unison, horrified, and drew back quickly, falling over each other like dominos.

"It turned out that half the town had come to his funeral, because they were eager to see the man who'd terrorised half the world finally put in the ground. Now they thought his ghost was coming to terrorise them even more!

"Since PESTILENCE HORNET had already begun to decompose, they were even more convinced! God hadn't thought to make his body look as good as new again.

"PESTILENCE HORNET was horrified to realise he'd begun to decompose, and wondered how on earth he'd be able to do heroic things while he was decomposing and no one would want to go near him, but they'd all run away!

"He looked around and realised everyone there had run away already, except the priest! He yelled out in anguish, 'God, how can I possibly do what you told me and be heroic if I'm decomposing? No one will want to be near me! Perhaps you and the devil are having an affair, and you just wanted to fling me back to earth to stop me shouting about it in hell, because you knew I'd discover it and do that!'

"The priest thought the man must be a psychiatric case, for thinking he could talk to God like that, and imagining he'd been with him. He went into the church and phoned a psychiatric unit.

"Then he went back out and spoke soothingly to PESTILENCE HORNET while they came to take him away.

"When they arrived, they didn't tell Pestilence Hornet they were taking him to a psychiatric unit, but said they'd take him somewhere where he could get medical attention. So he went with them without a fuss.

"But when he realised where he'd been taken, he yelled out, and started making threats that they'd better let him go or else. They put him in a straitjacket and injected him with a powerful tranquilliser.

"PESTILENCE HORNET realised protesting and making threats wouldn't get him anywhere. On reflection, he didn't know if he wanted to be set free anyway, knowing he was decomposing and everyone would run away from him. Somehow the psychiatric hospital staff hadn't thought to get him medical treatment to cure him of his flesh rotting problem. If he was ever going to get to be heroic, he thought, it might have to be in the psychiatric hospital. He decided to work out how he could.

"First he started behaving himself, till they decided it was safe to take him out of the straitjacket. They gave it a good wash to get the decomposing bits of him that had rubbed off on it off.

"It turned out that there were a number of people there who didn't have anything much wrong with them, but they were too lazy to work, just malingering, and fooling the psychologists and nurses there into thinking they had real problems, so they could stay there instead of being pressured by the government and their families to get work on the outside. Once PESTILENCE HORNET discovered that, he decided his heroism could consist of scaring them into leaving and getting decent jobs.

"So he decided to make that his life's project. Whenever he felt sure someone was just malingering, he would walk up behind them and say, 'I'm a zombie, you know. Did you hear about how I rose up from the grave?'

"Unfortunately, that didn't work on everyone. After all, it *was* a psychiatric hospital, so people could be expected to say weird things! But when some of them looked at his decomposing body, they could very well believe he was telling the truth. He told them they'd better get out and get a good job, or he'd eat them or haunt them all their lives.

"Three dozen malingerers became reformed characters and started contributing to the good of their country through PESTILENCE HORNET's efforts.

"Then he'd decomposed so much he couldn't do anything but die. His body hadn't stopped decomposing even though he'd been miraculously brought back to life. But on his deathbed, he hoped God would let him into heaven for being as close to heroic as he thought he could get.

"But that hadn't been part of the deal, as far as God was concerned. He'd only said Pestilence Hornet could go to heaven if he could do something heroic in hell. He'd agreed to him doing something heroic on earth, but only because he thought it would be a way he could make himself useful for once; he hadn't specifically said he'd let him into heaven if he did. He'd just let Pestilence Hornet think he meant that. When he met him again, he did congratulate him for at least intending to be heroic, but he told him he was still a reprobate who'd have to go to hell again.

"Pestilence Hornet yelled all kinds of abuse at God, accusing him of deceiving him. God said that just proved he needed to be in hell. But after Pestilence Hornet knelt down and apologised, pleading pitifully with him, and God started worrying he was about to start sloppily kissing his feet, he did promise that he'd make sure he was put on light duties from then on, for making the effort to be heroic.

"So PESTILENCE HORNET was swept up by the strong wind that had carried him to hell before, and dumped there again. But *this* time, he wasn't made to carry rocks up a hill. The devil personally informed him he'd be on light duties for eternity. ... Then he told him to get to one of the ironing boards, since the devil and all his millions of demons wanted all their clothes ironed.

" 'You barbaric savage hooligan!' PESTILENCE HORNET yelled at the devil as he went off. But he thought he'd better not say anything else, since after all, the devil was still holding that poker, and also he knew God could always change his mind about him being on light duties.

"So from then on, PESTILENCE HORNET did whatever ironing the devil told him to, and he'll have to for eternity now. He did one day manage to bravely sneak out to tell me all about what happened to him, with the help of a demon he became friends with, who thought the devil was so busy that day he probably wouldn't notice if Pestilence Hornet was gone for just a few hours. But I don't think he'll risk trying to escape for a holiday again, for fear that the devil will punish him by making him carry rocks up the hill forever again."

The friends liked Luke's story, and said they thought it would be fun if he told it to Becky on her birthday. They all came up with stories of their own, and had a good laugh telling them to each other.

The Argument's Still Going On, But There's an Amusing Interlude When a Few People Find Something to Joke About

Meanwhile though, Becky was in the middle of the argument she was having, feeling angry. She wasn't enjoying being mocked by the pugnacious Joe about the things she was saying. Since he'd just ridiculed her for saying she was fed up of hearing people say things she thought were stupid, when she hadn't given the group enough examples to prove she'd heard any more than one or two stupid things, she decided to tell them about a couple more. She said,

"OK, another stupid conversation at that group I visited, where people were saying they thought people ought to be punched for just saying something annoying, happened when one of the nicer ones said she'd been out with her guide dog, and a little boy had wanted to stroke it, and his mum said something to him in another language, and the boy told her she'd told him not to stroke it, saying it might have fleas. She said she just told the mum that actually the dog was very clean and didn't have fleas. But some of the people in the group were getting really bitchy, saying things like, 'That woman's a disgrace! You should have told her you bet she had fleas herself!'

"I was annoyed, because I thought, 'Why can't these people try and see things from the mum's point of view? She might have really been worrying that the dog had fleas, not just being nasty! If a mum told her son she thought I might have fleas, I might feel a bit insulted, but I'd probably just make a joke of it, saying something like, 'Actually I have! Great big ones! And not only that, I've got the plague! You'd better run, quick!' "

Malcolm's older brother Jim, who was there to guide him, smiled and joked, "I think the same way about babies, actually – that they've probably got something horrible and catching and it's best not to go near them! Whenever I see a politician going to kiss a baby when it's coming up to an election and he's trying to win votes, I tend to think, 'Be careful old chap! You're gambling with your health here! You don't know what kind of damage you might end up walking away with!' "

The others chuckled, and Esther joked, "I'd be more worried about the health of the baby!"

Most of them laughed and said they agreed.

Then Barbara grinned and joked, "Hey imagine if the way

babies screech was a kind of medical condition that was transmissible by touch, so a politician who kissed and cuddled babies in the hope of making people think he must be a nice friendly family man so they'd be more likely to vote for him might catch the crying noise, and he might not realise he had it, so next time he stood up in the House of Commons, or somewhere public, to give a speech, he might open his mouth, and instead of the speech, all that might come out would be a loud noise that went, 'Whaaaaaaaaaaaaaaaaaaaaaaa!' "

The others giggled. Then Becky said, "But if the noise was contagious, all the other people who touched babies would catch it as well, like their mums and dads. So everyone would be used to people going 'Whaaaaaaaaaaaaa', and people would keep opening their mouths to speak to each other and argue, or talk about important plans in business meetings, and all that would come out would be, 'Whaaaaaaaaaaaaaaaaa!' People wouldn't dare talk in the end; they'd probably decide to just write most of the things they ever wanted to say down, and hand each other little notes all the time."

Most of them grinned.

The Argument Gets Heated Again

The mood could have turned light-hearted at that point, but unfortunately, it soon became bad-tempered again when Becky saw a scornful look in Joe's eyes and became irritated again. She said, "Anyway, about what I was saying before, I was annoyed with the people in the group I've been talking about, for being so bitchy about that woman who warned her little boy not to touch the guide dog in case it had fleas. I was around some of their guide dogs, and afterwards my legs felt a bit itchy, and I myself wondered if one or two of them could have had fleas that bit me!"

Barbara said with a little irritation, "If you'd caught fleas, you'd probably know about it by now! The itching might have been to do with something psychological, the way some people say that if someone mentions head lice, they immediately notice an itch on their head."

Sheila said indignantly, "Thank goodness we haven't got the plague in this country any more, or fleas would be sucking Our blood and killing us! Honestly Becky, that supposed joke you said you'd make if someone said you yourself might have fleas doesn't sound much better than what you told us the others in that group you went to were saying! Pretty tasteless, considering how much suffering the plague caused! If I was blind and had a guide dog, and someone said it might have fleas, I'd just tell them to shut their dirty mouth!"

Becky replied, "Don't you think joking would be better, if you were sure they were going to be able to tell it was a joke? It would be pretty obvious I was joking if I said I had the plague, since they would know we don't have that in this country any more. So it wouldn't be as if I might scare them or anything! So I don't see what would be wrong with it. But I can see what would be wrong with insulting them, like you say You would! What do you think would happen next, if you said what you told me you'd say? It would hardly make them want to be nicer to you, would it! But I'd expect some of the people here to say ignorant things like that!"

Sheila was annoyed, and said spitefully, "I've been listening to you going on and on all evening, and you sound like a right little know-it-all!"

Becky responded, "Well I might know a lot more than you do, for all you know!"

Sheila replied, "I think that's very unlikely, considering I must have over a decade's more life experience than you have, and a whole lot more education, even if you are advanced for your age! My boyfriend recently wanted to start a new business. I helped him plan things. Whenever he had a new idea, I was always ten steps ahead of him when it came to thinking about how well it would work and how we could put it into practice! So don't you start suggesting I'm less intelligent than you!"

Becky was indignant, and said, "I wasn't! But why would you be offended about me doing that, when you're perfectly happy to boast to us about how much more intelligent you think you are than your boyfriend? For one thing, it doesn't sound very intelligent to me to pick a boyfriend to have who's less intelligent than you; and for another, I wouldn't mind betting that the real reason you were better at him at planning how to start the business is because you've been on a business course and he hasn't! You're dressing this up as you being more intelligent than him so you can boast about it, but I bet the real reason you were better at thinking of things is because they were things you learned about on a course he didn't go on!"

Sheila blushed. She looked a bit sheepish and said, "OK, I did go on a business course. But ..."

She would have carried on talking, but Becky interrupted triumphantly, "Ha! My guess was right! You know, if you want to keep your boyfriend, I hope you don't criticise him in the irritable way you've been criticising me, or he might get fed up and leave!"

Sheila said angrily, "Oh shut up, you sanctimonious twit! My relationship with my boyfriend's none of your business!

Do you think you're qualified to give us all relationship advice now, even though you're so much younger than us?"

Becky replied in irritation, "What's my age got to do with it? I *am* on a psychology course, you know! Do you somehow imagine advice from a child who's learned a lot about psychology's worthless, when the exact same advice given by an older person would be valuable, just because of their age difference? That's illogical and stupid!"

A Few of the Group Make Fun of Becky, Before Some of Them Wonder If She's Arguing Because She's Sleep-Deprived

Barbara said wearily, "Becky, I was hoping to Enjoy myself with my friends this evening; I haven't spoken to them for the best part of a year! I don't want to have to listen to an argument for the whole evening instead! Can you just calm down, so we can change the subject and start enjoying ourselves again?"

Becky was irritated, and protested, "It wasn't me who started this argument! Why are you just blaming me?"

Malcolm joked sarcastically, "Oh don't worry, Barbara. When someone comes to close this place for the night and they stop serving drinks, we can always ask them not to do that for the next couple of hours so we can have some extra time to start having a laugh, and I'm sure they'll do what we want, just like that."

Vicky joked, "Yeah, and we can always ask the people who run the buses and trains to put ones on especially late just for us, and I'm sure they won't mind."

The people in the group were beginning to giggle, except Becky.

Barbara said, "Actually, you could probably all come and sit in the lounge in my hall of residence if this place really does close before we want to finish chatting, although it does close pretty late!"

Joy grinned and joked, "Has anyone got any blocks of polystyrene or something else we can sound-proof the walls with so the sound of our voices doesn't wake people up?"

Barbara grinned and replied, "I don't suppose we'll be talking That loud, and lots of people make some noise late into the night anyway, so I don't suppose anyone will mind."

Cheryl smirked and said, "But we don't know how loud Becky's going to shout! We might need to cover all the windows and the ceiling in something sound-proof, let alone the walls!"

Brenda said, "Hopefully Becky will have gone to bed by then!"

Bridie said, "Yes! Actually, I think it's probably coming up to her bedtime now! I don't think you should have come with her, Barbara. You must know what she's like! If you tell her to go back, one of us can guide you and someone else back later at the same time. If she often stays up late, maybe that's the reason she's so argumentative! My older sister's kids get bad-tempered if they haven't had enough sleep."

Barbara replied, "The problem is that if I tell her to go back and she doesn't want to, it'll just lead to more arguing; and if she gets too annoyed with me, she might decide not to help me again. I've got to be a bit careful what I say to her because of that."

To their surprise, they heard a song come over the loudspeakers in the bar next door just then that was actually about arguing. Some of Them giggled.

But Becky was annoyed that Barbara had said she had to be careful what she said to her, and that Bridie thought she was only arguing because she was bad-tempered from not having enough sleep. It wasn't later than she would normally stay out. They weren't really planning to stay there till late, which is why Barbara had thought it would be alright to ask Her to guide her. She protested, "I'm not tired! And I haven't been arguing because I'm grumpy from not having enough sleep. I've been arguing because people here keep saying annoying silly things!"

Becky Gets Controversial Again, as She Explains More About Her Point of View

Christopher said, "You know, this argument's been going on for so long, I don't think I can even remember who started it, or what it was even started about! Can you, Becky?"

Unfortunately for him, Becky said, "Yes! It started because some people were saying things that weren't fair about someone who got offended when Brenda pulled her guide dog away from them!"

Christopher responded, "Well, maybe one or two people overreacted; but it's easy to do that when you're annoyed. Maybe you can understand that, since I think you've been doing a bit of that yourself tonight."

Instead of thinking about whether that might be true, Becky had an urge to defend herself, and protested in annoyance, "Well at least I haven't been saying spiteful things about people without being sure they even did anything that wrong, and without knowing what their side of the story is, like some people have! I can see how easy it would have been in the old days for someone to raise a rabble against people they'd decided they didn't like, like I said before! All they would have had to do was spread around a few rumours about them that might not even have been true, but that they'd know would make people angry!"

Christopher replied thoughtfully, "Well, I suppose raising a rabble might have been a good or bad thing depending on who it was being raised against."

Becky became more thoughtful herself, and said, "True. But if people are so quick to decide people need to be punished, any old lies could have been made up just by people who had a grudge, and people could have quickly got fired up with anger and eagerness to attack the people they were being spread about. I think that wherever it's possible, at least when no one's been hurt and nothing that bad's happened, people should think more about what might have made the people they're annoyed with do what they did, or even whether it's certain they did the things they're being accused of, before they decide they need to be punished."

Christopher said with a smile, "Well, at least the only thing people here did was to make a few comments you didn't like."

Joe chimed in, "You take things too seriously, Becky! Like that conversation you were talking about where people were saying someone deserved to be punched. I don't suppose any of them would really punch them!"

Becky replied, "Well if that's the case, it's strange how they could only have been joking when they were talking about punching other people, but when they heard about someone else who said something a bit like that, they were all horrified and angry and said he ought to be reported to the authorities and banned from working with the public! If they joke about punching people, I don't know why they take it so seriously when they hear about someone else saying something like it, before they even know the full facts!

"Here's what I mean: One of the people in that disability group where some of them had been talking earlier about punching the person who told Maureen to guess who'd just sat down next to her said a friend of hers had told her that a taxi driver had asked her what her guide dog would do if he punched it in the face. Everyone was horrified, and some of them were saying he ought to be banned from being a taxi driver and reported to the police, and should never be allowed on the roads again.

"Well maybe they were right. But they shouldn't have been so sure they could make a definite judgment, just based on one thing they were told someone said. They should have tried to find out what led up to him saying it before feeling qualified to make a judgment, since for all they knew, it might not have been as bad as it sounded:

"I mean, what if what really happened was that the driver was having a conversation with the person's friend where he said he'd been told that guide dogs sometimes don't defend themselves if they get attacked, because they're trained to be concerned for their owner at all times and not be distracted by other dogs, so an aggressive dog could come towards them and their owner might not realise, and the guide dog will carry on taking them where they want to go instead of haring off in goodness knows what direction to avoid the other dog, so an aggressive dog could get right up to them before they do anything or their owner realises. And then if it attacks the guide dog, the guide dog might concentrate on getting their owner to safety, rather than getting into a fight.

"The taxi driver might have just been curious about what it would take for a guide dog to forget their owner and just drag them off in who knows what direction or attack someone or another dog. So for all we know, he might have said, 'Do you think your dog would just forget you and attack me or just drag you away and forget about your safety if I kicked it?' The owner might have said the dog probably wouldn't. The taxi driver might have said, 'What about if I punched it in the face?'

"The guide dog owner might have started getting a bit scared and creeped out, because they might have worried that the driver was thinking about doing that for real. But the driver might just have been curious about what it would take for a guide dog to go full out to defend itself.

"It's easy to just jump to conclusions when you hear that someone said something that doesn't sound nice; but I think people should ask questions and try to find out more facts before condemning them.

"And it's not just when people say horrible things that people jump to unfair conclusions. I was in a cafe once where I overheard a family talking. They'd got some ice cream. Their little boy wasn't keen on eating his at first, and when they asked him why, he said it was cold. They laughed and said, 'Of course it's cold; it's ice cream! It's supposed to be cold!'

"It sounded as if they just thought he was being daft. He didn't know what to say to that, and just got a bit upset. But actually, I had the ice cream too, and it was quite a bit colder than the ice cream you'd get from an ice cream van. It had probably been taken out the freezer just that minute, and freezers are about minus twelve degrees Centigrade, or even colder! No wonder it was cold! I don't think it was fair of them to just think he was being silly. I think they should have just advised him to wait a few minutes for it to warm up.

"I was with Barbara when someone told us she'd seen a blind man asking where the post office was, and people were just laughing at him because it was right in front of him. But she didn't think that was fair, because he was blind so that wouldn't have been obvious to him, so she just told him where it was.

"And I was with some of my family not long ago, when one of them said he'd seen a woman ask someone at the station how to get to a particular place, when there were signs directing people to it right in front of her. The person telling us about it thought that was funny. But I didn't. I was just wondering, 'Why might she have done that then?' You know, there will always be a reason why someone's doing something, even if it isn't a good one. Who knows, maybe she had a sight problem; maybe she was in such a rush she hadn't been looking around; maybe she hadn't managed to learn to read properly at school; maybe the signs weren't all that clear, and so on. I prefer to puzzle over things like that instead of laughing at them."

Barbara's Friends Tell Stories About Embarrassing Experiences That Are Amusing in Hindsight

Vicky said, "Fair enough, but the woman who did that might have laughed at herself when she realised what she'd done, for all you know. I've got some blind friends who laugh at themselves when they have whoops moments. Just the other day, one of them was walking towards a bus stop when he banged into something. Well it was quite soft, so he thought it must be a person and said sorry. The people at the bus stop started laughing. It turned out that he'd said sorry to a big rubbish bag. But he was laughing himself when he told me about it, even though he'd been embarrassed at the time."

Malcolm said, "Yeah, I've done embarrassing things myself because I can't see, but I've laughed about them afterwards. I was once with a blind girl I wanted to impress, and I thought I knew the area I was in better than I obviously did, because I led her into a shoe shop, thinking it was the cafe next door; and before I thought about how it couldn't really be because it didn't sound like it, or smell like it, I ordered something to eat, and ordered something for her too. The salesman told me it was a shoe shop. I think he thought I must have been insane; and I think the girl thought I was stupid. They were probably both right. I had only been in the cafe once before though, so I wasn't that familiar with it."

The people in the group laughed.

Esther said, "I play the flute. I was going to play it with someone else who was playing the guitar in one of the bars in our college for an event not long ago, and before we started, I was eating peanuts and crisps that had been put on a table I was sitting at. They were in a bowl in the middle of it, so I kept reaching out to take some. Unbeknownst to me, there was a bowl of sauce on the table for people to dip bits of food in, and that bowl felt just the same as the bowl of crisps. I think someone might have moved them a bit after a while, maybe because they wanted to reach the peanuts and crisps more easily and move the bowl of dip at the same time to get it out of the way. Hopefully they didn't do it to trick me. Or maybe the bowls were next to each other without me realising.

"But one time when I reached out, I put my fingers in the bowl of dip by mistake, and got them covered in sauce; and just at that moment, we were called up to play our instruments, and I didn't have anything to wipe my fingers on! It was awkward at the time, but I can laugh about it now."

Joy told a story next, saying, "I thought it would be nice to buy a fur coat once, and I was in a shop with a group of other blind people and sighted helpers who'd come to guide us around, and I was feeling some fur coats on a rack to see which one I liked the texture of best, and then I felt one and said, 'Ooh, this one's nice!' Then I heard a voice saying, 'You can't have this one love, I'm wearing it!'

"That was embarrassing, but we all had a good laugh about it."

Becky said, "Those stories are funny. But I wasn't saying people shouldn't laugh at themselves or that that kind of thing can never be funny. I just don't like it when people laugh at other people or mock them because they think they're being silly, when they might not be. It just seems mean to me. I mean, it's sometimes fair enough to laugh at someone on the spur of the moment, because people can't help laughing at things when they happen. But the kind of thing I mean is where I've heard people talking about things other people have done, laughing at them scornfully, as if they're thinking they must have just been doing them because they're stupid, when really, there must often have been some kind of other reason, so it wasn't fair to just laugh and make fun of them.

"I think making a snap judgment that someone must just be a bit stupid is as bad as making these unfairly harsh judgments I've been talking about."

One of the Group Manages to Calm the Atmosphere With a Bit of Good Humour

Jim, worried that Becky's last comment would cause the argument to erupt again, stood up and joked, "I think some of us have had a bit too much to drink tonight! Becky, have you been at the whisky?"

Becky shouted, "No!"

Jim joked, "Perhaps you've had a crate of gin then? It's just that I can't believe you're always as argumentative as you've been tonight! Anyway, I think it's about time we all had healthier things to drink than alcohol! It might calm the mood down. I'm buying! What do you all want? ... A pint of cod liver oil, anyone? A gallon of beetroot juice, anyone? A bottle of chilli sauce, anyone? ... Well, that might not be too healthy actually, but it might be fun to witness someone trying to be brave enough to drink it! Becky, would you like a go?"

Becky calmed down and laughed. She said, "No thanks!"

Everyone in the group told Jim what they'd really like, and he went off to buy them all some drinks.

Eventually, the People in the Group Start Enjoying Themselves Again, as The Conversation Returns to Stories of Old School Memories

The mood became more relaxed.

Barbara yawned and commented, "You know, I'm feeling a bit tired now!"

Cheryl said, "I remember at school, I kept yawning in a lesson one day, and the teacher – the one some of us liked to call Miss bad-Tempered – ordered me to go and rinse my head under a cold tap to wake myself up. I went out, but I just wet a bit of my hair very slightly and pretended I'd done what she asked me to. I thought afterwards that I should have really done it, and then gone back into the classroom and wrung my hair out all over her desk."

The others laughed, and Joy said, "You might have wrung it out all over her books and notes! Then she would have angrily said, 'How can I teach the class now when all my books have gone soggy?' "

Barbara said for fun, "Wow, soaking her books could have got you out of the rest of the lesson! Then you might have been tempted to do it some more. You might have started yawning deliberately in some boring lessons after that, in the hope the teacher would tell you to rinse your head under the tap again so you'd have an excuse to wring your hair out over her desk again!"

Cheryl laughed and then said, "I remember when Miss Bad-Tempered was our form teacher, and one day I brought my coat downstairs because we were going to go outside, and I didn't realise, but one of my school blouses was tucked into it. I'd put it on the same hanger as the coat, and it must have come off with it without me realising. I think I'd even forgotten I'd put it on the same hanger by then. Miss Bad-Tempered immediately spotted it when she saw me though, and scolded angrily, 'What was the point of bringing your blouse down here? What a stupid thing to do! Go and put it upstairs again immediately!'

"It obviously didn't occur to her that I might have done it by accident. But maybe doing that deliberately from then on would have got me out of part of her lessons!"

Barbara grinned and joked, "Yeah, you could have kept saying things like, 'Whoops, Sorry Miss Bad-Tempered, I don't know why I brought this pile of socks down here ... again! I must be an idiot! I'll just go and put them back.' "

Malcolm chuckled and said, "She'd probably have got fed up of you doing it after a while though and started saying, 'No, just leave them on your desk. You can go and put them back in your break time!' "

Then Esther said, "I can't remember how they found out, but someone told me the headmistress – Miss Mouldy, as some of us sometimes called her – was chatting in her office with the deputy head one day, who told her she was intending to take some of the pupils to a magistrates' court the next day so they could hear some cases and find out what went on. The headmistress pleaded with her to postpone it, since she was due to appear there herself the next day for a driving offence.

"She tried to come across as so prim and proper with us, disciplining us for the slightest thing. She even gave me a long lecture once because my mum sent me a parcel in the kind of box people normally put braille books in. The headmistress was convinced my mum was trying to deceive the school into thinking it was books, and that I must be her co-conspirator! Never mind that the parcel just contained things like a vest and a packet of sweets! She made me take out the contents of the box one by one in front of her. And then we find out she's committed a driving offence! I did think it was funny!"

The others did too.

They talked about some more funny memories. Then they decided it was about time they went home.

The next day, Becky thought about what had happened the evening before. She thought maybe she had got carried away and done far too much talking, and been too argumentative, and probably spoiled a large part of Barbara's evening, plus ruining things for a while for other people in the group who didn't deserve it. She started to feel a bit guilty and miserable.

So she emailed Barbara and apologised for talking and arguing too much and spoiling part of her evening.

Barbara emailed her back, reassuring her not to worry about it, saying she'd at least got to have fun with her friends for some of the time, and that she knew the argument hadn't been all Becky's fault. She said she'd actually found a bit of the conversation interesting too. So Becky felt a bit better.

Thankfully, the rest of the time she spent with Barbara was trouble-free.

About the Author

Diana Holbourn has written self-help articles and is the author of *The Early Life of Becky Bexley the Child Genius* and other books about the same character. Taking short psychology courses, working on a helpline and reading psychology books has prepared her for writing the self-help information that appears as part of the story in the Becky Bexley series. Diana lives and works on the south coast of England, where the sun shines ... sometimes.

For more about the author and her books, visit:

www.DianaHolbourn.com

Other Books in this Series

Becky Bexley, Book One

Even from the moment she was born, it was clear that Becky Bexley was not like other children. Her family were shocked by her behaviour!

Just a few years later, and she's in secondary school, often seeming wiser than her teachers. She does her best to help people, whether they like it or not. She has advice for her teachers when they want to give up smoking, gives a boy advice he uses to stop himself being teased, and even gives the headmaster some advice on improving the school's anti-bullying strategy.

She helps people outside school too, including rescuing her mum from a con artist. She even gets to go to the White House, where she ends up giving the president advice about his behaviour!

He invites her to help some politicians with the depression they have. But will a few tactless remarks she makes and their own fierce disagreements unwittingly stirred up by some of the insights she tries to pass on ruin her efforts?

Becky's advice is based on genuine therapy techniques and psychological research, and the books in this series combine humour with handy information.

Becky Bexley, Book Two

Becky Bexley the child genius goes to university at a much younger age than most people do. She copes with the coursework, but has a few unexpected difficulties.

Things begin well, as she makes friends she has fun with, and finds herself giving one of her psychology tutors some psychological help.

She has a laugh working on a local community radio station with other students, and interviews the brother of a founder member of the pop group Fleetwood Mac.

The paranormal comes up for skeptical and sometimes amusing discussion after a student tells the others about scary night-time experiences he's been having that seem to be supernatural.

However, at a Christmas party in the psychology department, a succession of stressful events begins involving tutors behaving badly that makes Becky worry she risks being thrown out of university.

Becky's advice is based on genuine therapy techniques and psychological research, and the books in this series combine humour with handy information.

Becky Bexley, Book Three

Child genius Becky Bexley entices a group of her fellow university students to play a rowdy game in class for fun one day that has worried tutors coming to investigate what's going on.

On another day, she and a group of other students have a long long discussion where they talk about such things as world leaders taking foolish risks, false rumours, and interviews with transsexuals, and they tell stories about scams and broken friendships.

The discussion often becomes humorous though, as they tell each other funny news stories, make up jokes, and think up wacky ideas for fun.

Becky Bexley, Book Four

Child genius Becky Bexley helps to organise a lot of fun at university, some for charity. She turns out to have a talent for stand-up comedy.

Alcohol comes up for discussion one day as students talk about embarrassing things they did while drunk and the harmful effects of alcohol on the body.

Becky helps a girl overcome post-traumatic stress disorder, and a little boy with an anxiety problem that's blighting his life.

Becky's advice is based on genuine therapy techniques and psychological research, and the books in this series combine humour with handy information.

More Stories About Becky

There are stories about the experiences of Becky Bexley the child genius at university and afterwards that can be read free online here:

www.broadcaster.org.uk/beckycontents.html

Printed in Great Britain
by Amazon

56535731R00202